Financial Integration in East Asia

Financial Integration in East Asia examines the degree of domestic and international financial openness in ten Asian countries (Japan, Australia, Hong Kong, Indonesia, South Korea, Malaysia, and the Philippines, Singapore, Taiwan and Thailand) and the effect financial openness has on the structure of the macroeconomy. After examining the reasons behind the 1997–8 financial crisis, Dr de Brouwer puts these in context by summarising the literature on the costs and benefits of financial reform. He then assesses the information that interest rate parity conditions and consumption smoothing have for financial openness, and sets out theoretical and empirical models to explore the link between market interest rates and intermediated interest rates on deposits and loans. *Financial Integration in East Asia* also contains reviews of the literature and regional developments, with clear policy analysis throughout.

Financial Integration in East Asia is the latest title in the Cambridge series Trade and Development.

GORDON DE BROUWER is Chief Manager, International Markets and Relations, at the Reserve Bank of Australia. He has previously worked for the Department of Treasury in Australia, the University of Melbourne and Westpac Bank in Tokyo. He has published papers on money markets in east Asia and Japan, and on topics including inflation modelling, output determination and monetary policy.

TRADE AND DEVELOPMENT

A series of books on international economic relations and economic issues in development

Academic editor
Ron Duncan, *National Centre for Development Studies,*
The Australian National University

Advisory editors
Ross Garnaut, *The Australian National University*
Reuven Glick, *Federal Reserve Bank of San Francisco*
Enzo R. Grilli, *The World Bank*
Mario B. Lamberte, *Philippine Institute for Development Studies*

Executive editor
Maree Tait, *National Centre for Development Studies,*
The Australian National University

Other titles in the series
Helen Hughes (ed.), *Achieving Industrialization in East Asia*
Yun-Wing Sung, *The China–Hong Kong Connection: The Key to China's Open Door Policy*
Kym Anderson (ed.), *New Silk Roads: East Asia and World Textile Markets*
Rod Tyers and Kym Anderson, *Disarray in World Food Markets: A Quantitative Assessment*
Enzo R. Grilli, *The European Community and Developing Countries*
Peter Warr (ed.), *The Thai Economy in Transition*
Ross Garnaut, Enzo Grilli, and James Riedel (eds.), *Sustaining Export-Oriented Developments: Ideas from East Asia*
Donald O. Mitchell, Merlinda D. Ingco, and Ronald C. Duncan, *The World Food Outlook*
David C. Cole and Betty F. Slade, *Building a Modern Financial System: The Indonesian Experience*
Ross Garnaut, Guo Shutian and Ma Guonan (eds.), *The Third Revolution in the Chinese Countryside*
David Robertson (ed.), *East Asian Trade After the Uruguay Round*
Chris Manning, *Indonesian Labour in Transition*
Yiping Huang, *Agricultural Reform in China*
Richard Bird and François Vaillancourt, *Fiscal Decentralisation in Developing Countries*

Financial Integration in East Asia

GORDON DE BROUWER

CAMBRIDGE
UNIVERSITY PRESS

CAMBRIDGE UNIVERSITY PRESS
Cambridge, New York, Melbourne, Madrid, Cape Town, Singapore, São Paulo, Delhi

Cambridge University Press
The Edinburgh Building, Cambridge CB2 8RU, UK

Published in the United States of America by Cambridge University Press, New York

www.cambridge.org
Information on this title: www.cambridge.org/9780521121101

First published 1999
This digitally printed version 2009

A catalogue record for this publication is available from the British Library

Library of Congress Cataloguing in Publication data

De Brouwer, Gordon
      Financial integration in East Asia / Gordon de Brouwer.
          p.   cm. – (Trade and development)
      ISBN 0 521 65148 4
1. Finance–East Asia.   2. Financial crises–East Asia.
I. Title   II. Series: Trade and development (Cambridge, England)
HG187.E3704   1999   332´.095–dc21   98-33985   CIP

ISBN 978-0-521-65148-6 hardback
ISBN 978-0-521-12110-1 paperback

Contents

Preface and acknowledgements

I am indebted to many people for their help and support in the process of writing this book. I owe a special and deep debt to Peter Drysdale. I would never have started the book without his encouragement and active support, he has continually pushed me to explore and expand my research and has offered valuable counsel and friendship. Warwick McKibbin and Adrian Pagan have also provided important substantive comments and guidance. Warwick spent considerable time working through the book, especially chapters 4, 6 and 7, and I am grateful for his enthusiasm and insights. Adrian also provided many valuable comments, particularly about econometric and research methodology.

I have received much from the staff at the Australian National University. I am grateful to the administrative staff of the Australia–Japan Research Centre in the Research School of Pacific and Asian Studies, particularly Margitta Acker, Lynne Colley, Marilyn Popp, Sue Marks and Denise Ryan. I am also indebted to Maree Tait for editorial advice and assistance. I also owe thanks to Ron Duncan, Mardi Dungey, Ross Garnaut, Luke Gower, Steve Husted (now back at Pittsburgh), Shun Ikeda, Kali Kalirajan, Heather Smith, Neil Vousden and Graeme Wells for helpful comments. While completing the book, I have also been an Officer of the Reserve Bank of Australia. I received much support and encouragement from my fellow Officers, particularly Palle Andersen (now back at the BIS), Steve Grenville, David Gruen, Philip Lowe and Chris Ryan (now at the IMF). I am also grateful to the Bank for financial assistance and access to facilities it provided during my study leave. The views expressed in this book are my own and should not be ascribed to the Reserve Bank. The university also provided funds for which I am grateful, and I hope taxpayers' money has not been wasted. I spent five months, from October 1994 to March 1995, in Japan and am grateful to the Japan Foundation for very generous support.

During the course of the book I had the opportunity to visit a number of institutions. My time in Japan was spent at the Bank of Japan and I am grateful for the opportunity to do this and for the Bank's hospitality. I am especially indebted to Kunio Okina, Makoto Ohsawa and Masahiro Fukao for comments and support; the Japan connection will always remain dear to me. Michael Dooley also provided valuable advice at the time. I owe thanks to a large number of economists at the Hong Kong Monetary Authority, the Bank of Korea, the Federal Reserve Bank of San Francisco and the World Bank for discussions. Economists at Hitotsubashi University, the Research Department of the International Monetary Fund, the International Division of the Board of Governors of the Federal Reserve Bank System, the Economics Department of the University of California at Santa Cruz and the Institute of International Economics listened to me with patience and provided valuable comments at seminars at those institutions. I especially thank Menzie Chinn and Neil Ericsson.

Final thanks go to where they belong – to my family, and two members in particular. The first is my brother-in-law, Alan Marshall, who started the whole thing in 1982 when he encouraged me to study economics at the University of Melbourne. He bears the ultimate responsibility for everything in this book! The other is Michael Sparks, who has provided unwavering support and shown endless tolerance. This book is dedicated to him.

1

Financial integration

> 'Sit down, Shepherd Oak,' continued the ancient man of malt. 'And how was the old place at Norcombe, when ye went for your dog? I should like to see the old familiar spot; but faith, I shouldn't know a soul there now.'
>
> 'I suppose you wouldn't. 'Tis altered very much.'
>
> 'Is it true that Dicky Hill's wooden cider-house is pilled down?'
>
> 'Oh yes – years ago, and Dicky's cottage just above it.'
>
> 'Well, to be sure!'
>
> 'Yes; and Tompkin's old apple-tree is rooted that used to bear two hogsheads of cider, and no help from the other trees.'
>
> 'Rooted? – you don't say it! Ah! stirring times we live in – stirring times.'
>
> 'And you mind the old well that used to be in the middle of the place? That's turned into a solid iron pump with a large stone trough, and all complete.'
>
> 'Dear, dear – how the face of nations alter, and what we live to see nowadays! Yes – and t'is the same here.' [1]

People have always had to cope with the fact that the world around them is changing, and often in unexpected ways. This book deals with one aspect of change: how financial markets in particular countries in east Asia and the western Pacific have developed, become more open and integrated with the world, and what this has meant for the structure and operation of their economies.

In general terms, 'integration' is the process by which segmented markets become open and unified so that participants enjoy the same unimpeded access. It can occur through the removal of domestic and international controls on trade in the asset, good or service under consideration – for example, by implementing policies to deregulate and liberalise markets. Or it can occur simply by a reduction in the effectiveness of controls in a market – for example, by avoidance or non-enforcement. In either case, the key driving force for integration is the amalgam of the private interests of consumers, investors and financial institutions.

---

[1] Thomas Hardy, *Far From the Madding Crowd* (1874) (Harmondsworth: Penguin, 1978: 156–7).

The integration of markets implies, on the face of it, an increase in transactions in those markets and a tendency for prices to converge in common-currency terms; integration can also radically change the dynamics of the market. Financial integration is simply the application of this process to markets in financial instruments. The integration of financial markets thus implies an increase in capital flows and a tendency for the prices and returns on traded financial assets in different countries to equalise on a common-currency basis.

The aim of this book is to assess the degree to which selected economies in east Asia and the western Pacific are becoming more financially integrated with the rest of the world, and to explore some of the implications of integration for fundamental economic structure in these economies. The first part of this chapter explains why the book focuses on east Asia and the western Pacific. The second addresses the question of why financial integration is of interest to people interested in understanding how the world works, and then outlines the structure of the book.

Focus on east Asia

The economies examined in this book are Australia, Hong Kong, Indonesia, Japan, (South) Korea, Malaysia, the Philippines, Singapore, Taiwan and Thailand. These countries are grouped together under the shorthand description of 'east Asia'. This grouping excludes Cambodia, China, Laos, Mongolia, Myanmar, North Korea and Vietnam which are obviously part of east Asia. These economies are not examined because much of the data required for empirical analysis is either not available for a sufficiently long period or else is not of adequate quality. Their exclusion should not be construed as meaning that they are unimportant, or that the insights gained in this study are not applicable to them. China, in particular, presents an interesting and important case in financial development and warrants a separate study. The grouping is also controversial in that it includes Australia, which is close to east Asia but is a geographically separate continent in the western Pacific. This rather technical observation ignores the fact that the Australian economy is deeply integrated with those of east Asia and that much of Australia's economic diplomacy is focused on east Asia. Indeed, as is apparent in governments' response to the financial crisis in Thailand and Indonesia in the second half of 1997, and in discussions about an umbrella organisation for east Asian central banks, it is increasingly standard to include Australia in a loose east Asian grouping.

This region is chosen as the object of analysis of financial integration for a number of reasons. In the first place, it is a region of growing importance in the world economy and polity but the financial markets of its members have yet to be fully analysed. The ten countries are part of the Asia Pacific Economic Co-operation (APEC) group. They constitute a large economic area, accounting for about a quarter of world income and trade in the mid-1990s, up from about 11 per cent in 1970. The countries are also a dynamic group, with expanding intra- and extra-regional trade. There is a substantial body of applied research on trade and investment linkages in the APEC region and a growing body of literature on macroeconomic structure and policy. But the literature on financial structure and integration is relatively small, even if expanding. There is scope for contributing to this analysis in measuring the degree of integration of financial markets in the region; finance in east Asia has probably not been explored in as much detail as other issues since the quality and availability of data are generally lower than for trade and investment analysis. It is also more natural to focus, at least initially, on real variables since they are more obviously related to welfare. The consensus appears to be that financial development underpins rather than generates growth (Patrick and Park 1994), and so the proper focus, at least at early stages of development, is on the real economy and trade. In a similar vein, integration has been a major topic of analysis in Europe for decades but the focus on financial integration is only relatively recent.

There has also been substantial reform and growth in the domestic financial system and liberalisation of the capital account in many of these economies over the past decade, and this has occurred at a time when international financial markets have also changed notably. East Asian economies are, in their own right, interesting case studies on the effects of financial integration on macroeconomic structure and the implications for policy. More recently, of course, many of these economies have experienced a financial crisis, with sharp downward movements in asset and financial prices and economic contraction. The sources of these shocks need to be explained and the implications for financial reform pursued. At the same time, it is important to keep perspective, and so the discussion also includes a broader literature review of the costs and benefits of financial reform, with particular focus on east Asia.

The literature tends to be dominated by North American research and, while this has made a major contribution to the advancement of theoretical and applied economics, North American economists tend to focus on mainstream economies in constructing and testing theory. A different insight or perspective may be gained from examining smaller economies with different regulatory regimes and which are at different stages of economic development. To quote Solow (1986: S23), one 'of the few good ways we have to test analytical ideas is to see whether they can make sense of international differences in outcomes by appealing to international differences in institutional structure and historical environment'.

This is *not* to say that there is an 'Asian economic way' or that east Asian economies are inherently 'different' and not subject to the principles of standard economic analysis; the book in fact applies conventional analytical techniques to these economies. But the insights and views based on the experience of G7 economies should be examined in different regimes, and east Asia provides an exciting collection of economies with which to do this. As argued later, this analysis challenges some non-conventional views and enriches an understanding of the effects of repression and liberalisation on the real economy. In this context, it is worth noting that the focus here is financial integration *in* east Asia, not *of* east Asia. The focus of the former is on the openness of domestic financial systems to the rest of the world, the nuance of the latter is that there is an emerging east Asian financial grouping, such as a yen bloc. These two notions are distinct, and the focus in this book is clearly on the former.

Two of the foundations of the literature on integration are that integration is a *process*, and not an end in itself, and that there is no optimal region or integrated area other than the world itself (Cooper 1974); this is particularly so with financial markets. In this case, the process is the convergence of prices on financial assets throughout the world in support of the efficient allocation of capital. Restricting openness to a region rather than the whole world implies an inefficiency. The notion of the integration of east Asia seems to mimic the European literature and paradigm, which does focus on the integration *of* Europe. European analysts address issues such as which country dominates the regional monetary and financial system and how monetary union is to be achieved. It is possible to talk of Europe as a deutschemark bloc because European countries are aiming at economic convergence – that is, common economic growth, inflation and structural features such as budget and debt ratios – based on anchoring their economies to that of Germany. Despite the relatively high degree of economic interdependence in east Asia (Goto and Hamada 1994), integration of east Asian economies is not an issue, at least for the foreseeable future, since there is no aim to achieve convergence by structurally aligning and anchoring economies to Japan or any other regional economy. The focus is not on financial markets which are more open to some players or countries than to others, but on uniformly open markets. Accordingly, 'financial integration' and 'financial openness' are used interchangeably throughout the book.

Focus on financial integration

Much of the current discussion on financial integration is in terms of the interest of policymakers, but this growing interest has largely been motivated by what is happening in markets. It is reactive rather than proactive: it is a response to the private interests of consumers and investors and to the actions of financial institutions. It may well now be trite to say that the world is a smaller place, but the fact of the matter is that communications and technological advances over the past decade have radically changed access to information and markets and, consequently, business and personal strategies. The underlying force for integration is that people want freedom to make economic decisions and to access different forms of finance, risk management techniques and investment and portfolio diversification opportunities. It is now much easier to circumvent restrictions which people regard as inimical to their private interests, and this throws policymakers into a reactive role, forcing them to reassess their policy processes. While there is a focus in the book on the policy implications of financial integration, this should not detract from the assessment that much of the phenomenon is market driven.

There are several reasons why policymakers and economists focus on financial integration. In the first place, it is axiomatic that the macroeconomic policy mix depends crucially on the openness of the financial system (Fleming 1962; Mundell 1963). The more mobile is capital, the more substitutable are financial assets and the less flexible is the exchange rate, the more difficult it is for a country to set its interest rates independently of interest rates in the rest of the world. The degree of financial openness is an empirical question which needs to be resolved if policymakers are to know the structure of their economies and implement policies that will be effective in achieving their aims. This book seeks to present a simple and relatively general measure of financial openness.

One implication of integration is that the price of the good or asset is determined by the market, and economists generally argue that outcomes in competitive markets tend to be more efficient and equitable than otherwise. The degree of integration would seem to indicate whether there are efficiency gains to be had by liberalisation; the argument that financial integration promotes economic development and welfare is not, however, uncontroversial, and there are arguments that transitional costs can be high and that the gains from openness are overstated. The events of 1997 might be used to buttress these types of arguments. This book reviews the literature and presents new evidence to assess whether, and how, financial integration affects the real economy.

Financial integration induces change in basic economic structure and in the operating environment for policy, business and households. This change can also make it confusing and difficult to determine what is happening in an economy in transition, and so some view is necessary on what happens to an economy when it liberalises its capital account. Liberalisation of the capital account in Korea, for example, has been impeded by concerns that international financial integration will stimulate capital inflows, induce an appreciation in the real exchange rate and thereby reduce international competitiveness (Dornbusch and Park 1994; Kim 1994; Park 1994). This book seeks to present a simple model of the real economy which can be used as a reference for interpreting changes in the real economy brought about by financial integration.

Finally, policymakers in APEC economies are interested in identifying the openness of markets as part of negotiating and defining an agenda of reform and liberalisation in the region (PECC 1995). This is particularly difficult for trade and investment in services, since it is hard to identify legal restrictions and impediments to market access in this sector. An alternative to identifying legal restrictions explicitly is to deduce the existence of restrictions by identifying outcomes which indicate restrictions. Moreover, even if legal restrictions can be identified, what is important to policy is whether these restrictions *matter* – that is, whether they affect outcomes. This book draws inferences about the openness of the capital account and domestic financial system based on tests of financial integration. As such, it complements and enhances work on impediments to trade and investment in financial services in the APEC region.

This book addresses a range of issues related to the measurement and analysis of financial integration. It does not seek to answer every question about integration, but it does address key aspects of financial integration by examining measurement of the phenomenon and exploring, both in theory and applied analysis, the implications of integration for the real economy.

The book falls into four parts. Chapter 2 starts with an analysis of recent events in east Asian financial markets and economies. The financial disturbances that affected these economies have had a profound effect on the macroeconomies in east Asia, and on the way people think about financial markets and reform. Chapter 2 examines what happened, and then tries to set out the fundamentals that lay behind the financial crises, assess some policy implications and review the literature on financial liberalisation more broadly, in order to put these events in some longer-term perspective.

The focus then shifts to broader conceptual issues associated with financial liberalisation. The second issue taken up in the book is the measurement of financial openness. Chapter 3 reviews some of the summary measures of financial integration for east Asia, including the nature of legal restrictions that operate on the capital account of these countries, capital flows, interest rate relations, saving, investment and consumption relationships. Chapter 4 then examines international interest parity relationships in considerable detail. There are many different sorts of traded financial assets but it is not necessary to examine the interaction of domestic and foreign rates in all of these markets if their prices are linked through arbitrage in open markets. Hence, it is valid to assess integration by focusing on the prices in one market – which, in chapter 4, is the money market. Chapter 5 shifts the focus to the integration of domestic bank-intermediated markets with domestic money markets: even if money markets are internationally integrated, the impact of foreign monetary shocks on the home economy will depend on the extent to which *domestic* financial markets are integrated – that is, the extent to which changes in the prices of traded financial assets are transmitted to the prices of non-traded financial assets such as bank loans and deposits. (Chapter 7 takes a different tack, and looks at the effect of financial openness on consumption patterns.)

The third theme of the book is to understand more clearly the impact of financial integration on the real (as opposed to the financial) economy. Chapter 6 assesses the effects of financial integration on the real economy in the context of a two-good Ramsey model. The focus here is the effect of integration on the steady-state values of basic macroeconomic variables such as the real exchange rate, physical capital formation and net foreign liabilities. Chapter 7 looks at the effect of financial integration in a simple intertemporal model with demographic change, and assesses this model empirically. A model of intertemporal optimisation by an aging population with restricted access to financial markets is outlined and estimated.

The fourth stream in the book is to provide an overall policy assessment of financial integration. Chapter 8 summarises the results of earlier chapters and returns to some of the policy implications of integration discussed throughout the book; in particular, some implications for the operation of domestic policy and the relevance of consumption and debt for policy are examined.

2

Developments in east Asia, 1997–1998

The extreme financial volatility in east Asian markets in the second half of 1997 and early 1998 needs to be explained and put into context. This chapter does this in four sections. The first summarises recent developments, describing what happened to key financial variables. The second examines the fundamental factors that lay behind these events. The third is an assessment of what these fundamental factors and financial market dynamics imply for financial liberalisation and reform policies. The fourth tries to put these events in a broader, more long-term focus, by reviewing the empirical literature on the costs and benefits of financial reform.

What happened?

In the second half of 1997 and early 1998, there was a severe loss of confidence in east Asian financial markets. Table 2.1 presents a chronology of events in markets over this period. The crisis began with a deterioration of confidence in the Thai baht that spread through to other markets in the region (IMF 1997a). The baht, which had been a currency pegged largely to the US dollar, came under selling pressure in early May 1997, as forecasts for economic growth weakened, on the back of a sharp excess supply of semiconductors, a rising current account deficit (fuelled in part by the baht being tied to the US dollar which had been steadily appreciating against other major currencies since mid-1995) and an emerging expectation of a rise in Japanese interest rates.

The fall in the baht revealed further, more fundamental, problems in the Thai financial system. In the first place, Thai interest rates were higher than US interest rates, and banks and other financial institutions in Thailand had borrowed in US dollars and lent these funds to Thai businesses and individuals without taking forward cover in the foreign exchange market. This meant that domestic borrowers had taken on a foreign currency risk, which became an actuality when the baht, contrary to general expectations, was floated and depreciated. On top of this, financial institutions

Table 2.1. *Chronology of events, May 1977–March 1998*

Date	Country	Comments
1997		
7 May	Thailand	baht under selling pressure
May	Thailand	introduction of selective capital controls and extensive forward foreign exchange intervention
2 July	Thailand	baht floated
11 July	Philippines	peso trading band widened, devaluation
	Indonesia	rupiah trading band widened, devaluation
13 July	Malaysia	Bank Negara Malaysia (BNM) stops defending the ringgit
18 July	Philippines	IMF approves US$1bn loan to replenish reserves
11 August	Thailand	agreement reached on US$17.2bn IMF-led financial package
14 August	Indonesia	rupiah floated
14 October	Thailand	financial restructuring package released; restrictions on foreign investment in financial sector relaxed
17–21 October	Taiwan	NT$ devalued 7 per cent
22 October	Korea	intervention to support won
28 October		large share price movements around the world
31 October	Indonesia	US$18bn IMF-led package announced
19 November	Korea	won trading band widened
end-November	Korea	operations of 14 merchant banks suspended; two commercial banks nationalised
3 December	Korea	US$57bn IMF-led agreement announced
8 December	Thailand	two of 58 suspended finance companies allowed to reopen
16 December	Korea	trading band on won abolished
18 December	Korea	Kim Dae-Jung elected President
end-December	Korea	debt rollover negotiations commence
1998		
6 January	Indonesia	budget released
23 January	Indonesia	revised budget released
27 January	Indonesia	bank deposit guarantees and restructuring agency announced
January	Thailand	two-tier exchange rate system introduced in May 1997 abolished, allowing baht loans to non-residents
end-January	Korea	agreement to reschedule US$24bn in short-term debt
end-January	Korea	10 merchant banks closed (25 per cent of assets) and flagged closure of a further 20 institutions
February	Korea	labour market reforms announced
February	Thailand	two banks taken over by the Financial Institutions Development Fund
February	Malaysia	statutory reserve requirement reduced by 3.5 percentage points to 10 per cent
25 February	Thailand	IMF agreement revised
26 February	Korea	two merchant banks closed (taking the number to 12, with 15 of the 30 institutions assessed to be financially viable)
4 March	Thailand	IMF loan instalment paid
early March	Indonesia	speculation about presidential and vice-presidential nominations
5 March	Indonesia	announcement that IMF package to be delayed from mid-March to April
9 March	Indonesia	speculation that the government would renounce IMF-led package

(particularly merchant banks) had been increasing loans for real estate and shares, and as the economy started to slow on the back of a moderate weakening in fundamentals, real estate and share prices also fell. These assets had been used as collateral for lending by financial institutions and so weakened the strength of the financial system as a whole. The market's recognition of these fundamental problems in the financial system changed the credit risk associated with lending to Thailand, which induced a further portfolio shift away from Thai assets. As a result, the exchange rate fell further, which in turn compounded the problem. This pattern was repeated elsewhere.

These concerns about the Thai economy and currency caused a broader reconsideration of lending to other industrialising economies, particularly in south-east Asia (Indonesia, Malaysia and the Philippines) and Europe (the Czech Republic). In the face of this pressure, countries tried a range of measures to support their currencies. The Thai authorities had initially imposed capital controls on particular transactions and market participants in order to stop speculation which would force the currency to be devalued. These included restricting the access of foreign speculators to baht-denominated credits. Speculators had borrowed in baht and sold the currency in the expectation that they would be able to buy baht more cheaply after the currency had been devalued; by restricting the access of non-residents to baht, the authorities were able to increase the cost of maintaining baht positions. Indeed, interest rates in short-term offshore markets reached 1,300 per cent, forcing speculators to square their positions and buy baht, and the IMF reported that market losses were between US$1bn and US$1.5bn (IMF 1997a). The authorities also intervened actively in the foreign exchange market, with the loss of most of the Bank of Thailand's foreign exchange reserves. With few resources to defend the currency peg, the authorities floated the currency on 2 July and it immediately depreciated by 16 per cent.

The authorities elsewhere in Indonesia, Malaysia and the Philippines recognised that defending their currencies at the prevailing rates would only delay the inevitable, and so did not stand in the way of the market. They soon floated their currencies, which then depreciated substantially. There were broader spillovers in the region. The Singapore dollar depreciated, but more moderately. The Hong Kong monetary authorities were able to hold the peg of the HK dollar to the US dollar, largely because of the strong backing of foreign exchange reserves and the perception that the Chinese authorities would not devalue the rembimbi. In October and November 1997, the Korean financial and economic system came under market scrutiny, because events elsewhere in Asia drew attention to the concentration of lending to the Korean conglomerates, the *chaebol*, which had high debt exposure but had been performing increasingly poorly. Consequently, the won was sold down by the market. As currencies came under more pressure and the financial and macroeconomic outlook deteriorated, the governments of Thailand, Korea and Indonesia entered into negotiations with the IMF and other countries for financial support to aid economic and financial restructuring.

Figure 2.1 shows the currencies of selected cast Asian countries. The rates are shown in log form, so the movement on the vertical axis approximates the percentage change in the series. By mid-March 1998, the Indonesian currency had depreciated by about 80 per cent over the year, and the won and baht had depreciated by about 45 and 40 per cent, respectively. The Malay ringgit and Philippine peso fell by amounts similar to the baht and won, while the New Taiwan dollar and Singapore dollar depreciated by a more moderate 15 per cent or so (like the Australian dollar). These are large movements but they are, with the exception of the depreciation of the rupiah this time round, not unprecedented in the region – the baht, for example, was devalued by about 20 per cent in November 1984, and the rupiah was devalued by over 40 per cent in September 1986.

Other asset markets, such as stock markets, have also been affected. Figure 2.2 shows stock market indices in log form for a selection of east Asian countries. In the year to March 1998, the key stock market index in Malaysia had fallen about 40 per cent, those in Indonesia and the Philippines by about 30 per cent and those in Singapore and Thailand by about 25 per cent. The Thai stock market began falling in early 1996, and in the two years to March 1998 had fallen by over 60 per cent. (The weakness in the Thai stock market in 1996 was a reflection of weaker fundamentals.) Like the exchange rate movements, these are large changes.

This crisis has also had a very substantial macroeconomic impact on the countries involved, although the exact extent of this is still evolving. Forecasts for economic growth over 1998 and 1999 in Indonesia, Korea and Thailand, for example, have been steadily revised downwards, with the economies expected to shrink in absolute terms. This is in stark contrast to the high single-digit growth enjoyed over the past decade or so. The crisis also affected the region in general, with growth forecasts in Australia, Hong Kong, Japan and Singapore, for example, downgraded.

The 'fundamentals' behind what happened

As events unfolded in east Asia, the characterisation of the crisis changed. It was described first of all as a *currency crisis*, but many countries have

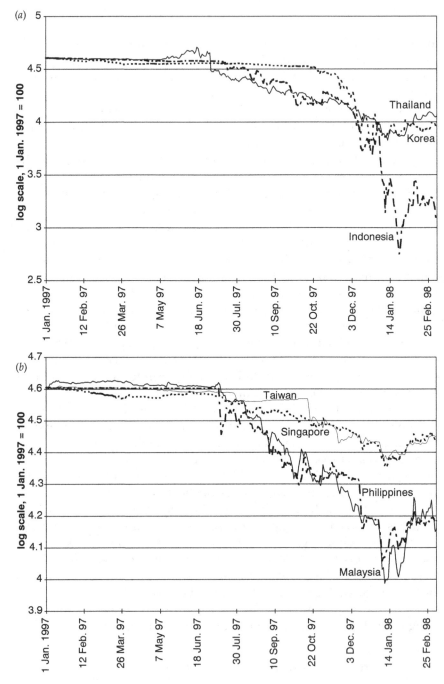

Fig. 2.1. Exchange rate indices, selected east Asian economies, January
1997–February 1998 (log scale), daily
a Thailand, Korea, Indonesia   b Taiwan, Singapore, the
Philippines, Malaysia

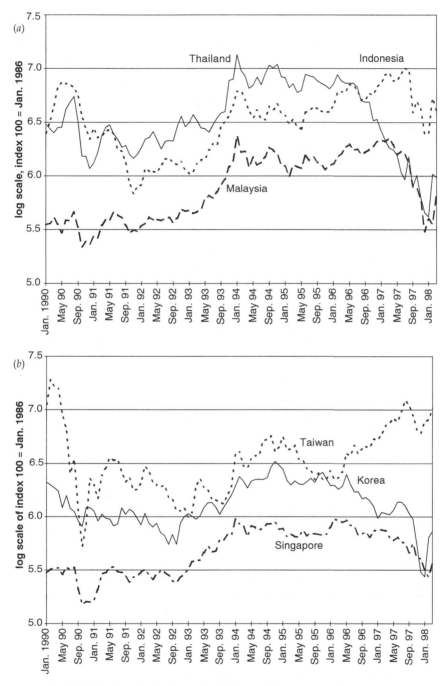

Fig. 2.2. Stock price indices, selected east Asian economies, January 1990–January 1998 (log scale), monthly
a Thailand, Korea, Indonesia   b Taiwan, Singapore, the Philippines, Malaysia

experienced sharp movements in their currencies without it causing a major revision of growth forecasts. Indeed, if the initial price effects of a depreciation can be contained, such that the impact of the currency movement is only a temporary rise in the inflation rate, then the real exchange rate can depreciate and short-term competitiveness be enhanced. The Australian dollar, for example, depreciated by about 40 per cent in the mid-1980s, and this was credited with helping transform Australian manufacturing exports and disciplining domestic economic policy.

The more apt, and now more common, description of what happened is that these countries faced a *financial crisis*. It was not a conventional macroeconomic crisis, in the sense that it was caused by poor fiscal or monetary policies. Table 2.2 sets out some key macroeconomic indicators of the east Asian economies. In general, these countries had strong growth, tight fiscal positions, low and stable inflation rates, high and roughly equal saving and investment rates, and substantial foreign exchange reserves. Indeed, these were precisely the indicators quoted by everyone in support of the argument that growth in east Asian economies was balanced and sustainable. While weakening economic growth and deteriorating net exports in Thailand sparked the market's concern about that country, this was not a major concern for other economies and the general expectation for Thailand was that the baht would only undergo some correction, certainly not lose about half its value.

The explanation lies more in these countries' financial systems in the interaction of rapid financial development, rising and speculative price rises on assets which are used as collateral for lending, inadequate understanding of risk, poor credit allocation and deficient supervision of the financial system. The financial sectors in these countries grew rapidly throughout the second half of the 1980s and first half of the 1990s. The money: GDP ratio (which is a standard indicator of financial development) in Thailand rose from about 50 per cent in 1985 to about 80 per cent in 1995, a period over which the real economy more than doubled. This is not a problem in itself but, at the same time, lending practices were deficient, which meant that the problems caused by bad banking were magnified.

The problems in the banking systems in Indonesia, Korea, Malaysia and Thailand are now well publicised. In the first place, government-directed lending, sometimes with implicit government guarantees, has been prevalent in these countries, including directives or persuasion to lend for government-sponsored large-scale projects. Links between business and financial intermediaries have also been strong in some countries, especially Korea, which, when it leads to extensive related-party lending, concentrates exposure to particular groups and increases risk. These sorts of

Table 2.2. *East Asian macroeconomic fundamentals, 1986–96*

	1986–90	1991–5	1996
Indonesia			
Real GDP growth (per cent)	6.3	7.1	7.8
Saving, investment (per cent GDP)	34, 33	35, 33	34, 33
Inflation (per cent)	7.5	8.9	8.0
Credit growth (per cent)	45	20	23
Foreign exchange reserves (USD)	5,412	11,089	17,820
Fiscal deficit (per cent GDP, − is deficit)	−1.8	0.8	1.2
Korea			
Real GDP growth (per cent)	10.0	7.5	7.1
Saving, investment (per cent GDP)	37, 32	36, 37	35, 38
Inflation (per cent)	5.4	6.2	5.0
Credit growth (per cent)	18	16	−27
Foreign exchange reserves (USD)	9,729	21,322	33,237
Fiscal deficit (per cent GDP, − is deficit)	0.3	−0.2	0.1
Malaysia			
Real GDP growth (per cent)	6.6	8.7	8.6
Saving, investment (per cent GDP)	35, 27	35, 36	40, 42
Inflation (per cent)	1.8	4.3	3.6
Credit growth (per cent)	11	18	27
Foreign exchange reserves (USD)	7,121	20,370	26,156
Fiscal deficit (per cent GDP, − is deficit)	−6.5	−1.0	0.7
Philippines			
Real GDP growth (per cent)	4.7	2.2	5.5
Saving, investment (per cent GDP)	20, 19	15, 22	16, 25
Inflation (per cent)	7.8	10.4	8.4
Credit growth (per cent)	5	33	40
Foreign exchange reserves (USD)	1,154	4,823	9,902
Fiscal deficit (per cent GDP, − is deficit)	−3.2	−0.6	0.3
Singapore			
Real GDP growth (per cent)	8.4	8.5	7.3
Saving, investment (per cent GDP)	42, 36	48, 35	50, 35
Inflation (per cent)	1.3	2.6	1.3
Credit growth (per cent)	7	12	17
Foreign exchange reserves (USD)	18,457	49,579	76,491
Fiscal deficit (per cent GDP, − is deficit)	5.2	13.4	8.4
Taiwan			
Real GDP growth (per cent)	9.1	6.6	5.7
Saving, investment (per cent GDP)	35, 21	28, 24	26, 21
Inflation (per cent)	2.2	3.8	3.1

Table 2.2. (*cont.*)

	1986–90	1991–5	1996
Taiwan (cont.)			
Credit growth (per cent)	19	20	9
Foreign exchange reserves (USD)	68,524	86,210	88,038
Fiscal deficit (per cent GDP, − is deficit)	−2.3	−7.4	−5.4
Thailand			
Real GDP growth (per cent)	10.4	8.4	6.7
Saving, investment (per cent GDP)	32, 33	36, 42	36, 42
Inflation (per cent)	3.9	4.8	5.9
Credit growth (per cent)	17	22	14
Foreign exchange reserves (USD)	7,069	25,145	37,192
Fiscal deficit (per cent GDP, − is deficit)	0.3	2.9	2.3

Source: IMF, *International Financial Statistics*; Central Bank of China (Taipei) *Statistical Bulletin.*

links also induce companies to finance through debt rather than equity, and so make business more vulnerable to movements in interest rates and dependent on the willingness of lenders to roll over funding. The business sectors in Korea and Thailand were both heavily geared, and so more vulnerable to adverse shocks. There was also a focus on developing particular key industries, such as semiconductors and motor vehicles, which led to concentrated – and excess – capacity in these industries.

At the same time, asset prices rose strongly, and this encouraged individuals and firms to borrow and purchase assets in the expectation of making capital gains. Share and property prices grew rapidly through this period. Figure 2.2 shows share prices and figure 2.3 residential and commercial property prices in Singapore. (Data on property prices in the region are patchy and the profile of Singaporean property prices broadly matches those in other east Asian countries.) High double-digit growth in asset prices was a feature of these markets, reflecting the increase in actual and expected wealth in the region and the easier availability of funds. Asset price inflation is not necessarily a cause for concern in itself, but it is a problem when the assets are used as collateral for loans, especially when those loans are used to finance speculation. Asset price rises which are short-lived, but which also underpin the value of collateral for new loans, can undermine the strength and stability of the financial system.

In the case of east Asia, there was a rapid expansion of credit. As shown

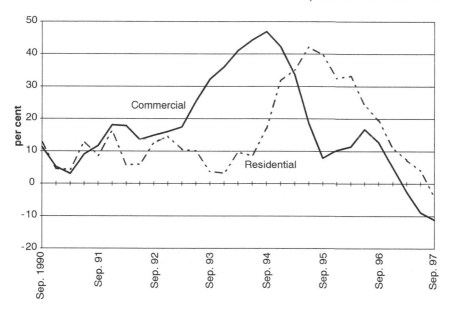

Fig. 2.3. Singapore, property prices, September 1990–September 1997
(annual rate of growth)

in table 2.2, credit growth had reached double digit levels, often over 20 per cent a year for several years, at a time when their nominal economies grew at markedly lower rates. What table 2.2 does not show, however, is that credit growth for property has been considerably faster than average credit growth. Figure 2.4 shows annual credit growth for real-estate and finance-related lending by banks in Thailand and Malaysia over the past decade or so. Property-related lending by banks rose faster than average lending in Malaysia in the early 1990s and in Thailand in the mid-1990s. These rates of growth are remarkable, and imply a rapid expansion of real-estate capacity in these countries, and east Asian economies more generally. Figure 2.5 provides an example of the rapid expansion of capacity in property in Indonesia, with a doubling of the share of investment in real estate and finance (although this does not necessarily 'prove' that this was *excess* capacity, the judgement of most observers is that it was). In this respect, there was overinvestment in non-productive and speculation-prone sectors of the economy, and excessive lending by financial intermediaries to these sectors.

The lack of information about non-performing loans and the lack of credibility in official statistics in most east Asian countries also increased uncertainty. Official estimates of the proportion of non-performing to total

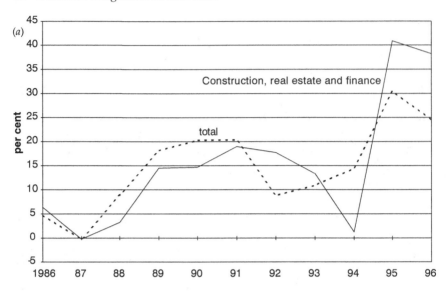

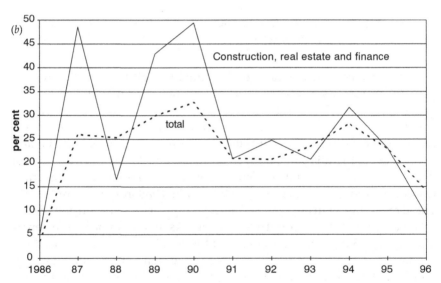

Fig. 2.4.　Thailand and Malaysia, bank credit growth, 1986–1996
a Thailand　b Malaysia

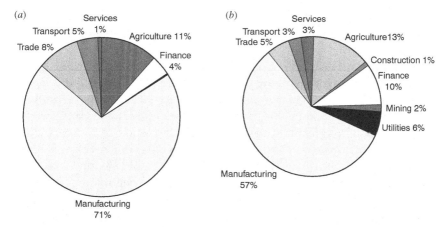

Fig. 2.5. Indonesia, approved investment plans
a 1990–64,029 bn rupiah   b 1996–130,647 bn rupiah

loans, if available, were low single-digit numbers – the Korean Ministry of Finance published data on non-performing loans only at the end of 1997, stating at the time that about 7 per cent of bank loans were non-performing. But the criteria for defining loans as 'non-performing' were less stringent in most east Asian countries than is typically the case elsewhere, and *market* estimates placed non-performing loans in double-digit figures, up to about 20 per cent of banks' loans in several cases.

Moreover, some of the expansion of domestic bank credit and investment was funded by overseas sources. This compounded the problem in two ways. First, most of the borrowing was in foreign currency, largely US dollars. The currencies in a number of these countries (especially Thailand, but also Indonesia) were regarded as relatively 'fixed' by the monetary authorities, and so financial institutions, companies and individuals did not take out forward cover to insure themselves against a depreciation of the local currency. The interest differentials between local and US interest rates were sizeable, and so forward cover would have been expensive – and, by definition, eliminated the gain from borrowing in US dollars. People ignored this because they thought the authorities had 'guaranteed' that the currency pegs would be firm, so that they could reasonably ignore this risk. This foreign currency exposure meant that when the currencies fell, they increased the domestic currency burden of debt, which reduced earnings and the viability of operations. At the extreme, the massive depreciation of the rupiah was said to increase the debt burden to such a degree that it made many firms which had previously been viable and solvent, no longer so. A depreciation – which usually boosts the traded sector and so stimulates the economy – can in fact damage growth when the foreign debt burden is large.

This problem was compounded further when foreign borrowing was made on a short-term revolving basis, as occurred in Korea and Indonesia. Calling in short-term loans would force firms to sell off assets, typically at well under 'true' market value, or declare bankruptcy. It was crucial in this context to obtain agreement to roll over existing short-term loans. As it turned out, this was easier to do in the case of Korea since much of the borrowing from overseas was done through banks, which tended to reduce the number of parties that needed to be called to negotiations for debt refinancing. But in the case of Indonesia, a considerable amount of borrowing had been done directly by the business sector, which is a larger, more disparate group and much harder to organise logistically.

Putting all this together, the events can be seen essentially as a financial crisis. A rapid expansion of credit (especially for real estate and particular manufacturing industries such as semiconductors and motor vehicles), asset price speculation, overcapacity in particular sectors and large, unhedged short-term foreign loan exposures left the financial system weak and an overborrowed business sector exposed. In these circumstances, an adverse shock, especially one which involved currency realignment, would be expected to have a relatively substantial impact on the economy. As markets became aware of these problems, credit risk was assessed to be higher, and portfolios were restructured. In many cases, the fall in the exchange rate increased the credit risk and induced further adverse currency movements.

The actual trigger for the crisis was probably a combination of events. Most proximately, it was the depreciation in the baht, which was induced by the deterioration in exports owing to the weakening of the semiconductor market and general loss of competitiveness from the baht being pegged to the rising US dollar. Less proximately, the causes were low interest rates in Japan (caused, in part, by the failure of the authorities to deal with a weak banking system) and the reversal of the interest rate cycle in US rates in 1994. But even if these were the triggering events, they were not the fundamental causes, since even if they had not happened, the structural imbalances in the financial sector would have caused problems through some other triggering event.

What does it mean?

The fact that the market sold off the currencies of countries in which the perceived risk of lending had increased is not a surprise. Indeed, the exchange rate depreciations have been largest in those countries with the largest perceived risks. What is a surprise, however, is the *extent* of the response, especially the extraordinary fall in exchange rates in Indonesia and lesser but still dramatic falls in Korea, Malaysia and Thailand. Many economists over a long period of time have spoken about the problems of having exchange rates which are too rigid and about the importance of maintaining sound domestic financial systems. But no one predicted the timing or the extent of the market's response. In its outlook for 1997 and 1998, the Asian Development Bank (ADB) forecast stable growth in 1997 and an acceleration of growth in south-east Asia in 1998 (ADB 1997). The IMF's October 1997 *World Economic Outlook* was equally sanguine, but did discuss the need, in general, for some flexibility in exchange rate arrangements and maintaining stable and resilient financial sectors. Clearly, economists have been humbled by the episode.

To the extent that the crisis in east Asia can be explained as a financial crisis, it has a number of implications for financial, macroeconomic and development policies.

Development strategies

East Asian countries have generally regarded export growth as the key to development and economic growth. This is probably fine as a development strategy, but not as a growth strategy for an industrialised economy, as the experience of Japan over the 1980s and 1990s would suggest. Growth in net exports (that is, exports *less* imports) cannot be an engine for *world* growth: industrialising countries need to restructure growth to domestic demand as they move closer to the industrialised countries' frontier.

Exchange rate policy

As part of the policy of encouraging exports, however, a number of east Asian countries tried to manage their exchange rates. They did so in two – sometimes contradictory – ways. On the one hand, they wanted their real exchange rate to be 'low' enough to maintain international trade competitiveness. Accordingly, the authorities in much of south-east Asia sought to minimise the appreciation in their *nominal* exchange rates in the face of very strong capital inflows in the first half of the 1990s to maintain their *real* exchange rate. This strategy does not work in the longer run, since the capital inflow under fixed nominal exchange rates boosts liquidity and tends to increase inflation, which then just appreciates the real exchange rate. The real exchange rate ends up appreciating, but the process is generally slower when it works through higher inflation than through a nominal exchange rate appreciation, since goods and services prices are much more sticky than asset prices. As a country moves from promoting growth through exports to domestic demand, policymakers are less likely to resist a real exchange rate appreciation. Indeed, Korea and Taiwan lessened their resistance to currency fluctuations progressively over the 1990s precisely because they were making this shift. Thailand, however, stands out as a country which was particularly rigid in resisting currency movements.

Policymakers' concerns with losing competitiveness are real but the argument contains a number of fallacies which militate against the position that a real exchange rate appreciation is to be avoided at all cost. In the first place, an appreciation of the real exchange rate reflects the comparative advantage and competitive strength of the home country: it is usually an indication of fundamental strength, not weakness. It is also a relative price change determined by the relative state of macroeconomic fundamentals. Foreign capital is attracted to higher domestic real returns and an appreciation of the real exchange rate is *part* of the equalisation of returns. Naturally enough, home governments want returns to be equalised through a reduction in the marginal product of capital caused by an expansion of the capital stock and national income at a given exchange rate, rather than a simple relative price change which eradicates returns to capital in one fell swoop and leaves the capital stock and national income unchanged. But some change in the real exchange rate is inevitable, as discussed above.

As a relative price, the real exchange rate is part of the allocative mechanism and so the change in the real exchange rate is an indicator to the market of where resources should be directed to ensure the structural change necessary for a balanced economy. The real appreciation makes exports less competitive in a static sense – that is, a real exchange rate appreciation is a one-off adverse relative price movement for exporters. But, in a dynamic sense, the real appreciation is a signal that the economy needs balance. Growth lies in more than just exports but also in services and home goods. Growth is not necessarily impeded by a real appreciation if the marginal returns are higher in non-traded or domestic sectors. Preventing the real exchange rate from appreciating in response to capital inflows is not generally feasible, since full sterilisation of capital inflows is not possible. It is also not desirable in the sense that it impedes structural adjustment and may generate macroeconomic instability in the form of inflation and financial fragility. Moderating the capital flows by some appreciation is also likely to reduce bottlenecks in investment, inflationary pressure and speculative capital inflows. Moreover, balance of payments models of the real exchange rate (Mussa 1984, 1986) predict that it depreciates over time in response to net total capital inflows, and so the appreciation is only temporary. These arguments, which had been made by economists before the crisis, are perhaps even more forceful with the benefit of hindsight.

On the other hand, policymakers in a number of countries also thought it important to fix or peg their currencies to a major currency or basket of currencies, with the US dollar typically playing the key role. This was regarded as important in obtaining anti-inflation credibility (although there are other ways to obtain credibility – for example, by having, and meeting, an inflation target). But it also meant that policy was tied to the fortunes of the US dollar, which itself can fluctuate substantially, and that policymakers could be forced to defend the currency against speculation. This turned out to be part of the problem in the mid-1990s, especially for Thailand which tried to maintain its peg to the US dollar more than any other economy in the region (with the exception of Hong Kong, which explicitly fixes its currency to the US dollar). As the US dollar started to appreciate against other major currencies from mid-1995, the baht and Thai exports lost some of their competitiveness. The sharp fall in semiconductor prices in 1996 also hit the economy, and the Thai current account started to widen. In the normal scheme of things, the baht should have been devalued but the authorities resisted this. When the economic fundamentals and the existing exchange rate are incompatible, and the authorities indicate that they will defend the current rate, speculation is inevitable, and Thailand spent most of its reserves trying to defend an indefensible exchange rate. The lesson is clear: some flexibility in exchange rates is necessary.

Financial system fragility

Many countries – including many in east Asia – have had large depreciations in the past, but these have not generated the almost cataclysmic effects of the depreciations in east Asia in 1997 and 1998. The difference in this case was the fundamentally weak structure of these countries' financial systems. Financial institutions in east Asia were weakened by large non-performing or bad loans, excessive investment in property or non-productive sectors, asset price speculation and extensive uncovered borrowing in foreign currencies, often on a short-term revolving credit basis. Combine this with a corporate sector which has high debt:equity ratios and a rising share of non-productive assets, and the economy is in a poor state to cope with any adverse shock. It just happened in this case that the initial shock was a currency adjustment in Thailand. The obvious implication is that countries must ensure that they have proper and sound financial systems in place before and after opening their economies to capital flows, and this entails changing the systems of preferred, directed and concentrated lending that gave rise to the problems in the first place. It is also a responsibility that lies with both financial institutions and policymakers.

What is unfortunate about this crisis is that some of the financial problems were avoidable since they were known to the authorities and financial institutions involved. In the late 1980s, Australia, Japan, Scandinavia and the United Kingdom experienced major asset price bubbles, financial sector difficulties and excessive corporate indebtedness after financial liberalisation. In Australia, too, in the mid-1980s, there had been problems for people and institutions which had taken out uncovered loans overseas in low-interest currencies when the Australian dollar depreciated substantially. In short, the sorts of financial-sector problems that arose in east Asia were not new, and the painful experience of other countries was not heeded sufficiently by policymakers and financial institutions in the region.

If the experience of other countries is anything to go by, it is fundamentally important that non-performing loan problems be addressed quickly and resolutely if the economy is to recover as soon as possible. Australia and Scandinavia responded quickly to the crisis, giving the market full information, closing some institutions and parcelling off the bad loans into a separate institution. As a result, the financial sector and real economy recovered. Contrast this to Japan, where policymakers and institutions tried to hide the problem and hope the economy would grow out of it. This failed, and since the banks' capital base was eroded they could not obtain capital to support new assets and confidence in the system was weak. In turn, this engendered a supply-side credit crunch on the economy.

The current account

There has also been some discussion of the role of the current account in the crisis but it is difficult to identify this as a key factor, with the possible exception of Thailand. More generally, the current account deficit embodies countries' intertemporal preferences, and the transfer of resources is not a matter of concern if the transfer is to repay borrowings or if the country already has (or expects to have) the resources to repay them. Basic economic theory indicates that what matters is whether the country has the ability to *service the debt over time*. Debt is sustainable as long as the country does not, over the long haul, just add the interest to its debt principal. In this regard – and contrary to popular wisdom – theory indicates that using capital inflows to finance current consumption is not necessarily 'bad' policy. If a country has low income this period but high income in later periods, for example, it is optimal for it to borrow now to finance consumption; it repays the debt in later periods when income is high. This is analogous to the life-cycle behaviour of households: when they are young, people borrow to buy a house, which is a form of consumption, and repay the loan as they get older. Obviously, this is good policy only when the prospects for future income are good. There is also a stream of theory which points to the possibility of excessive consumption and investment, or equivalently overborrowing, in the period just after liberalisation. This is more likely to occur when the cost of borrowing increases as debt rises, or when structural reforms are not credible.

So much for basic theory – what about practicalities? The empirical evidence suggests that theory is basically right. In general, running a current account deficit is *not* a signal that policy is unsustainable or that the country is likely to suffer a financial crisis. Sachs, Tornell and Velasco (1996), for example, found that current accounts did not help predict whether a country would also experience a currency shock after the Mexican crisis in 1994. Indeed, some countries which now have large current account surpluses once had large current account deficits. Singapore, for example, ran substantial current account deficits, up to 30 per cent of GDP, in the 1970s! Big current account-surplus countries, such as Japan and Germany, have also had big current account deficits at some stage in the post-war period.

That said, however, there is a fair degree of uncertainty in the real world, and lenders are entitled to be wary of countries which claim to have a large, but as of yet unproven, earnings potential. Country credibility matters. Accordingly, a current account deficit is more likely to appear sustainable when capital inflow is used for well directed, productive purposes than for unspecified projects or current consumption. This restriction is likely to be tighter, the less stable and more corrupt the political environment, and the smaller and narrower the country's resource endowments. In this case, high savings rates are likely to be a good indicator that borrowing is sustainable, given that the domestic financial system is stable. In fact, the countries that ran large current account deficits in the past usually did so because they were building up productive capacity to increase future output and income.

This carries an important implication for how policymakers and markets assess the financial crisis in east Asia: the crisis was not essentially a problem of large current account deficits. It would be a mistake for policymakers or markets to now say that countries should always have relatively small current account deficits. What matters is not the size of a deficit, but what the deficit is used for, and what it reflects about the structure of the economy: there is no 'right' number for a deficit that can be applied as a rule across all countries.

Market dynamics

The discussion above has concentrated on the perceived macroeconomic fundamentals lying behind the east Asian financial crisis. But the fact that economic and regional specialists have been so surprised by the extent of the asset and currency price movements is important information in itself. In the first place, economists now know that they know so little: we really have to exhibit more humility in our prognostications. Moreover, it may be that economists were simply wrong about the scale of the effects of shocks when financial structure is vulnerable. Economists do, after all, lack reliable models for predicting the timing and extent of currency and financial crises.

But, more fundamentally, the extent of the currency depreciations (especially in Indonesia) and the changeable – and sometimes inconsistent – market sentiment suggest that there may be problems in the market mechanism. For example, it is very difficult to explain how the rupiah, which before the crisis people were saying was largely at fair value (or, if overvalued, then by 10 per cent at most, Grenville 1998), could lose three-quarters of its value within a matter of weeks and then still be properly valued. The argument that the rupiah was especially susceptible because Indonesia is not a democracy does not ring true since the argument that Indonesia is not a democracy was used before the crisis to justify why Indonesia would be less affected than Thailand or Korea. Although there were concerns about the transition of the political leadership in Indonesia, the argument that the currency movement was bigger there because there were greater prospects for political and social instability is relatively circuitous since the prospects for turmoil were greater only because the currency fall was so large.

This particular outcome poses a challenge. It may be, for example, that the theory that economists have been using is inadequate. Most people tend to think that there is order to the world: if the economy experiences a shock, then there are corrective forces and a structure which bring the economy back to equilibrium on the same path. But this may not always be the case. There may be multiple equilibria, some of which are vastly worse than others, with even small shocks capable of sending the economy over the edge. The interaction of uncovered and short-term foreign borrowing, currency depreciation and negative sentiment, for example, may have been enough to shift an economy like Indonesia from being on a high-growth path to being on a low-growth one (only time will tell how permanent is the effect of the financial shock). The trigger here is a set of imbalances in the financial sector. The financial system is more important to the well-being of the economy than previously thought; if the possibilities of undesirable equilibria exist, then policymakers and institutions need to be well attuned to imbalances and ensure that the domestic financial system is structurally healthy before opening it up to international forces. We cannot be so blasé about the sequence of reform.

But also certainly part of what happened was that markets overreacted and overshot to an unexpected degree. Volatility is a feature of most asset markets, with even the currencies of the biggest economies fluctuating by up to 30 per cent over a year or two. One problem in east Asia, though, was the thinness of the market and the tendency for small foreign exchange transactions to move the market by disproportionately large amounts. The collapse of capital inflows was, in some sense, like a bank run, in which the psychology and panic of the group can affect decisionmaking and even objectively strong and solvent institutions can be affected.

If markets do not function in these circumstances, and if protracted downward movements have the potential to undo the fabric of an economy, then sticking by the pure market mechanism all the time hardly seems appropriate. It may be better to intervene in these circumstances or affect the flow of transactions in other ways, such as through the temporary imposition of capital controls. On occasions like this, the dangers are simply too big to ignore, and it may be reckless to leave the solution to the market when the market is not functioning.

As will be argued in the next section, the bulk of the evidence indicates that financial liberalisation is a necessary condition for full economic development, and that certainly there are substantial long-run benefits. But recent events have shown that if this process is not well managed in the transition path, events can arise which cause huge economic and social damage, and policymakers need to have the resources and wherewithal to deal with them. Management of the market's overreactions may include interventions in markets or the temporary imposition of capital controls. The difficulty is whether the movement in markets is really an overreaction or just a reaction that policymakers do not like, and this can be decided only on a case-by-case basis.

Despite the severity of recent events, it is still probably not desirable or possible to permanently reverse the process of financial liberalisation. Governments, of course, have the power to do this; but it is probably not easy to turn back the clock now without major disruption, because advances in technology and communications have made it so much easier to avoid regulations than before. Not only is financial capital fungible and mobile, so also is physical capital: factories in one country can be shifted to another much more easily – the sensitivity of physical capital in Japan to exchange rate movements during the early 1990s is a good example of this. The empirical evidence suggests that when the authorities impose capital controls in the face of deteriorating or misaligned economic fundamentals – such as in Malaysia in 1986 and Spain, Portugal and Ireland in 1992–3 – they are ultimately unsuccessful. But this does not appear to be the case when temporary controls are imposed to slow down 'hot money' – as in Chile in the early 1990s and Malaysia in early 1994.

Moreover, a reversion to *systematic* controls would not seem to be viable, because there is substantial evidence that capital controls were not generally effective in the first place since they created strong incentives to evade them. Evasion is fairly straightforward and can be achieved by misinvoicing trade payments, by internal transfers of funds by multinational companies, by corruption and fraud and by the creation of black markets (Mathieson and Rojas-Suarez 1993; Johnston and Ryan 1994). Moreover, when there is an expectation of a depreciation, capital flows are difficult to stop and they sometimes undermine confidence in the system and controls in this case can give rise to capital flight. Controls also tend to be inequitable since they are more likely to affect the poor than the rich because the rich generally have better access to avoidance mechanisms – through corruption, knowing the 'right people' and the right techniques, or otherwise.

A further upshot of the events in east Asian financial markets is that policymakers need to be flexible and lateral in their thinking, especially in not being too tied to the stock of thinking and practice in their own country. The way central banks think can matter to the outcome, because it conditions the way they respond under pressure. In hindsight, central banks were too wedded to their existing practice; in Thailand, fixed or pegged exchange rates were regarded almost as an article of faith, such that the authorities thought they had to defend the currency, which they did until their foreign exchange reserves were all but gone. By resisting some initial depreciation, they might have made the eventual depreciation after the float worse, although this is speculative since the counterfactual is unknowable. In Indonesia, by way of contrast, the authorities were proud that they had maintained an open capital account, and they did not impose short-term capital controls or even close the market when movements were extreme. They did not intervene in the market to buy rupiah when trades were going the other way, with small transactions having a substantial impact on the market rate. But by resisting the depreciation at some points, they may have provided some depth to the market and reduced the fall in the rupiah. The response was different again in Korea. There, the authorities had progressively widened the trading band for the won over the 1990s, and reacted to selling pressure by widening, but not abolishing, the fluctuation bands. At one stage, the market was closing just seconds after it had opened, which caused people to panic and unload won for dollars while they could, just in case. While the counterfactual is unknowable, it is arguable that this pushed the won down further than it otherwise would have gone: policymakers need to be flexible enough not to be prisoners of their ideology or practice.

A longer-term assessment of the benefits of financial integration

It is worthwhile standing back from what happened in financial markets in east Asia over 1997 and 1998 to consider the costs and benefits of financial reform from a longer-term perspective. These events highlight the importance of managing the transition to financial openness, but they do not necessarily negate the longer-run advantages of reform. In the literature, there are two basic arguments against financial openness.

Costs of financial liberalisation

The first focuses on the possible costs. If something goes wrong in the process of liberalisation, this may affect the long-run outcome if shocks to the adjustment path have permanent effects (that is, if there is hysteresis). Even if this is not the case, the effects of liberalisation may fall unfairly on some members of society. Consider the effect of the financial shock in Mexico in 1994. While the economy contracted sharply straight after the financial crisis, output recovered quickly but real wages did not. Figure 2.6 plots IMF data on consumer prices and wages from 1990, which shows that the purchasing power of wages has fallen by about 20 per cent since the crisis: ordinary people bear the cost.

Moreover, markets may be more volatile after liberalisation. Edey and Hviding (1995) found that while financial markets in the OECD were stable after deregulation, in the sense that trend volatility in financial markets did not increase, there have been episodes of greater volatility in

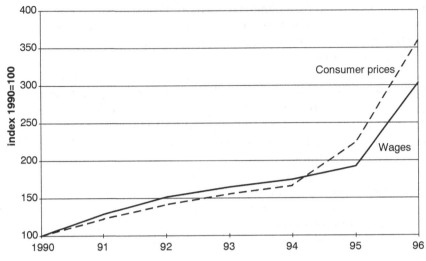

Fig. 2.6. Mexico, consumer prices and wages, 1990–1996

both developed markets (as in stock markets in October 1987), and in small or relatively new markets (as in the junk bond market in 1989, the Mexican financial markets in 1994–5 and the financial crisis in east Asia over 1997 and 1998). Moreover, there have been severe crises in banking and non-banking financial systems, notably in Australia, Japan, Scandinavia, the United Kingdom and the United States. It is not uncommon to read that liberalisation should be deferred because of the possibility of speculative bubbles or financial fragility (Kim 1994; Park 1994). Capital flows can be large and volatile, which may induce unnecessary fluctuations in financial prices – and, accordingly, output and general prices.

It has been well documented that financial markets can be too focused on the short term, be excessively sensitive to new information, or get caught up in fads that drive financial prices away from the economic 'fundamentals' which are thought to lie behind them.[1] Markets also sometimes follow trading rules that are not aligned to macroeconomic fundamentals,

[1] For example, Gruen and Kortian (1996) provide evidence that the foreign exchange market prices near-term expected changes in the terms of trade into the Australian dollar, but not medium and long-term changes. Isard (1995) concludes that covered interest parity is less likely to hold on long-dated instruments than on short-dated ones. Davidson, Okunev and Tippett (1996) present evidence that the US and UK stock markets overdiscount longer-term corporate earnings, arguing that this may be due to excessive focus on the short term. Cutler, Poterba and Summers (1990a, 1990b) find significant short-term positive autocorrelation in excess returns on a range of financial assets, which they interpret as evidence of feedback trading, such as charting, and short-term inefficiencies.

such as charting, technical analysis, programme trading, stop-loss orders and dynamic hedging techniques (Argy 1996).

The response to this argument is that crises in the quality of bank assets have also occurred in repressed east Asian markets, and they often tend to occur as a result of the incentives for corruption and lax management that are generated by repression itself (Haggard, Lee and Maxfield 1993). The crises that have occurred in open economies have generally been associated with lax management and poor internal control and review mechanisms within the banks themselves and with inadequate monitoring and regulation by bank supervisors. The inference to be drawn, then, is that it is necessary to strengthen prudential policy and bank management and to establish the institutions, resources and communication links between countries to deal with financial crises as they arise in order to secure the gains from liberalisation; it is not an excuse for retaining the status quo. The policy literature on financial liberalisation through the years has repeatedly emphasised that a healthy stable banking system is a necessary precondition for effective international financial liberalisation (Caprio, Atiyas and Hanson 1994). But if flows are judged to be excessively volatile or destabilising – and this is *not* an easy call – then what is the appropriate response? Are there ways to modify capital flows in order to temper their perceived destabilising effects?

On the international policy level, some commentators recommend a broad-sweeping tax on international financial transactions to slow the adjustment speed of international capital, thereby increasing monetary autonomy and reducing destabilising capital flows (Tobin 1978). There are a number of problems with this proposal, most especially that slowing capital flows may interfere with 'proper' private commercial decisions, that transactions taxes do not affect volatility in a range of financial markets, and that such a tax must be enforced by most, if not all, countries if it is to be effective (Dooley 1996). Whatever the case, the Tobin tax is not a policy choice for *individual* countries.

On the national level, policymakers face a number of choices. At the most elementary, one of the best ways to insure against sharp, volatile capital movements is to maintain 'good' macroeconomic fundamentals, which implies sustainable, well-focused fiscal, monetary and financial-system policies. While volatile capital flows and currency crises are usually associated with a marked deterioration in the macroeconomy or major political uncertainty, this is not the whole story. Volatile capital flows, for example, may be generated by speculation against a fixed exchange rate. If a devaluation of the currency is expected, say, speculators will sell the currency in anticipation of capital gains after the devaluation. Foreign

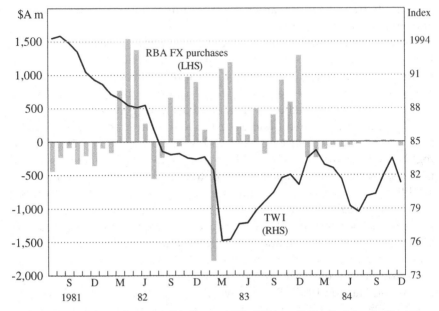

Fig. 2.7. Australia, capital inflows, 1981–1984, and the decision to float the
Australian dollar

exchange reserves fall, and the central bank is forced to devalue. The speculators then buy the home currency, gaining a profit because the foreign
exchange buys them more domestic currency than they had initially to sell
to obtain the foreign currency. Under a fixed exchange rate system, the
speculators make these gains at the expense of the central bank – and ultimately, therefore, taxpayers. One response to capital flows of this nature is
simply to float the exchange rate, as Australia did in December 1983 and
New Zealand in March 1985. In this case, speculators speculate against
themselves, not the central bank. As shown in figure 2.7, substantial capital
outflows in February 1983 induced a 10 per cent devaluation of the
Australian dollar; capital inflows and pressures for a revaluation arose at
the end of that year, and the authorities chose to float the currency. The UK
experience in 1994 was similar.

Policymakers also have the choice of imposing controls, and on short-
term, 'hot' capital in particular. Chile, Malaysia and Taiwan are examples
of economies which have done this in the 1990s. The Malaysian experience
is described in relative detail in chapter 4. The short-term restrictions
imposed in 1994 were judged to have been successful in controlling capital
inflow and an appreciation of the ringgit. Moreover, the event had no

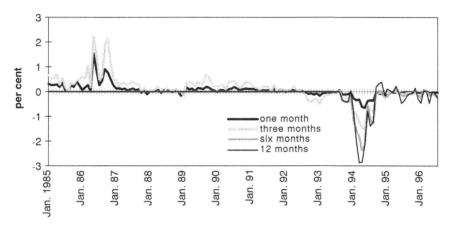

Fig. 2.8. Malaysia, covered interest differentials, January 1985–January 1986

lasting effect on the perceived political risk of investing in Malaysia. For example, covered interest differentials, which are a measure of capital controls and political risk, returned to about zero after the episode, as shown in figure 2.8.[2] This highlights the point that temporary controls can achieve their purpose.

Controls on short-term capital flows, however, may not always be the best response:

- Closing or controlling markets is probably not *effective* over longer periods of time, since financial instruments are highly fungible and markets are able to avoid controls when they have a sufficiently strong incentive to do so. Controls on financial markets tend to be effective only in the short term, since markets can avoid them by creating substitutes or using avoidance mechanisms.
- Controls are unlikely to work when they are inconsistent with economic fundamentals. Malaysia is a case in point. Short-term controls on capital inflow were put in place in 1994 in response to a rush of hot money. The inflow was subdued and the controls removed soon after: the controls were judged successful. Contrast this with the events of 1986, when controls were put in place against continued outflows in the face of speculation of ringgit devaluation. The devaluation was not

[2] The covered interest differential (cid) is calculated as $cid_t = i_t^* + f_{t,t+k} - i_t$, where i is the interest rate on a k-period security, an asterisk denotes a foreign variable, and f is the forward discount.

prevented since it reflected a necessary relative price adjustment in response to a deterioration in the national and trade accounts because of a weakening in Malaysia's terms of trade. The controls only delayed adjustment – and, more generally, delay may be costly if it exacerbates an underlying structural problem.

- If controls are effective, they may inadvertently prevent 'legitimate' transactions and so reduce economic efficiency. This cost, however, should be compared to the possible gains made by reducing destabilisation associated with 'hot money'.
- Even if controls are effective in the short run, their continued use may undermine confidence in economic management. Such a break in confidence is likely to be discontinuous, in the sense that imposing controls may not disturb investor confidence for a while – but, at some point in time, it may lead to a reversal of sentiment that is difficult to correct.
- The events which are described as a 'market failure' may, in fact, not be the failure of markets but of policy itself; the market may simply have been doing its job. This view is obviously controversial, but two events can be interpreted in this light. Consider, first, the events in Europe in 1992. German reunification was tantamount to a major negative supply shock and positive demand shock for Germany. The only way to contain the sharp increase in demand for capital and incipient inflation was to raise local interest rates and revalue the German mark. But revaluation was not possible within the framework of fixed exchange rates in the European Monetary System (EMS), and so all countries in the system were bound to undergo rising interest rates at a time when demand in *their* economies was weak. For some countries (such as the United Kingdom, Italy and Spain) this was not a credible policy and savers acted accordingly by restructuring their investment portfolios.

Consider, also, the Mexican crisis of 1994. This occurred against a backdrop of rapid accumulation of short-term US dollar-denominated liabilities, without a build-up of foreign exchange reserves, but with a marked deterioration in Mexico's fiscal position and increased political uncertainty (IMF 1995: 90–7). Masson and Agenor (1996) argue, moreover, that the devaluation itself revealed new information that the government's commitment to inflation and exchange rate stability had weakened. In both cases, one interpretation is that markets acted to protect the financial interests of savers many of whom are 'ordinary' people. If events like this occur because of inconsistent or non-credible policies, it may be better to change policy, rather than try and suppress the market.

Whether or not market responses are a signal of fundamental inconsistency in macroeconomic structure or policy is usually going to be a hard call. It is especially complicated since, at times, policymakers do think that markets are interpreting events incorrectly. There can be a dynamic tension between market and official views of events, and either side is not always right or wrong. The more credible and respected is the central bank within the financial sector, the more likely it is to be able to stand apart from and lead the financial markets. This is particularly so when financial markets are unsure about future directions or turning points in the business cycle. In these instances, markets rely more heavily on central bank economic analysis. But there is a need for analysis within the central bank to understand – but not be a slave to – the analysis of the financial markets.

The size of the benefits from financial liberalisation

The second argument against financial liberalisation is that the overall gains may be small. Barro, Mankiw and Sala-i-Martin (1995), for example, constructed a neo-classical growth model to assess the convergence of *per capita* output across countries. They argued that while convergence is faster for open than for closed economies, greater capital mobility is unlikely to substantially hasten convergence when the share of human capital is high (as expected) since only real capital can be used as collateral and so financed using external funds.

At face value, the Barro, Mankiw and Sala-i-Martin model implies that in the early stages of development, policies which favour real capital accumulation may be necessary. But at later stages, once productive capital is in place and access to foreign markets secured, policies which impede the access of households to financial markets are likely to retard the accumulation of human capital, since this also depends on obtaining funds to finance better education, better housing and higher living standards. In this sense, real gains are expected to flow from financial liberalisation even during the process of development.

Moreover, it does not necessarily follow, as Barro, Mankiw and Sala-i-Martin's (1995) model would have one believe, that human capital is not financed externally: human capital accumulation may be funded through the domestic banking system which has access to foreign funds; considerable human capital accumulation is provided by state education and training which may be funded externally since the government is a sovereign borrower; and, finally, considerable human capital accumulation is provided as an externality to direct foreign investment.

Krugman (1992) has also entered the debate on the size of the gains from financial liberalisation. He presented some unpleasant neo-classical arithmetic to support the argument that the contribution to growth from capital is small and that the contribution from imported capital is even smaller. Assuming that it takes 3 dollars of capital to produce 1 dollar of output, a current account deficit of 5 per cent of GDP which is used to fund the capital stock would increase capital only by 1.67 per cent and output by about half a per cent a year. Krugman added that this is not negligible but it suggests that it is not a major source of growth. Moreover, he argued that developing regions are generally unable to attract substantial external finance – as occurred, for example, in the period before the First World War when capital was highly mobile but flowed only from Europe to North America, Australasia and Argentina. Even in the early 1980s when petro-dollars were being recycled to developing countries, net inflows were limited to about 3 per cent of GNP. In short, capital does not generally flow from developed to developing country but *between* developed countries. So why bother to liberalise if it does so little?

Krugman's analysis is inadequate in that it is a simple extrapolation of the past to the future. The trade and investment relationship between the developed and developing countries of east Asia is more akin to the Europe–North American/Australasian relationship of the pre-First World War period than the European/North American–South American relationship of the 1980s. The recent development of east Asia is related to the sharp rise in Japanese FDI in the region, spurred by favourable relative prices, macroeconomic stability, geographic proximity and some cultural affinity. This is not standard North–South development.

Moreover, as shown in chapter 3, private net capital flows to the region were relatively high in the mid-1990s and are higher than current account positions would indicate. In fact, net capital inflows have been at double-digit levels for some countries, which implies a stimulus to output of up to 2 per cent a year for these countries in terms of Krugman's back-of-the-envelope arithmetic. This is *not* insignificant. Cohen (1994: 222–6) has also presented evidence that foreign capital increased investment and output in developing countries, particularly those with medium rather than low income levels, in the 1970s but less so in the 1980s. He estimated, for example, that foreign finance contributed 1.25 percentage points of the 2.54 per cent average growth of middle-income debtor countries in the 1970s.

The benefits of financial reform

In one sense, the issue of whether financial reform is beneficial is strange since all developed economies now have open capital accounts and liberalised domestic financial systems, and policymakers in these countries view this as necessary to supporting and maintaining economic growth. In their study on the effects of financial liberalisation on OECD economies, for example, Edey and Hviding (1995) argue that liberalisation provided three distinct benefits. In the first place, it improved internal efficiency in banking firms, as shown by declining operating costs and some fall in interest margins. It also improved allocative efficiency, in the sense that it removed distortions in relative funding costs and provided greater opportunities for international portfolio diversification. Finally, it reduced liquidity constraints and so enabled households to better smooth consumption over time. The consumption insurance literature predicts that people are unambiguously better off when they have access to financial markets since they are able to smooth consumption over their lives by borrowing and lending. In comparative static analysis, financial liberalisation is always better than financial repression. Financial repression affects the distribution of wealth, preferring borrowers over savers and those with assets over those without. It also delivers power to the bureaucracy which may be driven its own sectional interests, rather than the 'national interest' (Patrick 1994: 366).

To put some flesh on this, consider how the effects outlined by Edey and Hviding (1995) have emerged in Australia:

- Competition in the banking sector, especially for commercial wholesale finance and, more recently, housing finance, has substantially increased. As a result, average margins in banking have declined moderately, as shown in figure 2.9. Operating expenses have also fallen from about 4 per cent of assets in 1980 to around 3 per cent. The decline in interest margins on personal loans, however, occurred only in 1996, as loan securitisation became more popular. Competition has had an effect, even though it has been slower to make an impact than expected.
- Liberalisation has also increased allocative efficiency, in the sense that savers and investors have more choice. Figure 2.10 shows how the institutional structure of the financial system has changed with deregulation. The bank sector, which was declining under regulation, has expanded, particularly through the entry of new banks. New sectors, especially those involved with long-term saving, have grown substantially. This suggests that risk diversification has improved.
- Liberalisation has had a big impact on the ability of firms and households to smooth investment and consumption. For example, there is strong evidence that households are now more able to maintain consumption when there are temporary changes in their current

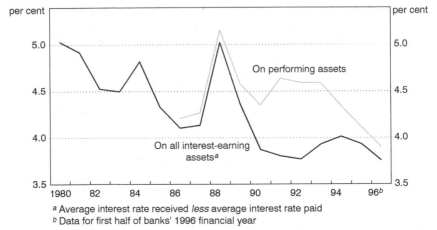

a Average interest rate received *less* average interest rate paid
b Data for first half of banks' 1996 financial year

Fig. 2.9. Australia, average interest margins, 1980–1996[a]

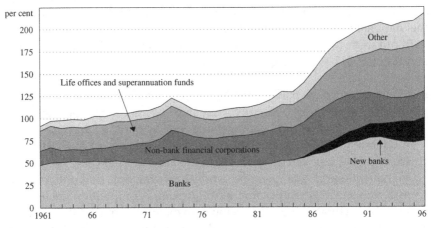

Fig. 2.10. Australia, structure of the financial system, 1961–1996

income (Debelle and Preston 1995; de Brouwer 1996). The effect of financial liberalisation on investment and consumption smoothing is evident in how the current account and composition of capital flows have altered over time. As shown in figure 2.11, the current account deficit increased in the early 1980s, and the nature of capital flows shifted markedly from direct investment to more 'general-purpose' portfolio investment.

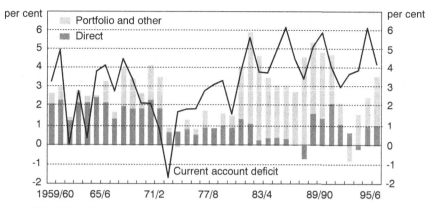

Fig. 2.11. Australia, current account and composition of capital inflows, 1959/60 to 1995/6 (per cent of GDP)

The evidence for favourable microeconomic effects from financial liberalisation in east Asia is relatively clear and strong. Repression distorts the allocation of credit, with the risk that funds go to those with connections rather than to the most efficient projects (Haggard, Lee and Maxfield 1993). Micro-evidence for Indonesia (Harris, Schiantarelli and Siregar 1994) and Korea (Cho 1988) indicates that while the cost of funds was typically higher after reform, the funds were better spread between firms and that this improved efficiency. Because deposits are regarded as public property in Taiwan, bankers in Taiwan face criminal liability in the event of bad loans and are, as a result, highly risk averse (Cheng 1993). Fry (1995) reported an unpublished paper by Chou (1991) which concluded that the forced risk aversion of Taiwanese banks is inefficient in the sense that banks lend on the basis of safety factors rather than performance. Fry (1995) also reported subsequent papers which show that banks in Taiwan lent excessively to large firms and state-owned firms with lower rates of return. Shea (1994) was unable to find evidence that banks in Taiwan made loans based on the productivity of the borrower. Financial repression in east Asian economies often tends to be accompanied by poor supervision of the banking system and poor management (Haggard, Lee and Maxfield 1993), and government-directed lending programmes have at times led to the deterioration of bank assets, as occurred with forced lending to heavy industry in Korea in the late 1970s and early 1980s (Choi 1993).

More generally, Fry (1995) has argued that it is generally harder to find macroeconomic effects of financial liberalisation. The early literature postulated that financial repression suppressed real interest rates and saving and predicted that liberalisation would boost saving and investment, but this effect was not evident, and sometimes saving actually fell after liberalisation (Edey and Hviding 1995), presumably because households reduced saving and increased borrowing (World Bank 1993: 17, 238–41; Park 1994: 142–4). While the savings rate may have been unchanged or even fallen, there is evidence that financial repression reduces the rate of growth (Roubini and Sala-i-Martin 1992; King and Levine 1993a, 1993b) and so the *level* of saving may not have declined even if the rate of saving did.[3] Liberalisation will also have no effect on saving if the rates under mildly repressed regimes mimic liberalised rates (World Bank 1993: 237–47) or if the formation of cartels or uncompetitive behaviour follows liberalisation, as occurred in the Philippines in the early 1980s (Hutchcroft 1993).

More recently, economists in the new growth school have provided evidence that financial openness adds to growth in other ways. King and Levine (1993a, 1993b) argued, for example, that financial development generates dynamic efficiency through improved information-gathering, evaluating innovators and pooling resources.[4] The pessimism in the standard neo-classical view has also been criticised on the ground that foreign capital is not a simple substitute for domestic capital since it brings with it large externalities in the form of technology transfer (Baldwin 1992), enhanced competition and macroeconomic structural adjustment associated with the implementation of financial reform (Branson 1992), and the need for developing countries to maintain open and stable macroeconomies in order to remain viable and competitive destinations for FDI (de Brouwer 1995). There is also a view that financial openness supports growth since it imposes a discipline on policymakers to follow 'sound' macroeconomic policies (Hanson 1994). Barro (1996), for example, reports that policies which promote education, the rule of law, low inflation and 'disciplined' government spending are positively correlated with economic growth, and these are the sorts of policies to which markets react favourably.

While King and Levine (1993a, 1993b) provided evidence that countries

---

[3] Park (1994) argues that the rise in saving rates in Korea in the 1980s was coincident with liberalisation but not caused by it. He argues instead that saving increased because the high rate of income growth (10 per cent a year) was unexpected and viewed as transitory, and that the rise in real interest rates, caused by lower than expected inflation combined with a posted rate system, was merely coincidental.

[4] Krugman (1992) argues that endogenous growth theory is inconsistent with capital mobility in that the sluggishness in the decline of returns to scale generated by special growth factors means that capital-rich countries would not have an incentive to export capital to capital-poor ones. This may be true to some extent but it is an exaggeration to say that the marginal efficiency of capital is the same in both cases.

with developed and efficient financial systems outperformed others, Park (1992, 1994) was unable to find real effects, notably on productivity and GDP, of financial liberalisation in Korea and Taiwan. Cohen (1994), on the other hand, found evidence that foreign finance aided the formation of human capital and stimulated growth in developing countries. Andersen (1993) reviewed the performance of Indonesia, Korea, the Philippines and Taiwan and argued that developed stable financial markets are helpful but not essential to growth in the early stages of development but crucial in later stages. Consistent with this, Kirakul, Jantarangs and Chantanahom (1993) reported Granger-causality tests for Thailand which favour the view that real economic development precedes and induces financial deepening in earlier stages of development but that feedback between the real economy and financial depth emerges in later stages of development. Gruen (1994) was unable to identify effects on Australian output from the substantial rise in capital flows since 1983. Gertler and Rose (1994) report that for a wide panel of developing countries, there is a robust positive relationship between output and financial depth (measured by money or credit: GDP). The relationship holds only in levels and not in first differences, which they interpret as indicating that the relationship is deep or structural; output and financial depth are correlated, but they do not address the causation between the two. Jung (1986) in fact found that Granger-causality tests ran both ways, although more often from output to finance. Patrick (1994) argued that even if financial deepening is accommodative rather than causal, financial development is still essential to achieving high growth.

While there is evidence that financial development and openness support growth, it is not surprising that this is less clear than the microeconomic effects. Consider, for example, Japan's recent economic history. Throughout the high-growth period of the 1950s and 1960s, Japan had a tightly regulated and closed financial system. Growth slowed down a notch after a series of unfavourable supply shocks, embodied in the oil price shocks of 1973 and 1979 and the yen appreciations of the mid-1980s and mid-1990s, and as Japan reached the technological frontier. These slowdowns also occurred as the financial system was being liberalised: growth and liberalisation are negatively correlated, even if no one believes that the fall in Japan's potential growth rate is due to financial liberalisation. In this framework, it is difficult to identify a clear positive relationship between growth and open, stable financial markets.

3

Measures of financial integration in east Asia

The enduring popular representation of financial market integration is the equalisation of the rates of return on similar financial assets. This has considerable intuitive appeal: as markets become more open and unified, differences in rates of return should reflect only fundamental factors such as differences in asset quality, risk and the like. But there are in fact a multiplicity of methods to measure the financial openness of an economy, ranging from simply looking at the various legal restrictions that operate on international finance in a country to using predictions of economic theory to infer the degree of financial integration.

This chapter reviews a number of measures of financial integration as they have been applied to selected east Asian economies. There are a number of standard, well established tests and analyses which provide a benchmark for assessing the degree of integration of markets (Obstfeld 1986a, 1994; Montiel 1993; Goldstein and Mussa 1993). Generally, these examine legal restrictions on the capital account, changes in capital flows, interest rate parity conditions, saving–investment correlations, inter-country consumption correlations and a range of other tests which seek to identify changes in real variables or structural economic relationships which are explicable in terms of financial integration.

Legal restrictions on the capital account

Emery (1991) and Cole, Scott and Wellons (1995a, 1995b) provide some information on the structure of money and foreign exchange markets in east Asia. The development of money markets in the countries examined in this chapter has sometimes been restricted, and the principal market is often the interbank market. This section focuses on the recent history of controls in exchange markets, drawing heavily on IMF (1997b). While most countries now have relatively open capital accounts, this is only recent for Korea, the Philippines, Taiwan and Thailand and, to varying degrees, controls still remain (or have been temporarily re-instituted) in these coun-

Table 3.1. *Summary of current and capital account liberalisation, 1980, 1990 and 1996*

	Current account restrictions			Capital account restrictions			Surrender export receipts		
	1980	1990	1996	1980	1990	1996	1980	1990	1996
Australia (*o*)	—	—	—	•			•		
Hong Kong (*o*)	—	—	—	—	—	—	—	—	—
Indonesia (*o*)	—	—	—	—	—	—	•	—	—
Japan (*o*)	—	—	—	•	—	—	—	—	—
Korea (*r*)	—	—	—	•	•	•	•	•	•
Malaysia (*o*)	—	—	—	—	—	—	•	•	•
Philippines (*r*)	•	•	—	•	•	•	•	•	—
Singapore (*o*)	—	—	—	—	—	—	—	—	—
Taiwan (*r*)	•	—	—	•	•	•	•	•	•
Thailand (*r*)	—	—	—	•	•	•	•	•	•

Notes:
 o = open capital account; *r* = restrictions on capital account.
 • = application of restrictions.
 — = not available.
Source: IMF, *Annual Report on Exchange Arrangements and Exchange Restrictions* (various years).

tries. The development of controls on payments in the current account, capital account and exchange proceeds for countries in the region is summarised in table 3.1.[1] In the first column, (*o*) and (*r*) indicate, respectively, that the capital account is relatively open (*o*) or restricted (*r*) based on the existence of legal restrictions.

Liberalisation has generally been pursued at times of macroeconomic stability in order to minimise possible destabilisation. The catalysts for reform have been recognition of the potential gains to national development from a more sophisticated and open financial system, the need to remain competitive as a location for foreign direct investment and a response to changes in world trading rules – indicated, for example, by the focus on trade and investment in services in the Uruguay Round (Wibulswasdi and Tanvanich 1992). Australia, Hong Kong, Indonesia, Japan and Singapore comprise the set of countries in this survey with what may be termed 'free capital markets', followed by Malaysia and Thailand

---

[1] Exchange restrictions on the capital account include restrictions on inward and outward FDI and other short- and long-term capital movements. Exchange restrictions on the current account include restrictions on foreign exchange transactions and sources of funding associated with imports, exports and invisibles. The requirement to surrender export receipts is separately identified.

with relatively free capital accounts, while the Philippines and, to a greater extent, Korea and Taiwan are countries which still maintain a relatively high degree of control over capital movements. The currencies of Australia and Japan are independently floating, while the currencies of other countries are managed floats with varying weights given to major trade currencies.[2] (Since 1992, the Philippines has stated that its currency is independently floating but, until 1997, it demonstrated very little movement.) Indonesia and Thailand floated their currencies in July 1997.

Hong Kong had a floating exchange rate from 1974 to October 1983, and the Hong Kong dollar was effectively fixed to the US dollar thereafter. It has had the longest and most consistently open exchange system in the region: the abolition of restrictions on the capital account in 1972, the lifting of the moratorium on bank licensing in 1978 and the consequent entry of foreign banks have ensured tight competition and expansion in both the domestic money market and the foreign exchange market (Ho, Lui and Cheung 1995). The sole, innocuous restriction in the capital account applies to the licensing of financial institutions.

The Australian dollar was floated and exchange controls removed in December 1983. The only controls that remain on the capital account relate to the Australian dollar investments of foreign governments and multilateral official organisations and to approval procedures for large-ticket (FDI) in particular sectors. The yen is also an independently floating currency determined by market supply and demand. Major capital account liberalisation took place in December 1980, when transactions were allowed unless explicitly prohibited and the requirement of an underlying real transaction was removed, and in June 1984 when controls on euro–yen transactions and exchange conversions (for example, allowing domestic banks to accept long-term foreign currency deposits) were eased (Suzuki 1987). Remaining controls relate to limits on FDI and notification requirements for outward investment. The authorities retain the right to re-instate emergency controls.

The Singaporean dollar is a managed float within a band set by the Monetary Authority of Singapore (MAS) against a basket of currencies of

---

[2] Guciano (1995) presents estimates of currency weights for various east Asian countries at mid-1995: the weights for the Singapore dollar are 0.5 for the US dollar (USD), 0.4 for the yen (Y) and 0.1 for the Deutschemark (DM) and Swiss Franc (SFR); the weights for the rupiah are 0.5 for Y, 0.4 for USD and 0.1 for DM and SFR; the weights for the ringgit are 0.4 Y, 0.3 USD, 0.2 DM and 0.1 other; the weights for the baht are 0.7 USD and 0.3 Y; and the weights for the New Taiwan dollar are 0.5 USD, 0.3 Y and 0.2 DM/SFR. Guciano argues that the weight given to the yen increased and that given to the US dollar decreased markedly in the first half of 1995, owing to the surge in the yen in early 1995, with the shift typically about a 10 per cent shift to the yen. The US dollar remains the key reserve currency in the region.

major trading partners. Singapore also has a relatively long history of an open capital account. The withholding tax on interest applied to non-residents was abolished in 1968 and the capital account was progressively liberalised in the wake of the float of sterling in 1972, culminating in the removal of almost all capital controls in June 1978. The remaining formal control is that domestic financial institutions not lend more than $S5mn to non-residents or residents for use outside Singapore without the permission of the MAS. This is a tool for the MAS to prevent speculation and maintain control over the exchange rate and, consequently, inflation. There is no offshore market in Singaporean dollars, and the MAS is reported to use other, more subtle, means to limit international use of the Singaporean dollar, including limiting the amount of local currency that banks can lend (raised from $S50mn to $S70mn in 1992) and the use of local currency funds to trade international stocks (Euromoney 1994: 25); it is also reported to use informal guidance. Arif, Kapur and Tyabji (1995: 371–5, 378–9), for example, note that institutions which operate in the Asian currency market do so under the aegis of the MAS and are subject to licensing requirements, and so are sensitive to informal guidance. They also cite a 1982 episode when Singaporean banks which accepted Singaporean dollar funds in Hong Kong (avoiding Singaporean reserve requirements) and on-lent those funds in Singapore were penalised by the MAS and the practice stopped. They argue that supervision is now used to prevent similar transactions with forward cover to limit the international use of the Singaporean dollar.

Indonesia is well known for its open capital account and has employed a liberal exchange system with minimal controls since August 1971 (Cole and Slade 1995: 152). Remaining restrictions are limited to FDI, controls on which have declined substantially over time, and on foreign borrowing by government bodies and state banks. There are no limitations on the international or domestic remittance of foreign exchange or rupiah. Bank Indonesia determined the exchange rate under a system of managed float against a basket of currencies (with widening fluctuation bands) until July 1997, after which the currency was floated.

The ringgit is a managed float currency whose value is based on a basket weighted by trading partner shares and currencies of settlement. While it is a managed currency, in recent years it has typically moved in line with foreign exchange market sentiment. Malaysia's capital account has been progressively liberalised since the float of the ringgit in June 1973, and spot and forward exchange transactions are free. Approval is required for a wide range of inward FDI and for all outward FDI which is financed within Malaysia. Foreign borrowing by residents is controlled but permission is forthcoming for borrowing for productive purposes, while borrowing in ringgit by non-residents also requires permission but is usually not granted (IMF 1997b). Exporters must repatriate foreign exchange within six months (Lin and Chung 1995: 247). The authorities have imposed temporary restrictions on exchange markets when the ringgit has been under pressure – as, for example, in 1986 and 1993–4 as discussed in more detail below.

From November 1984 to the start of July 1997, the baht was determined by the Exchange Equalisation Fund, which is part of the Bank of Thailand (BOT), on the basis of a peg to a composite of currencies. This allowed a degree of flexibility not available when the baht was pegged to the US dollar. The baht was floated on 2 July 1997, in response to speculation. While payments on the current account are unrestricted, some payments restrictions still apply on the capital account and foreign exchange export proceeds must be converted or deposited in foreign exchange deposits with authorised banks. Most remittances are uncontrolled and inward FDI is permitted freely, but outward FDI over US$5mn and portfolio and property investments abroad by residents require approval. A major liberalisation of the capital account was implemented in May 1990 (commercial banks were allowed to process trade-related foreign exchange transactions without BOT approval), April 1991 (official approval was no longer required for capital outflow except when over a certain limit or for investment in foreign stock or property markets) and April 1992 (exporters were allowed to transfer foreign currency deposits for overseas debt payment or make payment in baht using non-resident accounts) (Wibulswasdi and Tanvanich 1992). Apart from existing controls on capital outflow, banks' allowable net foreign exchange positions and variations in withholding taxes on foreign borrowing are reputedly used to control capital inflows (Warr and Nidhiprabha 1995). Officials from the BOT describe the Thai capital account as 'one that is formally open but not fully' (Nijathaworn and Dejthamrong 1994: 2). While the BOT had stated its intention to remove remaining capital controls, the currency crisis from mid-1997 saw the reform program put on ice. Various short-term capital controls were introduced in May and June 1997 to stymie speculation against the baht, including barring foreigners from conducting baht-denominated transactions with Thai banks without a 'legitimate' commercial purpose, and forbidding securities lending on Thai stocks (to stop short-selling of Thai stocks).

The Philippine peso has been classified as independently floating since September 1992 (before which it was a managed rate tied largely to the US dollar), but payments restrictions still apply on both the Philippine current and capital accounts. Inward FDI must be registered and approval is required for outward FDI over US$1mn and foreign borrowing. Preference is given to export-oriented and priority sectors. There has been substantial easing of controls on the capital account since 1991 (Yap *et al.* 1995). Foreign exchange receipts can now be retained, authorised banks can buy and sell foreign exchange without official approval, residents and non-residents are allowed to maintain foreign currency deposits in the Philippines, and residents are allowed to maintain deposits abroad (although some limitations apply to the peso deposits of non-residents).

Korea follows a liberal managed float, introduced in March 1990, by which the exchange rate varies within a band around a rate posted by the Bank of Korea (since November 1994, 1.5 per cent), where the rate posted is the average of the previous day's rate. The authorities maintain some restrictions on capital transactions and require the surrender of export proceeds. The form of controls has varied with the direction of capital flows, with current controls directed at stymieing inflows and easing upward pressure on the won. Major reforms were instituted in 1988 but were subsequently reversed in 1989 when economic conditions deteriorated. Controls remain on inward FDI and on foreign borrowing by Korean firms and banks. Portfolio investment abroad is limited. In the first half of the 1990s, there was progressive reduction in documentation requirements for spot and forward exchange transactions (although the in-principle requirement of trade backing still applies for forward transactions), a progressive relaxation in controls on foreign exchange positions and an apparent shift in the mindset with the introduction of a negative list in September 1992 under which transactions were allowed unless expressly prohibited (Kim and Lee 1994). Foreign borrowing limits and restrictions in investing in overseas stock were partially eased in 1994.

The New Taiwan dollar was formally floated in July 1978 but a market was established only in February 1979 and the rate remained strongly influenced by the Central Bank of China (Taiwan Province). From April 1989, the rate was allowed to fluctuate within a band set by the Foreign Exchange Center (Chen 1990). The capital account was partially liberalised in 1986 and July 1987 when the Central Bank of China lifted controls on trade-related transactions in the current account and allowed residents to hold foreign currencies. Approval is still required, however, for large (> $US1mn) outward foreign exchange transactions, with an annual limit of $US5mn (Emery 1988) until February 1994 and $US10mn thereafter. The limit before July 1987 was $US5K. Limits remain on the foreign exchange position of banks. Capital controls in Taiwan appear to be still relatively tight.

Capital flows

Increasing integration of financial markets suggests, in the first instance, an increase in the trade of financial instruments and hence an increase in capital flows. This is not a necessary condition since financial markets may be open but net and even gross capital flows may be zero, as would occur if financial prices are fully equalised between the two markets (Barro, Mankiw and Sala-i-Martin 1995). Capital flows will occur in the transitional phase – and, arguably, the economy is always in transition – and when shocks hit the economy. But it is generally expected that integration is associated with more capital flows, and, indeed, this appears to be borne out by the data.

Information on net capital flows is contained in balance of payments data, and table 3.2 summarises net capital flows for countries in the region from 1980 to 1999 in US dollar real prices (estimated using the CPI deflator, 1990 = 100). In this case, net capital flows, presented in the first row, are defined as the surplus on the capital and financial accounts, which excludes changes in reserves (following the IMF's fifth *Balance of Payments Manual*, 1993). This contrasts with the standard method of using the current account deficit as a summary measure of net capital inflows. The current account deficit itself understates net capital inflows when reserves are increasing, as occurred in much of east Asia during the mid-1990s. The next four rows provide further detail: the second row is inward FDI, the third row is inward portfolio investment, the fourth row is financial inflow intermediated by banks and the fifth row is other non-bank private financial inflow.

There are two striking features of net capital flows for this group of countries. First, all countries for which data are available, with the very notable exception of Japan, are generally net importers of capital, often on a substantial basis. Japan's net capital outflow in 1993 was almost double the combined net inflow from Australia, Indonesia, Korea, Malaysia, the Philippines and Thailand. Second, there was a sharp increase in non-official capital flows to east Asian economies during the mid-1990s, particularly to Malaysia and Thailand, but also to the Philippines and Indonesia. In the former two countries, net capital inflows increased markedly in real terms in the first half of the 1990s and even exceeded 10 per cent of GDP. A notable increase is reported in FDI (Australia, Indonesia, Malaysia, the Philippines and Singapore), and portfolio investment (Korea – substituting out of short-term bank borrowing – and Thailand), although there have been notable increases in long-term bank borrowing in Australia, short-term bank borrowing in Malaysia, Singapore and

Thailand, and non-bank long-term borrowing in Indonesia, Malaysia, the Philippines and Thailand.[3] Given data collection and publication lags, table 3.2 does not show the reversal of capital flows that occurred in some countries in east Asia in late 1997.

Table 3.2 refers to net capital flows but gross capital flows may be more relevant in providing an insight into the greater mobility and fungibility of capital. One estimate of gross capital flows is provided by separately summing the inflows and outflows recorded in published balance of payments statistics. On this basis, the change in capital flows can be striking. For Australia, for example, private inflows rose from 5 per cent of GDP in 1980 to 60 per cent in 1990 and 75 per cent in 1993, although these flows were mostly offset by capital outflows in the form of repayments on loans. Thai non-bank private capital inflows rose more than 15-fold from less than B100bn (about US$4bn or about 5 per cent of annual GDP) in the first quarter of 1989 to B1500bn (about US$60bn or about 50 per cent of annual GDP) in the second quarter of 1994. These inflows are almost offset by outflows (Jantarangs 1994).[4]

The explanation for the increase in capital flows lies in the confluence of push and pull factors. On the one hand, the rise in net capital inflows was coincident with a rise in net capital outflows from Japan, where investment was driven offshore by relatively high local factor prices (partly a result of the sharp appreciation of the yen in the mid-1980s and 1990s) and the perceived need of Japanese firms to position themselves in Europe, the United States and other offshore markets to gain entry to markets and avoid trade sanctions. World interest rates were also lower in the 1990s and this has led to a push to find new, higher-yielding securities (Khan and Reinhart 1995). Moreover, as Ishii and Dunaway (1995) detail, there have been institutional push factors in the form of new debt rating agencies and east Asian mutual funds which promote investment in east Asia[5] and regulatory changes in lender countries, such as those which make it easier for foreign issuers to place capital in the US (Khan and Reinhart 1995). There are also pull

---

[3] Kohsaka (1995); Ishii and Dunaway (1995), Yasuhara *et al.*(1995) conduct similar analysis, but present more disaggregated data.

[4] Further insights into the turnover of capital may be gauged by looking at daily turnover figures for foreign exchange, stocks and derivatives.

[5] There were 34 funds managing US$2.4bn assets in east Asian emerging markets in 1988, but 219 funds managing US$13.9bn in 1993 (Ishii and Dunaway 1995: 68). Growth in mutual funds has been particularly strong in Korea and Thailand, which may explain the growth in portfolio investment in both countries. According to Kiriwat (1995), the Thai authorities liberalised the mutual fund system in 1993, increasing the number of mutual funds from one to eight and total assets under management increased ten-fold from mid-1992 to end-1993 to US$5bn. The Korean authorities have also implemented a policy to promote Korean mutual funds.

Table 3.2. *Capital flows, 1980–96*

(US dollar bn, 1990 constant prices)

		1980	1990	1993	1994	1995	1996
Australia	Net capital inflow	6.9 (2.9)[a]	14.8 (5.0)	9.6 (3.8)	9.3 (3.2)	17.5 (5.8)	15.5 (4.7)
	Direct investment inflows	3.0	6.5	2.7	3.4	12.2	5.0
	Portfolio inflows	3.0	6.3	5.6	12.8	1.9	6.4
	Bank inflows	0.3	4.6	2.4	1.9	6.2	7.5
	Private non-bank inflows	1.9	1.6	−2.4	−5.2	1.6	5.8
Indonesia	Net capital inflow	2.9 (2.0)	4.5 (4.2)	5.1 (3.6)	3.4 (2.2)	8.9 (5.2)	—
	Direct investment inflows	0.2	1.1	1.8	1.9	3.7	—
	Portfolio inflows	0.1	−0.1	1.6	3.4	3.5	—
	Bank inflows	0.0	0.0	1.2	0.5	1.7	—
	Private non-bank inflows	0.0	3.0	0.2	−1.9	0.4	—
Japan	Net capital inflow	29.9 (1.8)	−21.5 (0.7)	−92.4 (2.4)	−75.1 (1.2)	−54.9 (1.2)	−23.4 (0.6)
	Direct investment outflows	−3.8	−48.1	−12.5	−16.0	−19.3	−19.5
	Portfolio outflow	−5.9	−40.2	−58.1	−80.7	−74.8	−95.5
Korea	Net capital inflow	9.4 (9.5)	2.5 (1.0)	2.5 (0.8)	9.0 (2.7)	14.4 (3.7)	19.5 (4.8)
	Direct investment inflows	0.0	0.8	0.5	0.7	1.5	1.9
	Portfolio inflows	0.2	0.1	9.3	6.3	9.6	14.0
	Bank inflows	3.5	2.0	0.7	6.9	10.5	10.3
	Private non-bank inflows	5.9	4.0	−0.3	4.8	7.7	9.6
Malaysia	Net capital inflow	2.2 (5.8)	1.7 (4.1)	9.7 (17.1)	1.1 (1.7)	6.3 (8.6)	—
	Direct investment inflows	1.5	2.3	4.5	3.8	3.5	—
	Portfolio inflows	0.0	−0.3	−0.6	−1.5	−0.4	—
	Bank inflows	0.8	0.7	5.7	−3.3	0.4	—
	Private non-bank inflows	−0.1	−0.8	1.5	1.8	2.6	—
Philippines	Net capital inflow	4.3 (8.3)	2.1 (4.6)	3.0 (6.0)	4.5 (8.0)	4.6 (7.2)	—
	Direct investment inflows	−0.2	0.5	1.1	1.4	1.3	—
	Portfolio inflows	0.0	−0.1	0.8	0.8	2.2	—

Bank inflows	1.1	0.3	-0.2	1.5	1.4	—
Private non-bank inflows	1.9	0.4	1.5	2.6	1.5	—
Singapore Net capital inflow	2.5 (13.5)	3.9 (10.5)	-1.0 (1.9)	-10.1 (16.1)	-2.1 (2.9)	0.4 (0.6)
Direct investment inflows	2.0	5.6	4.2	7.4	7.0	7.9
Portfolio inflows	0.2	0.6	2.6	0.1	0.0	1.0
Bank inflows	0.8	-1.0	1.8	4.8	3.8	6.7
Private non-bank inflows	1.1	2.7	5.8	0.4	4.6	5.2
Thailand Net capital inflow	3.2 (6.3)	9.1 (10.6)	9.5 (8.4)	10.7 (8.5)	18.3 (13.3)	16.2 (—)
Direct investment inflows	0.3	2.4	1.6	1.2	1.8	1.9
Portfolio inflows	0.2	0.0	4.9	2.2	3.5	3.0
Bank inflows	-0.7	1.0	6.0	12.6	11.3	2.4
Private non-bank inflows	3.1	7.0	0.6	-3.3	5.2	7.5

Notes:
[a] Figures in parentheses are per cent of GDP.
— = not available.
Source: IMF, *International Financial Statistics.*

factors. Greater macroeconomic and political stability and cost competitiveness have been instrumental in attracting funds to east Asia (Nijathaworn 1993; Kiriwat 1995). Added to this has been the recognition that these economies contain a young and expanding middle class and so offer large potential markets. At the same time as these economies have become more attractive as destinations for FDI, they have also been liberalising and restructuring their domestic financial systems and opening their capital accounts. This makes them more attractive as destinations for portfolio investment and ensures that foreign capital which wants to enter these economies can do so. As examined below, formal and informal impediments to access still remain in some countries.

Interest rate parity conditions

As cross-border trade in financial instruments increases, returns on identical instruments should exhibit a greater tendency to equalise over time, and so it is natural to examine interest parity conditions for evidence of greater financial integration. The conventional definitions of interest rate parity – closed, covered, uncovered and real interest rate parity – are usually assessed to ascertain the information about the state of a country's international financial integration. These definitions are nested and cumulative, and the conditions for their existence become progressively more stringent and the information about international financial integration more diffuse (Frankel 1993a). On the other hand, real interest parity may hold overall even though the constitutive parity conditions fail simply because the sub-conditions fully offset each other, and so it is worth moving up through the parity conditions to determine whether real interest parity holds or not, and why.

Closed interest rate parity holds if the rates of return are the same on instruments which are denominated in the same currency and are otherwise identical except that they are traded in different jurisdictions. Denoting the interest rate on the k-period instrument traded domestically as $i_{t,k}$ and the interest rate on the k-period instrument traded offshore as $i_{t,k}^{offshore}$, closed interest parity holds when

$$i_{t,k} = i_{t,k}^{offshore}. \tag{3.1}$$

Given market efficiency, closed interest parity fails when domestic exchange controls are in place or when there is a country or political risk premium, and so it is a necessary condition for financial integration. When closed interest parity holds, covered interest parity will also hold when the difference between rates of return on instruments which are identical except for their currency denomination equals the forward discount on the home currency,

$$i_{t,k} = i^*_{t,k} + f_{t,t+k} \qquad (3.2)$$

where $f_{t,t+k}$ is the forward discount on the domestic currency. The exchange rate is quoted in units of domestic currency per unit of foreign currency, so the forward discount and depreciation of the spot rate are positive numbers and the forward premium and appreciation of the spot rate are negative numbers. Given that offshore domestic interest rates are usually not available, covered interest parity is the baseline for assessing the international integration of traded financial asset markets.

When covered interest parity holds, uncovered interest parity will also hold if investors are risk neutral, expectations are formed rationally and the expected future depreciation of the home currency, $\Delta s^e_{t,t+k}$, equals the forward discount,

$$i_{t,k} = i^*_{t,k} + \Delta s^e_{t,t+k}. \qquad (3.3)$$

Equations (3.2) and (3.3) imply that the forward discount equals the expected depreciation of the spot rate,[6] but this has not been empirically supported (Cumby and Obstfeld 1984; Hodrick 1987, and Frankel 1993b) because of factors such as a time-varying exchange risk premia,[7] the failure of rational expectations, a peso problem[8] or the effect of Jensen's inequality[9] (Frankel and Froot 1993; Taylor 1995). McCallum (1994) and Taylor

---

[6] The theoretical literature suggests that the forward discount is a biased measure of the expected depreciation, indicating that (3.3) does not necessarily follow from (3.2). Fama (1984), for example, derives a model in which optimising agents set the forward rate equal to the certainty equivalent of the future expected spot rate, with the certainty equivalent modelled as the sum of the expected future spot rate and the currency risk premium. Hodrick (1987:7–15) sets out an intertemporal optimisation model of asset pricing of forward exchange rates and expected future spot rates based on Lucas (1982), which shows that the forward rate is a biased predictor of the expected spot rate with the wedge between the two defined as the risk premium and equal to the covariance of the expected spot rate and interest rates weighted by intertemporal substitution parameters.

[7] Froot and Frankel (1989) present empirical evidence for a risk premium by regressing survey measures of the exchange rate on the forward discount and finding a negative and significant constant term which they interpret as evidence of a large risk premium in the forward rate.

[8] The 'peso problem' arises when there is a small probability of a discontinuously large event which does not in fact occur within the (relatively small) sample period. This increases the probability of Type 1 error – that is, it makes rejection of the null hypothesis that markets are efficient and rational more likely when the that null is true. It also generates sampling distributions which are not normal since the draws or the distribution of expected returns are fat-tailed, skewed and not independent of each other (Krasker 1980).

[9] For a stochastic variable (X) with positive variance, it follows that $E[1/X] > 1/E[X]$ and so the expected value of the future spot rate exceeds the forward rate when the exchange rate is quoted in terms of foreign currency per unit of domestic currency even if the investor is risk neutral (Siegel 1972). Attfield, Demery and Duck (1985: 166) and Taylor (1995:15)

(1995) modify (3.3) to account for the possibility that investors are risk averse and charge a possibly time-varying risk premium,[10]

$$i_{t,k} = i^*_{t,k} + \Delta s^e_{t,t+k} + rp_t. \tag{3.4}$$

When the Fisher effect holds, the nominal interest rate can be linearly approximated as

$$i_{t,k} = r_{t,k} + p^e_{t,t+k}, \tag{3.5}$$

where $p^e_{t,t+k}$ is the rate of inflation expected to prevail from time t to time $t+k$, and so (3.4) can be rewritten as

$$r_{t,k} = r^*_{t,k} + \Delta q^e_{t,t+k} + rp_t \tag{3.6}$$

where $\Delta q^e_{t,t+k} = p^{e*}_{t,t+k} + \Delta s^e_{t,t+k} + p^e_{t,t+k}$ and is the expected depreciation of the real exchange rate. If relative purchasing power parity (PPP) holds, then $\Delta q^e_{t,t+k}$ is zero since common-currency rates of inflation are expected to be the same. Only if the risk premium is zero and uncovered interest parity, the Fisher effect and relative purchasing power parity all hold are real interest rates equalised.

There is an extensive empirical literature on parity conditions for most OECD economies and a growing literature for east Asian and western Pacific economies. Goldsborough and Teja (1991) tested whether parity held in Australia, Hong Kong, Japan, Malaysia, New Zealand and Singapore from January 1987 to March 1990, and reported a significant degree of financial integration. Chinn and Frankel (1992, 1994a) assessed parity for Australia, Hong Kong, Japan, Malaysia, New Zealand and Singapore against the US dollar from 1982M9 to 1992M3, and found that the average covered interest differential for these countries moved from about minus 1 percentage point to about 0 over this time, indicating a shift from systematic control on capital inflow to a position of no evident systematic control. This conforms with the experience of open OECD economies but given that the tests are constrained to those countries which are already widely thought to be open and integrated, the information content is somewhat limited. Chapter 4 contributes to this literature by providing new data for countries not previously examined, updating tests to assess whether covered interest parity holds more closely in the 1990s, and looks in more detail at episodes of exchange

advocate estimation in natural logarithms to limit this problem since log(1/Z) equals - log(Z) and the paradox does not arise. McCulloch (1975) showed the operational importance of the convexity term to be negligible. In this book, exchange rates are transformed as natural logarithms, and the percentage change in the exchange rate is calculated as the first difference of the log values. Interest rates are in decimals.

[10] This assumes that the exchange risk is not fully diversifiable (Frankel 1993c).

control in east Asia, since controls are not always applied on a systematic basis.

The consensus seems to be that tests for uncovered interest parity fail to provide any information about the degree of financial integration (Makin 1994). Dooley and Isard (1980), Hansen and Hodrick (1980) and Cumby and Obstfeld (1984) are among the many papers which reject uncovered interest parity for open, developed markets, arguing that rejection would appear to be due to time-varying currency risk premia or non-rationally formed expectations about exchange rate movements. Indeed, in a survey of developments in exchange rate theory, Krugman (1993) concluded that 'there is no plausible way to reconcile' the predictions of uncovered interest parity with the data (1993: 9) and that the various 'ways to rationalise the apparent failure of exchange markets to meet efficiency criteria ... either lack plausibility or create as much trouble as they solve' (1993: 11).

The empirical literature on finance in east Asia tends to focus on the interaction of domestic and international interest rates by testing the influence of a foreign rate on the domestic rate, sometimes controlling for variables which are thought to explain country and exchange risk (such as current account imbalances, fiscal imbalance or domestic financial instability) (Glick and Moreno 1994; Das Gupta and Das Gupta 1994). Alternative tests seek to measure the relative importance of US vs. Japanese interest rates on domestic rates in the region (Chinn and Frankel 1994b; Glick and Moreno 1994; Phylaktis 1995). These papers generally find that the impact of foreign interest rates on domestic rates in the region has increased over time. Chapter 4 contributes to this literature by taking a somewhat contrary position and arguing that uncovered interest rate parity tests may in fact contain substantial information about the state of financial integration. It presents evidence which supports increasing linkages between nominal interest rates, particularly in the 1990s.

The empirical literature suggests that the real interest differential has narrowed as a result of greater financial openness (Fukao and Hanazaki 1986) but not by as much as expected (Mishkin 1984a, 1984b; Mark 1985; Cumby and Mishkin 1986; Gaab, Franziol and Horner 1986; Frankel and MacArthur 1988; Piggott 1994). This is perhaps not surprising given the widespread failure of uncovered interest parity. On the other hand, more recent work using cointegration techniques indicates that real interest rates for G10 countries are equalised over the long term (Kugler and Neusser 1993) and when transactions costs are taken into consideration (Goodwin and Grennes 1994). The empirical literature for the western Pacific region is similar. Glick and Hutchison (1990), Okuda (1993), Chinn and Frankel (1994b) and Phylaktis (1995), for example, find that real interest rate parity does not generally hold in the region but that there has been an increasing tendency for it to do so. Chapter 4 decomposes the real interest differential in order to isolate failure due to uncovered interest parity and purchasing power parity.

The test of parity can be applied to the rates on any set of financial instruments so long as they are traded in both markets and identical but for currency denomination. Tests can be conducted on short-term money market instruments, bonds and stocks. In general, tests are conducted using rates on money market instruments because these are the most comparable and available of assets, although there is also a growing literature which examines the relationship between stock prices (Gultekin, Gultekin and Penati 1989; Niederer 1994) and the cost of capital (Fukao and Hanazaki 1986; McCauley and Zimmer 1992; Fukao 1993). Gultekin, Gultekin and Penati (1989) were unable to find segmentation in returns and variances between Japanese and US stock markets in the four years after the enactment of the new Foreign Exchange and Foreign Trade Control Law in December 1980, but did before. Niederer (1994) observed that stock prices in Hong Kong, Singapore, Malaysia and, to a lesser extent, Thailand and Indonesia showed relatively high correlations with each other but, apart from Hong Kong and Singapore, not with stock prices in mature economies. Stocks in Korea and Taiwan appear poorly synchronised with other markets. McCauley and Zimmer (1992) present evidence that the cost of equity in the G3 and United Kingdom converged substantially in the early 1990s. Fukao (1993) presents evidence that the cost of capital across G10 countries did not converge in the 1980s but showed some tendency to do so at the start of the 1990s. Tests are not conducted on bond yields since government and corporate bond markets generally have developed only recently (Dalla and Khatkhate 1996).

As shown by the literature review above, tests of interest rate parity tend to focus on a narrow range of traded financial instruments. If the rates on traded assets in a country are market-determined and hence related to each other by arbitrage, then differences in return should reflect only asset differences such as term to maturity, liquidity, risk and such like. In this case, information about the integration of domestic and foreign financial markets can be obtained by examining just one market in traded financial instruments. Even though money markets are only a relatively small set of the menu of financial instruments available, tests of integration may reveal a considerable amount of information about the integration of traded assets overall. On the other hand, to the extent that non-traded financial instruments, such as deposits and loans, are important to portfolio choice and consumer and producer decisionmaking, then it follows that tests of international financial integration need to be supplemented by tests of domestic financial integration. This has not yet been applied to east Asia but is conducted in chapter 5 below.

Saving–investment correlations

Feldstein and Horioka (1980) proposed a test for capital mobility based on identifying a change in a basic structural macroeconomic relationship: saving and investment should be uncorrelated in a small country which produces a single good and is integrated in both the goods and financial markets since a shortfall in domestic savings can always be financed by foreign capital. The nexus between domestic saving and investment is broken by access to international finance. Feldstein and Horioka regressed investment on saving and estimated what they called a 'savings retention coefficient' – a term which simply means the correlation between saving and income – of about 0.9 for OECD economies from 1960 to 1974. This result has been replicated for different countries and historical time periods (Montiel 1993). Obstfeld (1994) reviews evidence that saving and investment links are negligible for domestic regions but not international regions, which suggests that borders are not irrelevant to capital flows. The Feldstein–Horioka approach, however, has been subject to substantial criticism.

In the first place, real interest parity and exogeneity of the real interest rate are necessary conditions for saving and investment to be uncorrelated (Frankel 1993a; Makin 1994), but these conditions do not generally both hold: the first because of the general failure of uncovered interest parity and relative PPP (as explained above), the second because some countries, notably the United States, are too large to be exogenous. To the extent that real interest rates are not equalised across countries, a shortfall in domestic savings, for example, will push up the domestic interest rate but not induce the capital inflow necessary to equalise real interest rates and provide the funds required for investment. Investment falls as a result of the savings shortfall (Goldsborough and Teja 1991: 6). Real interest rates tend to be equalised within countries but not between countries, and so it is not surprising that intra-country regional correlations of saving and investment tend to be lower than inter-country correlations.

Moreover, there is good reason to expect that saving and investment are correlated even when capital is perfectly mobile (Montiel 1993). Governments may respond to 'large' external imbalances by changing public saving and investment, for example, and this will tend to induce correlation between gross saving and investment (Tobin 1983; Westphal

1983; Bayoumi 1990). Similarly, investment and saving are both pro-cyclical and tend to move in the same direction in response to shocks to productivity and world real interest rates (Obstfeld 1986a). In short, saving is endogenous in both cross-section and time-series regressions (Montiel 1993: 16). Mendoza (1991, 1994) and Baxter and Crucini (1993) simulate dynamic stochastic general equilibrium models and show that high saving–investment correlations can be generated by productivity or terms of trade shocks, even when capital is perfectly mobile.

While saving and investment are positively and significantly correlated, there is evidence that correlations are declining over time. Obstfeld (1986a) reported a fall in the saving-retention coefficient for some OECD countries using time series analysis, and in a later paper (1994) presented cross-sectional evidence that the savings retention coefficient fell for OECD countries in the 1980s (0.64) relative to the 1970s (0.87). Frankel (1993a) reported a substantial decline in the retention coefficient for the United States in the 1980s, in fact not distinguishable from zero, arguably due to large and persistent current account deficits.

Dooley, Frankel and Mathieson (1987) reported that developing countries in general have a lower saving-retention rate than OECD economies. Goldsborough and Teja (1991) reported results for a pooled regression for 17 Pacific Basin countries[11] from 1980 to 1987, and estimated a saving-retention coefficient of 0.67 (OLS) for the full period and 0.62 (OLS) for 1984–7. Montiel (1993) reported a range of saving-retention ratios based on time-series analysis with OLS and IV estimation[12] in levels, first differences and error-correction specifications for developing countries, and his work suggests the following rough ranking of capital mobility from lowest to highest for countries in the region: the Philippines, Thailand, Indonesia, Korea, Malaysia and Singapore. This conforms broadly with the state of capital account and domestic financial system liberalisation (see chapters 4 and 5) and results from this study (see chapters 4 and 6).

Consumption correlations

An alternative approach to measuring integration is to examine changes in consumption patterns over time. In most economic models, consumption depends on income and wealth. Income and wealth vary over time, sometimes in a predictable way, as in the life-cycle model where individuals

---

[11] The countries are Australia, Canada, China, Fiji, Hong Kong, Indonesia, Japan, Korea, Malaysia, Mexico, New Zealand, Papua New Guinea, the Philippines, Singapore, Taiwan, Thailand and the United States.

[12] Montiel reports that inference is not generally affected by estimating in OLS rather than IV.

start with low income and few assets but gradually gain more income and accumulate assets. At other times, they move unpredictably. Accordingly, individuals try to smooth their consumption over their life-times and try to build up a stock of precautionary savings or reserve assets to deal with unforeseen events. Whatever the case, consumption will be tied to current income and the immediate vicissitudes of life unless there is access to borrowing and lending or, as otherwise stated, there is access to the market in state contingent claims. Financial integration enables countries to trade internationally in financial assets in order to eliminate local idiosyncratic consumption shocks and so should lead to smoother national consumption over time.

Obstfeld (1986a) shows that the efficient allocation of consumption risks implies that the marginal utility of consumption is equal in each country in each state of nature, and the inter temporal marginal rates of substitution of consumption across states of nature coincide. In 1994, he sets out a simple model to show the relationship between national consumption correlations and the information these contain about capital mobility. Assume that individuals consume a composite traded good (c), that there is a complete and free market in state-contingent assets, that individuals in each country can be aggregated into a representative national agent, and that there are a total of J countries. Each national agent maximises expected utility,

$$u_t = E\left[\int_t^\infty u(c_s)e^{-rs}ds\right],\tag{3.7}$$

where r is the subjective constant rate of time preference. A benevolent dictator maximises a social welfare functional with fixed country weights (w), yielding the necessary condition for efficient distribution of world tradeable consumption,

$$w^i u_c^i = w^j u_c^j \tag{3.8}$$

for all i and j country pairs, and where u_c refers to the marginal utility of consumption. This implies that marginal rates of substitution across states of nature are equalised internationally. Obstfeld gives this empirical content by assuming a constant elasticity of substitution utility function of the form,

$$u = \frac{1}{1-r}c^{1-r}.\tag{3.9}$$

Using (3.9) to obtain the marginal utility of consumption for country i and j, taking natural logarithms and the first differential of (3.8), yields the expression,

$$\hat{c}_t^i = (r^j / r^i)\hat{c}_t^i \qquad\qquad (3.10)$$

where a circumflex represents the growth rate calculated as the first-log difference. If subjective rates of time preference are identical across countries, then consumption growth rates are identical. If subjective time preference differs between countries, then real *per capita* consumption growth will be faster in the economy where individuals have a lower rate of time preference. Whatever the case, growth rates will be perfectly correlated as long as subjective time preference is constant. Obstfeld's model accords with the basic intuition that expanding the means by which people can smooth consumption over time tends to increase the correlation of consumption between countries. To the extent that state-contingent asset markets are incomplete, the correlation should be less than unity, with a tendency to move to unity strictly interpretable, *under the assumptions of the model*, as an increase in financial integration.

Obstfeld (1994) used the Summers and Heston (1991) data set to review correlations between consumption growth in a variety of developed and developing economies and that in the rest of the world from 1951 to 1988, splitting the sample in 1972–3 in order to capture changes in capital mobility. The consumption correlations were calculated using the annual change in the natural logarithm of a country's real *per capita* private consumption and that of the rest of the world (ROW, defined as the rest of the economies in his sample). He found that correlations are higher for developed than developing economies, and that they are higher in the latter period, particularly in developed economies. In terms of east Asia, the only countries Obstfeld investigated were Australia, Japan, New Zealand, the Philippines and Thailand, a restriction based on a judgement about the quality and the quantity of data. He concluded that capital mobility over the past three decades has risen in Japan and Thailand, but fallen in Australia, New Zealand and the Philippines. The result for Australia and New Zealand is counterintuitive. Montiel (1993) conducted a related test for developing countries from 1965 to 1985 using the same data set and concludes that the majority, including Korea, Malaysia, the Philippines, Singapore and Thailand, appear to enjoy relatively high capital mobility, a result which is similar to his tests on saving–investment correlations. He noted that the quality of the data is generally poor and the length of the time series short, and so cautioned against strong conclusions, although he did argue that relatively high capital mobility may appear because of aid flows.

Montiel's analysis does not provide insight into how capital mobility has evolved over time. While the effect of financial integration on consumption is examined more rigorously in chapter 7, table 3.3 presents

Table 3.3. *Consumption and income correlations*

	Private consumption			Total consumption			Income		
	1963–72	1973–82	1983–92	1963–72	1973–82	1983–92	1963–72	1973–82	1983–92
Australia	0.35	0.36	0.17	0.09	0.33	0.03	0.47	0.42	0.59
Hong Kong	—	0.31	0.47	—	0.22	0.52	—	0.61	0.62
Indonesia	0.15	−0.10	−0.34	0.35	−0.01	0.26	−0.32	0.27	0.14
Japan	0.31	0.57	0.73	0.14	0.54	0.74	0.62	0.68	0.46
Korea	−0.10	0.73	−0.69	0.11	0.75	−0.68	0.25	0.80	0.34
Malaysia	0.23	0.33	−0.38	0.14	−0.02	−0.44	0.34	0.87	−0.16
Philippines	0.24	0.40	0.24	0.12	0.42	0.30	0.28	0.58	0.27
Singapore	−0.11	0.11	0.28	0.15	−0.19	0.27	−0.26	−0.10	0.09
Taiwan	0.12	0.74	0.29	0.02	0.64	0.04	0.04	0.84	0.40
Thailand	−0.09	0.93	−0.42	−0.32	0.88	−0.43	0.16	0.91	0.29
New Zealand	0.28	0.43	0.53	0.07	0.33	0.56	0.03	0.39	0.18
PNG	—	0.24	0.73	—	0.31	0.62	—	0.56	0.59
Canada	0.29	0.42	0.92	0.10	0.37	0.85	−0.22	0.44	0.90
France	0.27	0.46	0.57	0.13	0.68	0.46	0.28	0.86	0.58
Germany	−0.57	0.53	0.63	−0.74	0.63	0.56	0.48	0.80	0.72
Italy	−0.46	0.52	0.28	−0.27	0.43	0.30	−0.18	0.71	0.50
UK	0.26	0.57	0.64	0.06	0.43	0.57	0.32	0.67	0.74
USA	−0.11	0.57	0.70	−0.37	0.48	0.65	−0.35	0.74	0.68

Note: — = not available.
Source: Estimations based on national accounts data published by IMF, *International Financial Statistics*.

consumption and income correlations for east Asian economies over decade sub-samples which are more consistent with the programme of domestic and international financial liberalisation in these countries. The correlations are calculated between annual domestic real *per capita* consumption growth and the geometric mean of annual real *per capita* consumption growth in the (rest of the) G7 industrialised economies, calculated with data drawn from the IMF's *International Finance Statistics* data base (see Appendix 3.1, p. 000, for details). Correlations are estimated for private and total (private *plus* public) consumption and national income for Australia, Indonesia, Japan, Korea, Malaysia, New Zealand, Papua New Guinea, the Philippines, Taiwan, Thailand and Singapore. Correlations for G7 countries are included for reference. Liberalisation of financial and capital markets in east Asia and the western Pacific occurred largely in the 1980s, and so Obstfeld's industrial country pre- and post-1973 division is inappropriate. The 1970s can also be separately identified in an attempt to isolate common shocks such as the 1973 and 1979 oil price hikes.

The correlations remain well below unity for all economies, and are higher for G7 countries, excluding Italy, than for east Asia (excluding Japan) and the western Pacific. The evidence of rising correlations for east Asian economies over the full period is stronger in this book than in Obstfeld (1994), though this study is different in its wider focus on east Asian industrialising economies (rather than those in Central and South America), the extension of the sample period into the early 1990s and the different consumption growth definitions and estimations. The results are generally robust to the definition of consumption. Of the east Asian and western Pacific economies, correlations steadily increased for Hong Kong, Japan, New Zealand, Papua New Guinea and Singapore, remained unchanged for Australia and Indonesia, and were volatile for Korea, Malaysia, the Philippines and Thailand (rising in the 1970s but falling in the 1980s). Obstfeld (1994) argues that changes in income correlations are the benchmark for assessing changes in consumption correlations: if consumption is a function of income and income is subject to shocks, then capital mobility can be said to have increased only when consumption correlations rise more than income correlations, for only in this case is there evidence of the use of insurance contracts, in the broad sense of the term, to smooth consumption. In this case, consumption appears to be dominated by income in Korea, Malaysia, the Philippines and Thailand, but increased capital mobility is evident for Hong Kong, Japan, New Zealand, Papua New Guinea and Singapore. This result largely conforms with expectations since, apart from Papua New Guinea, the countries in the latter group have all had open capital accounts for the past decade or more. In the rest of G7, increased capital mobility is evident in the cases of Germany and the United States. The tentative implication, therefore, is that capital mobility in east Asia has risen since the 1960s and that there is still considerable scope for a further rise. Both the putative increase in capital mobility and its imperfection are global phenomena.

That said, there are important caveats to this analysis and the results should be seen as tentative at best. In the first place, data for each country are subject to a range of local and common shocks, which can create noise and substantially affect the results when the period for which growth correlations are calculated is reduced. Moreover, the model assumes the existence of a single traded non-durable good, that risks have already been shared optimally within each country and that utility functions exist and have the form specified. The exclusion of non-traded goods is potentially important since their consumption is more difficult to smooth over time. Even if perfect capital markets exist, the larger is the share of non-traded goods in consumption and the greater the shocks to the non-traded sector, the less smooth is total consumption over time. Rising correlations in this context may just reflect growth in the traded sector.[13] If countries are subject to consumption-good preference shocks, or if pure time-preference rates or mortality rates change, then changing consumption correlations are neither necessary nor sufficient indicators of changes in financial integration. In most developed economies, the population has been aging, which implies that the discount factor and consumption growth will be declining. In most of east Asia, the populations are young, the probability of death at any specified age and discount rates have fallen, and so consumption growth is expanding. This renders changes in consumption growth correlations difficult to interpret as evidence of financial integration. This is particularly relevant here since European countries dominate Obstfeld's study; indeed, correlations for east Asian countries, excluding Japan, are weaker than for Europe. Montiel focused on developing countries but did not consider the effect of demographics, even though demographic change is arguably greater in such countries. There is evidence that consumption smoothing is imperfect even within countries, let alone between them (Obstfeld 1994). In Australia, for example, consumption insurance between the various states is substantial, but still incomplete, as indicated by the dependence of consumption on income in states which have suffered large financial shocks (de Brouwer and Preston 1996).

---

[13] Backus and Smith (1993), however, present evidence that the effect of non-traded goods on consumption correlations is small for the eight OECD economies they examine.

The literature on consumption correlations addresses the issue of consumption insurance – that is, whether individuals are able to eliminate idiosyncratic shocks such that consumption across individuals at any one time exhibits common behaviour. An alternative approach is to examine the ease with which one individual or set of individuals is able to smooth its consumption across time, an approach based on the standard classical or Fisherian analysis. This is addressed in detail in chapter 7 in a model which explicitly takes aging of the population, non-durability of consumption goods and liquidity constraints into consideration.

Miscellaneous measures

There is a variety of alternative methods of measuring financial integration which identify changes in financial integration through changes in structural economic relationships. In this context, the real limit to assessing financial integration is the invention of the economist in setting up tests to identify changes in variables associated with integration. Based on Haque and Montiel (1990), Reisen and Yeches (1993) seek to identify financial integration in Korea and Taiwan by calculating the time-varying coefficient from a regression of the differential between the domestic interest rate and the estimated closed-capital account domestic interest rate on the differential between the exchange rate-depreciation-adjusted world rate and the estimated closed-capital account domestic rate. They argue that if markets are perfectly integrated, the slope coefficient is one since both sides of the equation are identical. Conversely, if markets are not integrated at all, the world rate has no effect on the domestic rate and the coefficient is zero. They conclude that interest rates in Korea and Taiwan are not well integrated. Dooley and Mathieson (1994) use a similar framework but identify financial integration in the Pacific region by focusing on the responsiveness of money demand to the foreign as opposed to the domestic interest rate. They find a high degree of capital mobility for Korea, Malaysia, the Philippines and Thailand, limited mobility for Indonesia (and Sri Lanka) and no mobility for Myanmar. This finding does not rely on the premise that money demand functions exist and are stable, a claim which tends to be refuted by the data (for Australia, for example, see de Brouwer, Ng and Subbaraman 1993). Rather, it looks to find a change in a basic relation suggested by theory which is consistent with changing financial openness.

Faruquee (1992) takes a different approach, using maximum likelihood estimation to model nominal interest differentials for Korea, Malaysia, Singapore and Thailand as ARMA processes with conditional heteroscedasticity and interpreting a reduction in the variability of disturbances as evidence of increased capital mobility. He concludes that capital is more mobile in these countries, although the reduction is often episodic rather than systematic. These results are difficult to accept since his procedure does not control for expected changes in the exchange rate, and so lower conditional variance may simply reflect greater stability in the exchange rate.

Mendoza (1994) uses numerical methods to assess the implications of dynamic stochastic models for capital mobility and compares these with stylised facts on capital mobility. He argues that saving–investment correlations are unlikely to be informative about capital mobility if the magnitude or persistence of income disturbances changes and that consumption variability is not sensitive to capital mobility. The empirical analyses in chapter 7 on the effects of financial integration on non-durable consumption identify real effects of integration at the same time as providing evidence that structural changes are occurring in fundamental economic relationships. Hence, this chapter also 'measures' financial integration. What then, are the tentative conclusions about the region? Applied to the countries examined in the book, these tests generally show that the openness and development of financial markets increased markedly in the 1980s.

Conclusion

This chapter has reviewed the literature on the measurement and implications for macroeconomic performance, structure and policy of financial integration. Legal restrictions on the capital account, the size of capital flows, interest rates and saving and consumption correlations point to increased but still imperfect financial integration in the 1980s and 1980s for the ten east Asian economies examined. Chapter 4 extends research on the measurement of international financial integration by examining new evidence on interest parity conditions and extends analysis to the 1990s. Chapter 5 examines domestic financial integration, which is a necessary precondition for full financial integration.

4

Interest parity conditions as indicators of international financial integration

The integration of markets implies, on the face of it, an increase in transactions and a tendency for prices in those markets to converge. Hence, the international integration of financial markets implies an increase in capital flows and a greater tendency for the common-currency prices and returns on traded financial assets in different countries to converge. The convergence of returns is typically measured by closed, covered, uncovered and real interest parity over a set of traded assets including money market instruments, long-term securities and equity. This chapter examines covered, uncovered and real interest parity for money market instruments in Australia, Hong Kong, Indonesia, Japan, Korea, Malaysia, the Philippines, Singapore, Taiwan and Thailand to evaluate the financial integration of these economies with the world market.

In the first section, some issues concerning data are then discussed. New evidence is presented and assessed on covered interest parity relative to US traded assets for Australia, Hong Kong, Japan, Malaysia, Singapore, Taiwan and Thailand. Particular attention is paid to whether the 1990s are different from the 1980s (and if so, why) and the importance of periodic rather than systematic exchange controls is highlighted. Mean uncovered interest differentials are then estimated and standard tests of uncovered interest parity applied, yielding a striking difference in the results between financially open and closed economies. McCallum's (1994) model is used to explain this and the inference is drawn that tests of uncovered interest parity may in fact contain considerable information about financial openness. The time-varying influence of foreign interest rates on domestic nominal interest rates is assessed by examining the cointegration of interest rates and variance decompositions in vector autoregressions. The real interest differential is decomposed into the uncovered interest differential and relative purchasing power differential in order to explain the wedge between domestic and foreign real interest rates. Finally, the results are summarised and some policy implications are drawn in the conclusion.

Data and estimation issues

Definitions, sources and graphs of the data are presented in Appendix 4.1 (p. 183). In general, the interbank market rate is used as the representative money market rate, largely because of the relative lack of development of other money market instruments. Estimations are conducted using the Microfit β test version and RATS. Three econometric issues need to be addressed before progressing.

First, the tests in this chapter are mostly conducted using end-month data of three-month interest rates, forward discounts and depreciations, and the overlapping observations generate a moving-average error of order two in the error of the estimating equation. This biases the standard errors but is corrected by using the Newey–West estimator of the covariance matrix (Newey and West 1987). The lag in the Parzen window is set equal to the length of the induced MA process (Greene 1993). Unless otherwise stated, the standard errors reported in this chapter are Newey–West corrected.

Second, financial returns tend to exhibit periods of relative volatility and stability, and this suggests that estimation can be made more efficient by modelling the conditional variance of the error term (Bollerslev, Engle and Nelson 1994; Pagan 1995). In fact, generalised autoregressive conditional heteroscedasticity (GARCH) occurs with some data sets here. The order of GARCH is tested by examining the order of ARCH(q) in an OLS estimation, and the log-likelihood function is maximised with a parsimonious specification of the error variance using the Microfit β test version. Unless otherwise reported, estimations do *not* include GARCH errors.

Stationarity is the third issue that arises in the estimations. The results from a time-series analysis of money market interest rates are presented and discussed in detail in chapter 5, together with those for intermediated interest rates. The conclusion from that analysis is that money market rates in these countries are non-stationary and are I(1) processes in the full sample from 1975 to 1994 and in the four five-year sub-samples. The caveat is that standard tests have low power in discriminating between integrated and near-integrated, strongly autoregressive processes. The apparent first-order integration of interest rates motivates the search for cointegration between interest rates. Interest differentials and forward and spot exchange rate changes in general appear to be stationary (as reported in the text of this chapter, p. 70) and standard statistical tests are applied, but there are important exceptions, discussion of which is deferred until later.

Covered interest rate parity

The derivation of the interest parity conditions was comprehensively reviewed in chapter 3. It is generally assumed that markets are efficient in the sense that market participants search for arbitrage possibilities and conduct trade when it is profitable, and that efficiency rises as the collection, storage and analysis of information improve. If arbitrage possibilities are exploited, then the existence of a non-zero covered interest differential (CID), defined as

$$CID_t = i_t^* + f_{t,t+k} - i_t,$$ (4.1)

indicates either that assets are not fully comparable or that there are impediments to trade in them. Non-comparability may be due to differences in liquidity or maturity, or to political and default risk which give rise to a country or political risk premium. Impediments to trade may arise because of transactions costs (bid–ask spread and brokerage fees), financial constraints (margin requirements associated with forward transactions, illiquidity in a market and credit limits) and government regulation (taxation, market access controls, exchange controls, interest rate ceilings) (Rivera-Batiz and Rivera-Batiz 1994). In reality, CIDs are not zero, but in deep and liberalised financial markets impediments tend to be negligible and differentials close to zero (Ito 1986; Frankel 1993a). The average *absolute* CID from 1982M9 to 1988M4 for 'open' Atlantic developed economies was 0.24 percentage points, for example, in contrast to 1.15 percentage points for 'closed' Atlantic developed economies.[1] A positive CID occurs when the foreign covered rate, defined as the foreign interest rate *plus* the forward discount, is greater than the domestic rate, and so indicates domestic controls on capital outflow when access to the foreign market is free (which is the case since the foreign market is the US market). Conversely, a negative CID occurs when the foreign covered rate is smaller than the domestic rate, and so indicates domestic controls on capital inflow.

There are a number of studies which have examined covered interest parity in east Asian economies. Goldsborough and Teja (1991) tested whether parity held in Australia, Hong Kong, Japan, Malaysia, New Zealand and Singapore from 1987M1 to 1990M3, and reported a significant degree of financial integration. Chinn and Frankel (1992) assessed parity for Australia, Hong Kong, Japan, Malaysia, New Zealand and Singapore

---

[1] This is based on Frankel (1993a). Frankel calculates the CID for each region by summing the *actual* covered differentials, which gives insight more into the nature of capital controls in a region than whether impediments to arbitrage are relatively small or large.

against the US dollar from 1982M9 to 1992M3, and found that the average CID for these countries moved from about -1 percentage point to about 0 over this time, indicating a shift from a control on capital inflow to a neutral position. Given the liberalisation that has occurred, as discussed above, these results are not surprising.

While the previous studies are relatively recent, there is scope for expanding them in three ways. First, further advances in technology and information processing and the internationalisation of financial intermediation have made the identification and exploitation of arbitrage possibilities easier, and so markets may be even more integrated in the 1990s than previously. In Tokyo, Sydney, Hong Kong and elsewhere in the region, for example, financial institutions are employing more mathematicians and technicians, they are using ever-more high-powered computer hardware and ever-better storage, communications and processing software, and their dealers are scouring markets in a range of assets all day every day in the pursuit of arbitrage opportunities, creating what O'Brien (1992: 99) calls a 'seamless global financial market'.

Second, the earlier studies use regression analysis and focus on average changes in parity but do not examine episodes of exchange control. Chinn and Frankel (1992) for example, present recursive regressions with common break-points but do not identify influences which may be important in a particular market at a particular time. This chapter extends the regression analysis and examines events in markets. This is shown to be important since some countries have applied controls on capital selectively and episodically rather than systematically.

Third, the previous studies focus on the developed forward markets of the western Pacific, where the data are of high quality. The existence and depth of these markets is itself an indication of substantial integration and a tendency for covered interest parity is anticipated. Forward markets have existed for some time in countries such as Korea, Indonesia, Taiwan and Thailand, even if they are incomplete. This chapter assesses covered interest parity not just for Australia, Hong Kong, Japan, Malaysia and Singapore, but also for Taiwan and Thailand using new data, and so provides an opportunity to compare the integration of some of the most and some of the least developed markets in the region (Glick 1988; Emery 1991).

Covered interest parity holds when, as stated in chapter 3,

$$i_{t,k} = i_{tk}^* + f_{t,t+k}. \tag{4.2}$$

Covered interest parity is tested by re-arranging and parameterising (4.2) as

$$f_{t,t+k} = \alpha + \beta(i_t - i_t^*) + u_t, \tag{4.3}$$

and the null hypothesis of covered interest parity is $\alpha = 0$, $\beta = 1$.[2] Interest rate and exchange rate quotes are end-period when available, they are taken as close together in time as possible and an attempt was made to draw rates from assets which are as comparable as possible (Frenkel and Levich 1975). The interest differential and forward discount are stationary for all countries except Australia, which the standard tests indicate are I(1) and cointegrated, and Taiwan, which the tests indicate are I(1) but not cointegrated.[3] Table 4.1 summarises the results from estimating (4.3) using OLS in levels for all countries, except for Australia, for which the estimates are corrected for bias using the technique of Phillips and Hansen (1990) and Taiwan, for which estimation is in first differences.[4] The coefficients and standard error of the constant and slope are presented in columns (2) and (3) and their joint significance and marginal significance in column (4).

Covered interest parity is rejected for all countries in the sample (except Taiwan for which the standard errors are very large), in most instances because of the significance of the constant – that is, there is a non-zero CID. For all countries except Taiwan and Malaysia (full sample), the slope

[2] To the extent that (4.2) is an identity, it does not contain an error term and can be written with either variable as the dependent variable. Equation (4.2) is in fact an approximation of the true relationship between interest rates and the forward discount, with the error in the approximation equal to the difference of the remainder terms of the linear approximations of $\ln(1+i)$ and $\ln(1+i^*)$. Strictly speaking, therefore, the null hypothesis is not correctly stated, but if the difference term is negligible as expected (given that interest rates are in decimals), then the constant should be dominated by other effects which are of interest.

[3] The ADF(1) statistics for the interest differential and forward discount stated in table 4.1 are, respectively, -2.07 and -1.61 for Australia, -3.91^* and -3.29^* for Hong Kong, -2.80 and -2.91^* for Japan, -3.98^* and -3.58^* for Malaysia (with trend), -3.81^* and -4.45^* for Singapore, -2.35 and -2.44 for Taiwan, and -3.72^* and -3.36^* for Thailand, with the critical values based on Fuller (1976). The ADF(1) test on the error from a regression of the forward discount on the interest differential is -4.01^* for Australia and -2.21 for Taiwan, with the critical values based on MacKinnon (1991)

[4] Two points are relevant here. First, the outcomes for Australia and Taiwan are not very sensitive to the different specification. The constant and slope coefficients (and standard error) in uncorrected levels are, respectively, -0.07 (0.02) and 0.95 (0.02) for Australia, and 0.30 (0.10) and 0.58 (0.13) for Taiwan (including a dummy for market closure in mid-1992), although the slope coefficient in Taiwan's case is different from 1 and the joint null is rejected (chi-square (2) is 10.6) in levels estimation. Secondly, ARCH(q) was statistically significant in the estimations for Australia (ARCH(5)), Hong Kong (ARCH(5)), Malaysia (ARCH(1) full sample only) and Singapore (ARCH(2)). The results for Australia and Hong Kong were not corrected – in Australia's case because the coefficient on ARCH(5) was explosive and in Hong Kong's case because the coefficient on the ARCH(5) process was statistically insignificant. The standard errors for Malaysia (full sample) and Singapore are not corrected for the bias induced by overlapping observations. While the covariance matrix is affected by overlapping observations, the uncorrected and corrected standard errors are generally very similar and statistical inference is unaffected, and so the bias maintained in not adjusting the standard errors in these two cases is probably negligible.

Table 4.1. *Test of covered interest parity, 1985M12–1994M12*

Country	Period (1)	Constant ($\alpha = 0$) (percentage points) (2)	Interest differential ($\beta = 1$) (3)	$\alpha = 0, \beta = 1$ ($\chi^2(2)$) (4)
Australia (o)	1985M12–1994M12	−0.06 (0.04)	0.94* (0.03)	51.42* (0.000)
Hong Kong (o)	1984M1–1994M12	−0.04* (0.01)	0.97 (0.05)	26.7* (0.000)
Japan (o)	1984M1–1994M10	−0.01* (0.002)	1.01* (0.005)	40.1* (0.000)
Malaysia (o)	1985M1–1994M10	0.14* (0.03)	0.87* (0.03)	—
	1987M1–1992M6	0.20* (0.03)	0.93 (0.04)	90.2* (0.000)
Taiwan (r)	1991M11–1994M4	0.00 (0.04)	0.59 (0.20)	4.32 (0.115)
Thailand (r)	1985M1–1994M9	−0.30 (0.16)	0.99 (0.05)	7.6* (0.022)
Singapore (o)	1980M1–1994M5	0.20* (0.03)	0.96 (0.03)	—

Notes:
  * = statistical significance at the 5 per cent level.
  o = open capital account; r = restrictions on capital account.
  — = not available.

coefficient is numerically very close to 1, although it is marginally statistically different from 1 for Australia and Japan. The rejection covered interest parity is, apart from Taiwan, economically trivial. For all countries except Thailand,[5] the average three-month CID is significantly less than 1 percentage point in absolute terms.

The CID is smallest and the slope coefficient is numerically closest to 1 for Japan, which is not surprising given that the data are euro rates.[6] The results for Japan are important in two respects. First, the interest rates used are euro rates drawn from assets with identical maturity and risk and, along with the forward and spot exchange rates, they are drawn at approximately the same time on the same day so time-measurement errors are minimised: the only reason for covered interest parity not to hold in this case is that there are transactions costs (measured by the bid–offer spread) and these have a minor numerical effect. Secondly, to the extent that covered interest parity holds in east Asian countries against US dollar assets, it will also (very nearly) hold between them and traded yen assets.

Since the data used for Japan are euro rates, they are by definition not directly affected by domestic regulation, exchange control or political risk.

[5] The Thai data are one-month data and so the average three-month covered differential is −0.90.
[6] The differential before 1980 is positive, which is probably explained by the relatively unsophisticated technology of the time, the thinness of the market and the restriction on Japanese players from entering the euro market. The sample for Japan represents the modern period of free markets.

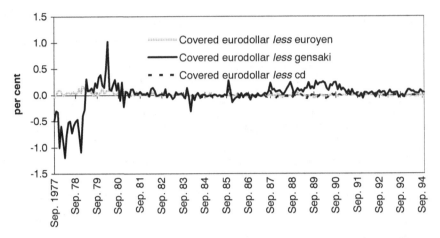

Fig. 4.1. US covered interest rates *less* Japanese interest rate, September
1977–September 1994

The extent of these effects can be seen by estimating the covered interest
differential using domestic onshore and covered foreign offshore returns.
Figure 4.1 plots the covered eurodollar rate and euroyen rate spread with
both the covered eurodollar–gensaki spread and, from 1980, the covered
eurodollar-certificate of deposit spread.[7] Measurement errors increase
when local rates are used, as shown by an increase in 'spikes', and episodes
of domestic market control are apparent. Until the late 1970s, controls were
maintained on gensaki transactions and drove domestic yen interest rates
above euro yen rates, suggesting controls on capital inflow aimed at stem-
ming yen appreciation (Ito 1986). After 1980, however, the covered interest differential settled mostly to zero, except in 1988–90, when there was a
sustained positive differential in the gensaki-based differential but not in
the CD-based differential, a fact which suggests that the 1988–90 episode
was peculiar to the gensaki market. This appears to reflect thinness in the
gensaki market at a time of market expectation of substantial capital gains
to be made by holding bonds on the balance sheet.[8] While the CD rate is

[7] While the CD rate is usually regarded as the more representative open market rate in Japan
in recent years (de Brouwer 1996), it developed only in the 1980s. In the 1970s, the gensaki
was the only open market in Japan, and it still remains relatively deep (outstandings at
September 1994 totalled Y12.5 trillion compared to Y18.7 trillion in CDs), although it is less
traded.

[8] Viewed in isolation, the jump in the covered eurodollar–gensaki spread could be interpreted as evidence of controls on capital outflow, possibly to stem yen depreciation (the yen
depreciated 18 per cent from Y125 at October 1988 to Y152.85 at June 1990). This interpretation is not consistent with the eurodollar–CD spread and the absence of formal capital
controls, and is better explained as a distortion peculiar to the gensaki market.

said to be manipulated by banks at times,[9] the distortion does not appear to be profitable in terms of arbitrage and the CD rate is essentially identical to the euroyen rate (and these rates are indistinguishable in figure 4.1).

Australia, Hong Kong and Singapore are similar in that while covered interest parity is rejected, the rejection is marginal and numerically insubstantial and their covered interest differentials appear to have declined in the 1990s. For Australia, the average differential declined from − 0.2 per cent from 1987M1 to 1990M12 to − 0.1 per cent from 1991M1 to 1994M12.[10] The euro covered differential, data for which are available only from mid-1992, is approximately 0. The average differential is smaller for Hong Kong and fell from − 0.035 from 1984–91 to − 0.021 from 1992–1994. For Singapore, the average differential declined from 0.26 in 1980M1–1990M12 to 0.11 in 1991M1–1994M6. The developments in technology and trading mentioned above suggest that markets can now conduct arbitrage more finely, and this improvement occurred largely around the turn of the decade. The result for Singapore is noteworthy in that the various controls used by the MAS to isolate the domestic Singapore dollar money market from the Asian (US) dollar market appear to have no obvious effect on the covered interest differential.

The results for Malaysia, Thailand and, especially, Taiwan are less supportive of parity. While covered interest parity is rejected for Malaysia over the full data period from 1985 to 1994, this is largely owing to two episodes of selective control in exchange markets in 1986 and 1994: once these episodes are excluded from the sample, the interest differential and the forward rate move one-for-one with each other. The average covered differential from 1987 to 1993 is 0.16 percentage points, in contrast to 0.93 in 1986 and − 1.46 from February to April 1994. In 1986, sustained weakening of commodity prices, exports and domestic output from 1984 placed downward pressure on the ringgit and induced speculation against the currency, especially in April and August. While interbank rates rose substantially during these episodes, the large positive covered differentials at these times indicate (undeclared) controls on capital outflow to support the ringgit. In contrast, from late 1993, the ringgit faced strong upward pressure as short-term capital flowed into the high-yielding money and

---

[9] Based on an interview in Tokyo on 20 February 1995; banks sometimes reduce the issue of CDs in order to put upward pressure on CD rates and, therefore, on short-term lending rates.

[10] The data were carefully selected as the last working day of the month for both Australia and the United States. Daily Australian Treasury Note data were not available before December 1985, although weekly auctions were held. Tests which include data before December 1985 are likely to contain large measurement errors, and inferences drawn from these tests are misleading.

share markets. In response, Bank Negara Malaysia prohibited banks from conducting swaps and forward transactions which were not related to trade, investment or inventory, raised and extended reserve requirements on all deposits from abroad (including the vostro accounts of foreign banks with Malaysian banks), set a ceiling on domestic banks' net external liabilities and prohibited residents from selling short-term financial instruments to foreigners in January and February 1994.[11] These restrictions were mostly eased by mid-1994 and the covered differential narrowed significantly.

Despite the thinness in the market and exchange controls applied over at least the 1980s, the statistical tests for Thailand are supportive of covered interest parity, although this seems to be caused by large standard errors (the standard error of the equation is 1 percentage point which is at least 10 times that for other countries except Taiwan).[12] The differential averaged − 0.34 percentage points over the past decade, which is only slightly greater in absolute terms than the average 0.24 for developed free markets in the 1980s. The average in the second half of the 1980s is − 0.49, compared to − 0.17 in the 1990s, which suggests increased integration and is consistent with the removal of some major capital controls in the early 1990s. These figures belie large variation in the covered interest differential at times – for example, − 0.85 per cent from 1986 to mid-1989 and − 1.7 per cent in the first half of 1993, both of which suggest controls on capital inflow and both of which were periods of baht appreciation. The fact that one of these episodes occurs after the May 1990 and April 1991 reforms suggests that liberalisation of the capital account is not complete.

Parity is formally accepted for Taiwan using 90-day data in first differences, but it is only just so and it is only because the standard errors are relatively very large. (Parity is strongly rejected in levels.) The standard errors are much wider than in the Australian, Malaysian and Singaporean cases, and the slope coefficient is substantially lower numerically.[13] The CID was largely negative from November 1991 until March 1993 (average of − 0.2 percentage points for 90-day assets), and positive thereafter (average of 0.15 percentage points). The particularly large negative differential from June to August 1992 is coincident with the record appreciation of the New Taiwan dollar around July 1992, when the $NT/$US rate broke the $NT25 barrier, falling to $NT24.65 from a peak of $NT40.4 at September 1985. A

---

[11] The 1986 episode is reported in Bank Negara Malaysia *Quarterly Bulletin*, 1 (1 and 2), and the 1993–94 episode is reported in the Bank Negara Malaysia *Quarterly Bulletin*, 9 (1).

[12] Moreover, Thai data are monthly averages.

[13] When estimated in levels, the slope coefficient is numerically similar to that estimated in first differences (0.58 compared to 0.59). Parity in levels is firmly rejected (the OLS standard error is 0.09).

negative differential implies controls on capital inflow, which is consistent with the authorities' stand against the appreciation of the New Taiwan dollar – indeed, the authorities closed the market during this time. This caused considerable uncertainty in the forward market, with the buy–sell spread widening substantially in August and September.

Uncovered interest rate parity

Basic tests of uncovered interest parity

The standard macroeconomic approach to analysing the impact of foreign interest rates on domestic interest rates is the uncovered interest parity condition,

$$i_{t,k} = i^*_{t,k} + \Delta s^e_{t,t+k}, \tag{4.4}$$

the usual test of which is the parameterisation of (4.4) as

$$\Delta s^e_{t,t+k} = \alpha + \beta(i_{t,k} - i^*_{t,k}) + \varepsilon_t. \tag{4.5}$$

The null hypothesis of uncovered interest parity is $\beta = 1$. In this specification, a possible exchange risk premium is subsumed into the constant and, to the extent that it is time-varying, into the error term. The expected depreciation is not directly observable but may be proxied by the forward rate, survey expectations or the actual depreciation over the period t to $t + k$ on the assumption that expectations are rational in the Muthian sense that they are formed using all available information (and so, accordingly, the market may err in its exchange rate predictions but not on a systematic basis). All methods have major drawbacks but the rational expectations approach is used here for comparability with the literature.[14] The actual depreciation may be decomposed into an expected depreciation, which is formed on the basis of all available information (Ω_t), and a forecast error term (ϖ_t) which has an expected mean of zero

$$\Delta s_{t,t+k} \equiv \Delta s^e_{t,t+k} + \varpi_t, \tag{4.6}$$

---

[14] On the assumption that expectations are formed rationally and that investors are risk neutral, the forward discount may be used as a proxy of the expected depreciation, but it is well known that in practice the forward discount is a biased and uninformative predictor of expected depreciation (Attfield, Demery and Duck 1985: 161–76; Hodrick 1987). Alternatively, expectations may be proxied by surveys of the expectations of currency dealers. Survey measures, however, are highly correlated with the forward rate (Froot and Frankel 1989), they tend to be biased, they may be unreliable (who knows whether the respondents are telling the truth and whether they plan to act on what they say?), or they may just not be available.

where $\Delta s^e_{t,t+k} = E_t[\Delta s_{t,t+k} \mid \Omega_t]$ and $E[\varpi_t \mid \Omega_t] = 0$, and is substituted into (4.6),

$$\Delta s_{t,t+k} = \alpha + \beta(i_{t,k} - i^*_{t,k}) + \omega_t \qquad (4.7)$$

where ω is a composite error term, $\omega_t = \varpi_t + \varepsilon_t$. Given (4.4) and (4.6), the uncovered interest differential (UID) is defined as

$$UID_{t,k} = i^*_{t,k} + \Delta s_{t,t+k} - i_{t,k}. \qquad (4.8)$$

The change in the log of the exchange rate and the estimated UID in all countries appear stationary (at the 1 per cent level) over the periods listed in table 4.3, but the evidence for stationarity of the interest differential is more ambiguous. The standard tests suggest that the interest differentials of Australia, Hong Kong, Indonesia, Singapore and Thailand are stationary at the 5 per cent critical level and those of Japan and Taiwan at the 10 per cent level, while those of Korea, Malaysia and the Philippines are not stationary.[15] This indicates that there is more persistence in interest differentials than in the depreciation, which suggests that the interest differential and depreciation may be different processes. This is more apparent for countries which have exercised substantial (even if occasional) control over the capital account. It also suggests that the domestic rate and US interest rate are not likely to be cointegrated for Korea, Malaysia and the Philippines at conventional levels.

The estimations of (4.7) and (4.8) are reported in table 4.2.[16] Given that (4.7) has performed very poorly in the literature, with an average coefficient of about -0.8 even in well developed and sophisticated markets (Froot and Thaler 1990), it is not expected to perform well with this data set. Indeed, looking at column (2), this expectation is met.[17] The

[15] The ADF(1) statistics for the interest differential, change in the exchange rate and uncovered interest differential are, respectively, -3.14^*, -6.88^* and -6.76^* for Australia; -3.87^*, -6.16^* and -4.65^* for Hong Kong; -3.75^*, -4.06^* and -3.86^* for Indonesia; $-2.78\#$, 6.83^* and -6.01^* for Japan; -2.37, -3.39^* and -3.30^* for Korea; -2.26, -6.50^* and -5.80^* for Malaysia; -2.36, -3.41^* and -3.27^* for the Philippines; -3.92^*, -7.04^* and -6.47^* for Singapore; $-2.83\#$, -4.18^* and -4.42^* for Taiwan; and -3.38^*, -6.67^* and -5.54^* for Thailand, where $\#$ and $^* =$ significance at the 10 and 5 per cent levels (Fuller 1976).

[16] The diagnostics of (4.7) were tested for ARCH(q) up to 12 lags and in all cases conditional variances were found to be ARCH(1). The equations were re-estimated with ARCH(1) for all countries except Korea and the Philippines for which the variances are explosive. If ARCH(1) errors are included, the slope coefficient is -0.04 (with a standard error of 0.12) in the Korea and -0.24 (with a standard error of 0.28) in the Philippines equation. The results and inference are *not* qualitatively different for the other countries when estimation is by OLS or by OLS with the Newey–West correction for overlapping observations.

[17] Chinn and Frankel (1992) test uncovered interest parity by regressing the domestic interest rate on a constant and the foreign (US) interest rate *less* the survey measure of expected depreciation. The slope coefficient is always significantly different from zero and the implied coefficient on the expected depreciation is negative in most cases.

Table 4.2. *Mean uncovered differential and uncovered interest parity,*
1980M1–1994M9

Country	Period	$\Delta s_{t,t+k}=\alpha+\beta id_{t,k}$ $\alpha=0$ (1)	$\Delta s_{t,t+k}=\alpha+\beta id_{t,k}$ $\beta=1$ (2)	Mean uncovered differential (3)
Australia (*o*)	1980M1–1994M9	−0.13 (0.55)	−0.53* (0.41)	−0.44 (0.57)
Hong Kong (*o*)	1984M1 1994M9	−0.04 (0.03)	0.29* (0.07)	0.06 (0.05)
Indonesia (*o*)	1987M1–1994M8	0.90* (0.12)	0.02* (0.07)	−0.69* (0.13)
Japan (*o*)	1980M1–1994M7	−2.80* (0.65)	−2.41* (0.75)	−0.71 (0.64)
Korea (*r*)	1980M1–1994M9	−0.10 (0.23)	0.58* (0.15)	−0.59* (0.22)
Malaysia (*o*)	1981M1–1994M7	−0.51* (0.19)	−1.04* (0.20)	0.49 (0.29)
Philippines (*r*)	1987M1–1994M2	0.34 (1.15)	0.23* (0.37)	−1.83* (0.55)
Singapore (*o*)	1980M1–1994M9	−2.03* (0.40)	−2.29* (0.47)	0.02 (0.25)
Taiwan (*r*)	1980M11–1994M3	0.14 (0.20)	1.25 (0.22)	−0.58* (0.24)
Thailand (*r*)	1986M1–1994M6	−0.34 (0.20)	0.14* (0.20)	−0.71* (0.16)

Notes:
* = statistical significance at the 5 per cent level.
o = open capital account; *r* = restrictions on capital account.

null that $\beta=1$ is rejected in all cases except Taiwan and the rejection is marginal for Korea (using OLS). The slope coefficient is also positive for Indonesia, the Philippines and Thailand but is negative otherwise, and significantly so for Hong Kong, Malaysia, Japan and Singapore. Herein lies the anomaly: if parity is conditional on arbitrage, it should hold in open markets but not in closed ones, but the countries with what are regarded as the more liberalised, developed and open financial markets in the region tend to be the ones which most strongly reject uncovered interest parity, while the countries with what are regarded as the more repressed and insular financial markets are the ones where parity holds, or is closer to holding. This is addressed below, but it is worth noting at this stage that the contrast is between economies with *open and closed capital accounts*, not between economies with flexible or fixed/managed exchange rates. Accordingly, the argument that the outcome simply reflects the 'fact' that exchange rate movements are more predictable in fixed or managed rate systems is not compelling. If this were the case, there should be no distinction between Hong Kong and Singapore on the one hand, and Korea and Taiwan on the other.

Now consider the UID in column (3). In his study of G7 countries, Marston (1993) found average UIDs (relative to the United States) from 1966 to 1989 to be negative but not significant, although the standard errors were large, and he interpreted this as evidence in support of uncovered interest parity in the long run. Montiel (1993) found that mean differentials are generally different from zero in developing countries. In the western Pacific economies, the average uncovered differential is not significantly different from zero over periods of several years for Australia, Hong Kong, Japan, Malaysia and Singapore, but *is* both significant and negative for Indonesia, Korea, the Philippines, Taiwan and Thailand. Note that the countries with significant negative uncovered differentials are also the ones with positive slope coefficients in the basic uncovered interest parity test equation.

A negative and significant UID arises because of *persistent* expectation errors, currency or country risk premia or impediments to capital inflow into the countries. Given the length of the sample period, expectation errors are likely to be netted out, and, moreover, if expectation errors are not systematically important for G7 countries (Marston 1993), they are unlikely to be so for non-G7 Asian countries.[18] The explanation for the significant differential, therefore, seems to lie with risk premia or impediments to capital inflows in these countries.[19] The New Taiwan dollar and won are relatively controlled rates not subject to sharp discrete changes, and Taiwan and Korea still employ capital controls, which suggests that the uncovered differential exists because of restrictions on capital flows. The numerical rejection of covered interest parity for Taiwan in the 1990s supports this view. Capital flows have also been controlled in both the Philippines and Thailand and the currencies in these countries have been subject to sharp discrete changes (the peso in 1983, 1984 and 1990, the baht in 1981 and 1984). This suggests that the UID in these countries may reflect a combination of controls and exchange risk premia. The uncovered differential on peso investments is about two and half times the size of that on rupiah and baht investments, which suggests an additional exchange risk, probably caused by the greater political and macroeconomic instability of the Philippines. The rupiah, on the other hand, is a market-determined rate subject to large depreciations (1983 and 1986) and capital controls do not exist, which suggests that the uncovered differential is

---

[18] Over shorter samples, the UIDs may sometimes be significantly different from 0. When the sample is broken into five-year sub-samples, for example, the results do not change dramatically and usually countries which have zero differentials over the full period also have zero differentials over sub-periods. For example, the differentials and standard errors (in per cent) for Australia over three five-year sub-periods are 1.59 (0.83), − 2.05 (1.19) and − 0.90 (0.67), none of which is significant at the 5 per cent level. The striking exception is Hong Kong, for which the differential is 0.24 (0.08) for 1985M1–1989M12 but − 0.12 ((0.05) for 1990M1–1994M12.

[19] The uncovered differential is positive for Malaysia and only barely insignificant, which is consistent with impediments to capital outflow on average. As discussed above, the Malaysian authorities used controls to limit capital outflow from 1984 to 1986 and capital inflow for a short period in 1994.

explained by an exchange risk premium. Das Gupta and Das Gupta (1994) present evidence that the margin between Indonesian and US interest rates is explained not by current account or fiscal imbalances but by domestic financial-sector risks. The tentative conclusion, then, is that the negative uncovered differential for Korea and Taiwan is due to controls, that for the Philippines and Thailand is due to a combination of controls and currency-risk premia, while that for Indonesia is due to a currency-risk premium.

Explaining the anomaly

This still leaves unresolved the issue of why changes in the interest differential have the expected positive effect on a currency depreciation only in repressed or riskier economies but a perverse negative effect in countries with developed and open financial systems. An explanation may lie in the arguments expounded by Isard (1988: 186) and McCallum (1994) about the reaction function of central banks.

Isard argued that a negative slope coefficient in (4.7) occurs when the monetary authority smooths interest rate movements over time. To see this, note that if covered interest parity holds, (4.7) can be restated as

$$\Delta s_{t,t+k} = \alpha + \beta f_{t,t+k} + \omega_t. \tag{4.9}$$

Following Fama (1984), β can be decomposed as

$$\beta = \frac{\text{cov}(\Delta s_{t,t+k}, f_{t,t+k})}{\sigma^2(f_{t,t+k})} = \frac{\sigma^2(\Delta s_{t,t+k}^e) + cov(rp_t, \Delta s_{t,t+k}^e)}{\sigma^2(rp_t) + \sigma^2(\Delta s_{t,t+k}^e) + 2cov(rp_t, \Delta s_{t,t+k}^e)}, \tag{4.10}$$

where the final expression follows from the decomposition of the forward rate as the sum of a risk premium and the future spot rate (Lucas 1982; Fama 1984; Hodrick 1987: 7–15):

$$f_{t,t+k} = rp_{t,t+k} + \Delta s_{t,t+k}^e. \tag{4.11}$$

As Fama pointed out, assuming rational expectations, $\beta < 0$ can occur only when the covariance between the risk premium and the expected depreciation of the exchange rate is negative and larger than the variance of the expected depreciation. He found that for the nine developed economies he examined, regardless of sub-sample or exchange rate regime, the slope coefficient was almost always negative and sometimes significant, and he was puzzled about the cause of the negative covariance: why is a larger depreciation associated with a fall in currency risk? Isard (1988: 186) argued that it may be caused by central bank smoothing of interest rates. Smoothing of interest rates induces smoothing in the forward discount but not in the expected depreciation of the exchange rate, since the underlying fundamentals have not changed, and so there must be negative correlation between the risk premium and expected depreciation as fundamentals change for (4.11) to hold. Intuitively, given a constant interest differential, greater currency risk can be offset only by a lower expected depreciation if the spot rate depreciated when currency risk increased, and so the smoothing of interest rates implies a different level of the exchange rate. This mechanism simply does not work if there are exchange controls, and so there is no reason for the exchange risk premium and expected depreciation to be negatively correlated.

McCallum (1994) takes a different tack. In the first place, he states that the monetary authority attempts to trade off movements in the exchange rate and the interest differential such that it sets the local interest rate lower than otherwise when the currency is appreciating and higher than otherwise when the currency is depreciating. He also states that the monetary authority tries to prevent the interest differential from departing too far from its recent value. These factors imply that the interest differential evolves as

$$id_t = \lambda \Delta s_t + \sigma id_{t-1} + \zeta_t, \tag{4.12}$$

where id is the interest differential (domestic *less* foreign rate), λ is positive since the depreciation is denoted by a positive Δs, σ is the stickiness in the interest differential and ζ is a random (policy) influence.

McCallum does not explain this reaction function further. At first glance, it would appear to be an unusual way to model a central bank's reaction function since central banks explicitly target domestic inflation and real income, not the interest differential. The specification can be rationalised, however, by the following line of argument. Assuming that inflation and real income are functions of the interest rate (among other things), when the central bank uses the local money market rate as its instrument, it can be said to be *implicitly* targeting this interest rate. Since the authorities try to smooth inflation and real output over the economic cycle, such targeting also implies interest rate smoothing. Moreover, central banks intervene in money markets to eliminate the effects of temporary but possibly large imbalances in the supply and demand for overnight cash, and this has an additional smoothing effect. When the foreign central bank has a similar target or operational rule, the foreign interest rate and hence the interest differential is also smoothed. The smoothing of the interest differential, therefore, follows from the combined operations of the two central banks. Central banks in the region also tend to be concerned with movements in the exchange rate, given the implications of changes in it for inflation or for the real exchange rate. This is particularly the case when the exchange rate is fixed or managed, as is the case for seven of the ten economies in this survey. Given that the differential is defined in regard to the US interest rate, this characterisation makes sense only as long as the US central bank is not concerned with adjusting US interest rates to influence the exchange rate. This would seem to be the case.

McCallum then considers uncovered interest parity, writing it with an error term, ξ, to represent 'the myriad of minor influences' (1994: 123) that prevent parity

$$\Delta s^e_{t,t+k} = id_t - \xi_t. \tag{4.13}$$

If there are systematic influences that drive a wedge between the expected depreciation and the interest differential, then the error term may be an ARMA process. Substituting (4.12) for the interest differential and assuming that the wedge term is AR(1)

$$\xi_t = \rho \xi_{t-1} + v_t, \tag{4.14}$$

(4.13) becomes

$$\Delta s^e_{t,t+k} = \lambda \Delta s_t + \sigma id_{t-1} + \zeta_t - v_t - \rho \xi_{t-1}. \tag{4.15}$$

As reproduced in appendix 4.2 (p. 199), McCallum then shows that the rational expectations solution of the exchange rate depreciation is

$$\Delta s_t = [(\rho - \sigma)/\lambda] id_{t-1} - (1/\lambda)\zeta_t + [1/(\lambda + \sigma - \rho)]v_t \tag{4.16}$$

McCallum argues that a negative coefficient on the interest differential is not inevitable but is likely since interest differentials are generally highly autocorrelated – that is, σ is close to 1 – and systematic wedges in the parity condition are probably small – that is, ρ is close to 0 – for his sample of the G3 (1994: 125).

How is this relevant to the anomalous results outlined above? In the first place, interest differentials do tend to be highly autocorrelated for the economies in this survey. The first-order autocorrelation coefficients for Australia, Japan and Taiwan, for example, are 0.92, 0.95 and 0.91, respectively, for the sample lengths outlined in table 4.1. But the key is ρ, the persistence in the wedge that prevents uncovered interest parity. When the UID is highly autocorrelated ρ is close to 1 and offsets σ. A partial offset implies that β is negative, a full offset implies that β is 0, and a more than complete offset implies that β is positive. ρ is positive when there are transactions costs, an exchange risk premium or capital controls. If the risk premium is time-varying rather than constant, then ρ is expected to be smaller, and if exchange controls are systematic rather than episodic, then ρ is expected to be closer to 1. This appears to fit well with the countries examined. β is positive and significant for Korea and Taiwan, both of which have historically enforced systematic capital controls. β is positive but not significant for the Philippines and Thailand, which have enforced capital controls but are also subject to bouts of currency weakness. is positive but insignificant for Indonesia, which has relatively open foreign exchange markets but recent experiences of major currency instability. β is negative, mostly significantly so, for Australia, Hong Kong, Japan, Malaysia and Singapore, which are countries with open capital accounts, relative exchange rate stability and hence low ρ. Exchange controls in Malaysia have been applied periodically but not systematically. In short, the results across different countries and exchange rate regimes dovetail with McCallum's exposition of the interaction between the standard uncovered interest parity condition and the central bank's policy function. This does not 'prove' McCallum's model but it is evidence in support of it, and it suggests that uncovered interest parity may contain information about the degree of financial integration. One extension of the analysis would be to use different ARMA specifications of the error term in (4.13).

If the model is correct, then two implications should follow. The first is that the behaviour of β over time should reflect changing openness in the capital account. Appendix 4.3 (p. 201) sets out plots of rolling regressions of β estimated by OLS with samples of 60 observations. β is mostly (if not always) negative for Australia, Hong Kong, Japan, Malaysia and Singapore and mostly positive for Korea and Taiwan (figures A4.3.1–A4.3.7). The movement in β appears to be consistent with priors about developments in the capital account in various countries. For example, β is positive for Malaysia only in 1986 and in early 1994, which coincides with the two episodes of exchange control. β gradually became negative in Korea in the second half of the 1980s, but sharply reversed and became positive in 1989, coincident with the reversal of capital account and financial reform. β has been consistently positive in Taiwan, indicating little easing in the true bind of controls. On the other hand, caution is advised in interpreting these results since there is some instability in this coefficient in all countries.

The other implication of the model is that, if it is correct, it should be possible to decompose β into underlying structural parameters estimating ρ and λ from (4.12) and, given β from (4.7), σ. This is not successful. For Korea and Taiwan, for example, the exchange rate targeting coefficient, λ, obtained by estimating (4.12), is not significantly different from 0. If this were the case, β would be indeterminate. In the case of Australia, the estimates of λ and σ from (4.12) are 0.007 and 0.92 which, for an estimate of β

of -0.53, implies that the stickiness in the wedge in the parity condition, ρ, is 0.99. This is implausibly high.

Cointegration of interest rates

Analysis of uncovered interest parity is typically conducted in terms of the relationship between the expected depreciation and the interest differential, but it can be restated with the focus on the relationship between domestic and foreign interest rates, given expectations about movements in the exchange rate. In particular, if interest rates and the exchange rate are I(1) processes, then it is interesting to ask whether domestic and foreign interest rates are cointegrated and, if so, does the cointegrating relation show a greater tendency for interest rates to equalise over time? In this framework, the expected depreciation is I(0) and does not enter the cointegrating relation but may be part of the dynamics of the relationship.[20] Chinn and Frankel (1992) and Glick and Moreno (1994) state that there is little evidence of cointegration between domestic and foreign rates, but it is worth exploring this issue in more depth.

The long-run relationship between rates is

$$i_{t,k} = \tilde{\alpha} + \tilde{\beta} i_{t,k}^{*} + \nu_{t}, \tag{4.17}$$

where the constant term is a wedge parameter between interest rates possibly caused by a risk premium or other asset differences. If interest rates are integrated processes of order 1, they are also cointegrated if the residual, ν_t, is I(0). The method used in this chapter to test for cointegration and estimate the cointegrating vector is the vector autoregression (VAR) maximum likelihood technique outlined by Johansen and Juselius (1990). Letting $X = [i^*,i]'$, the VAR is

$$X_t = \mu + \sum_{i=1}^{n} \Pi_i X_{t-i} + \varepsilon_t \tag{4.18}$$

which may be rewritten without loss of generality as a vector error-correction model,

$$\Delta X_t = \mu + \pi X_{t-1} + \sum_{i=1}^{n-1} \Gamma_i \Delta X_{t-i} + \varepsilon_t \text{ where } \pi = -[I - \Pi_1 - \ldots - \Pi_n]. \tag{4.19}$$

Given that π is a 2×2 matrix, i^* and i are cointegrated if π is of rank 1. If the matrix is of rank 2, then the interest rates are stationary, while if the

[20] McCallum's model does not affect this redefinition of uncovered interest parity. Rewriting (4.16) in terms of the domestic interest rate yields the equation,

$$i_t = i_t + \frac{\lambda}{\rho - \sigma} \Delta s_{t+1}$$

matrix is of rank 0, then the interest rates are integrated but not cointegrated. If the matrix is of rank 1, it can be decomposed as the product of two matrices, $\alpha\beta'$, with β' the cointegrating vector. The rank of π is assessed on the basis of two tests on the characteristic roots of π, the lambda max test statistic, which tests the null hypothesis of r cointegrating vectors against the alternative hypothesis that there are $r + 1$ cointegrating vectors, and the trace test statistic, which tests the null hypothesis that the number of cointegrating vectors is less than or equal to r against a general alternative (where the maximum value of r is the dimension of π).

The results for the ten countries in this study are presented in table 4.3. Columns (1) and (2) present the lambda max and trace test statistics for one cointegrating vector and, based on these statistics, column (3) summarises whether the domestic and foreign rate are cointegrated, with c indicating cointegration and nc indicating no cointegration. A constant term is included in the cointegrating relation and the estimate, equivalent to $\tilde{\alpha}$ in (4.17), is presented in column (4) (in percentages rather than decimals). The coefficient equivalent to $\tilde{\beta}$ in (4.17) is presented in column (5) and the chi-square (1) test statistic equivalent to the test that $\tilde{\beta}$ is 1 and the chi-square (2) test statistic equivalent to the joint test that $\tilde{\alpha} = 0$, $\tilde{\beta} = 1$ are presented in columns (6) and (7), respectively. The three-month-ahead change in the log of the exchange rate is included in the regression as an I(0) variable. Generally, a lag length of 4 was selected for the VAR.[21]

The claim that there is little evidence of cointegration between domestic and foreign interest rates would seem to be too strong. Over the full sample, domestic rates in Hong Kong, Indonesia, Japan, Singapore, Taiwan and Thailand are cointegrated with the US rate, although this is so in all sub-periods only for Hong Kong and Taiwan. For all countries except Indonesia and Korea, the local rate is cointegrated with the US rate in the 1990s. For all countries except Malaysia the US interest rate has a positive impact on the local interest rate, which indicates that capital controls do not succeed in isolating domestic rates from foreign rates entirely. This impact has been increasing numerically over time in Hong Kong, Indonesia, Singapore and Thailand but decreasing in Taiwan. In all cases of cointegration, the constant term in the cointegrating relation is significant, indicating that assets are not identical, and in all cases apart from Japan and Taiwan in the 1980s it is positive, indicating that local

---

[21] The exceptions are Thailand, for which a lag length of 2 was selected to reduce serial correlation in the residuals from the estimation, and Australia for the period 1985M1–1989M12, for which a lag length of 2 was selected since longer lag lengths produce bizarre results (for a lag length of 4, there is cointegration with a constant of 49 and a slope coefficient of 31.77).

assets generally require a premium over US assets. Some premium is expected since the US asset is US Treasury Bills and other country assets are interbank or non-official securities, but it is notably large for Indonesia and the Philippines, which are countries with episodes of currency and financial instability. It is not possible to identify a sensible long-run relationship between interest rates in Korea and Malaysia over the past 15 years, and in Malaysia's case, the impact of the US rate is negative from the mid-1980s.

One explanation of the insignificance of US interest rates on Malaysian rates may be that Malaysia is part of a 'yen bloc' but this explanation is not very persuasive. Arbitrage is by definition concerned with the relationship between a pair of interest rates, and arbitrage over a set of interest rates is simply the condition that arbitrage holds over all pairs in the set. If the theoretical motivation for testing for a long-run relationship between rates is that arbitrage drives the rates of comparable assets together, then there seems little additional information to be gleaned by testing for cointegration between more than two rates. Even if Malaysia were part of a yen bloc, it would still be tied to US interest rates by arbitrage. It also begs the question that if the ringgit is tied to the yen, why do US interest rate shocks have a positive effect on yen but not on ringgit interest rates? In terms of the long-run relationship between interest rates, the findings of Chinn and Frankel (1992) and Glick and Moreno (1994) that the influence of US and Japanese rates on east Asian rates changes over time is difficult to interpret. What those findings may point to, however, is that the *dynamics* of uncovered interest parity – the fact that the influence of the foreign rate on the domestic rate in the short term depends on expectations about changes in the exchange rate – are important and can reveal information about which exchange rate the monetary authority targets. But the point still holds that movements in the exchange rate would not be expected to reveal information about long-run or equilibrium parity relationships since the expected depreciation is stationary. This suggests that estimation of a cointegrating vector over short periods may not be informative – and, indeed, cointegration is most evident (and perhaps the vectors most plausible) in tests over the full sample. In this context, the evidence of cointegration is weaker for countries with managed exchange rates *and* capital controls, such as Korea, Malaysia, the Philippines and Thailand, and for countries which are thought to have large and time-varying risk premia, such as Indonesia and the Philippines.

Table 4.3. Cointegration of domestic and foreign interest rates, 1980M1–1994M12

Country	Period	λ $H_0:r=0$ $H_1:r=1$ (1)	Trace $H_0:r>=0$ $H_1:r>=1$ (2)	Cointeg. (3)	$\bar{\alpha}$ (4)	$\bar{\beta}$ (5)	$\bar{\beta}=1$ $\chi^2(1)$ (6)	$\bar{\alpha}=0, \bar{\beta}=1,$ $\chi^2(2)$ (7)
Australia (o)	1980M1–1994M12	11.80	14.85	nc	-0.94	2.23	3.48#	8.66*
	1980M1–1984M12	12.81	16.37	nc	0.00	1.13	0.08	3.34
	1985M1–1989M12	10.30	17.30	nc	-3.38	4.11	1.98	10.07*
	1990M1–1994M12	27.85*	32.04*	c	-0.15	1.63	3.72#	6.36*
Hong Kong (o)	1984M1–1994M12	23.44*	29.28*	c	0.21	0.80	3.38#	6.71*
	1985M1–1989M12	16.95*	19.39#	c	1.34	-0.91	1.83	8.50*
	1990M1–1994M12	29.86*	31.86*	c	0.00	1.06	4.18*	13.54*
Indonesia (o)	1983M1–1994M8	18.71*	20.03*	c	2.05	0.68	1.17	15.27*
	1985M1–1989M12	18.35*	24.72*	c	3.30	-0.02	2.59	13.91*
	1990M1–1994M8	13.52	16.22	nc	1.62	0.81	0.23	7.15*
Japan (o)	1980M1–1994M10	15.70*	19.00#	c	0.06	0.61	3.56#	9.97*
	1980M1–1984M12	11.78	13.99	nc	-0.01	0.62	1.29	8.49*
	1985M1–1989M12	7.02	12.48	nc	0.31	0.48	0.49	5.62#
	1990M1–1994M10	19.41*	34.00*	c	-0.20	0.98	0.01	13.51*
Korea (r)	1980M1–1994M12	7.43	11.90	nc	2.30	0.39	1.04	4.78#
	1980M1–1984M12	14.02#	15.14	nc	-0.79	1.37	1.59	2.76
	1985M1–1989M12	5.47	6.30	nc	-3.83	3.41	1.56	5.13#
	1990M1–1994M12	8.87	11.89	nc	3.45	-0.10	4.23*	8.72*
Malaysia (o)	1981M11–1994M10	9.44	13.86	nc	2.50	-0.53	4.39*	4.39
	1981M11–1984M12	4.47	8.55	nc	1.69	0.19	0.58	0.71
	1985M1–1989M12	8.02	12.42	nc	3.19	-0.86	2.14	6.41*
	1990M1–1994M10	19.54*	26.64*	c	2.50	-0.59	12.15*	12.34*
Philippines (r)	1980M1–1994M5	8.18	11.68	nc	4.02	-0.08	0.99	4.72#
	1980M1–1984M12	10.28	12.63	nc	6.16	-1.01	7.50*	7.95*
	1985M1–1989M12	15.24#	17.81	nc	-3.15	4.40	5.14*	12.02*
	1990M1–1994M5	17.08*	23.78*	c	1.67	2.17	8.06*	11.96*

Singapore (o)	1980M1–1994M12	14.95#	18.23#	c	−0.13	0.73	5.41*	11.56*
	1980M1–1984M12	8.61	14.07	nc	0.19	0.65	1.33	6.94*
	1985M1–1989M12	7.66	10.08	nc	0.03	0.56	3.09#	7.29*
	1990M1–1994M12	25.14*	29.16*	c	−0.09	0.79	11.05*	22.92*
Taiwan (r)	1980M11–1994M6	22.22*	26.83*	c	1.08	0.41	9.39*	9.45*
	1980M11–1984M12	15.56#	19.95#	c	−0.16	0.84	0.13	9.48*
	1985M1–1989M12	17.69*	19.24#	c	−0.45	1.06	0.05	8.60*
	1990M1–1994M7	18.08*	23.90*	c	1.16	0.65	4.46#	13.44*
Thailand (r)	1980M1–1994M12	20.82*	27.98*	c	0.87	0.86	0.80	11.24*
	1980M1–1984M12	8.93	14.24	nc	1.56	0.62	1.97	5.05#
	1985M1–1989M12	9.15	12.74	nc	−2.60	2.46	2.27	4.35
	1990M1–1994M12	15.62#	22.33*	c	0.54	1.30	1.50	8.96*

Notes:

= significance at the 10 per cent level; * = significance at the 5 per cent level.

o = open capital account; r = restrictions on capital account.

c = cointegration, nc = no cointegration.

Accounting for innovations over time

Another way to assess the time-varying influence of the foreign interest rate on the domestic interest rate is to decompose the forecast error variance of a vector autoregression of the three-month domestic and foreign interest rates and the three-month-ahead exchange rate depreciation (that is, decompose the forecast error variance of (4.18) where $X = [i^*_{t,k}, i_{t,k}, \Delta s_{t,t+k}]')$. Like Glick and Moreno (1994), the analysis is restricted to the domestic rate equation but, unlike Glick and Moreno (1994), the depreciation is included since it is a potentially important conditioning variable. In terms of the domestic rate equation, the variance decomposition isolates the proportion of the variance in the domestic rate caused by the innovation in the domestic rate itself and by the foreign rate and depreciation over specified time lengths, and so provides fresh insight into the source and persistence of shocks to the domestic interest rate (see Enders 1995: 294–312).

In order to identify the shocks, a recursive structure is imposed on the original system underlying the reduced system outlined in (4.18)

$$
\begin{bmatrix} 1 & 0 & 0 \\ a_{21} & 1 & 0 \\ a_{31} & a_{32} & 1 \end{bmatrix} \cdot \begin{bmatrix} i^*_{t,k} \\ i_{t,t} \\ \Delta s_{t,t+k} \end{bmatrix} = \mu' + \sum_{i=1}^{n} \Pi'_i \begin{bmatrix} i^*_{t-i,k} \\ i_{t-i,k} \\ \Delta s_{t-i,t-i+k} \end{bmatrix} + \varepsilon'_t.
\tag{4.20}
$$

The foreign interest rate is not determined contemporaneously by either the domestic rate or the expected depreciation, the domestic rate is determined contemporaneously by the foreign rate but not by the expected depreciation and the expected depreciation is determined contemporaneously by both the foreign and domestic interest rates. This ordering is one way to exactly identify the system. It is well known, however, that the assignment of the variance may vary with the ordering of the variables and so some explanation of why this ordering is appropriate is required. If the home country is relatively small, it is not unreasonable to assume that the US rate is unaffected by local conditions (Glick and Moreno 1994). But some feedback may be expected between the local rate and the expected depreciation. However, in McCallum's (1994) model the evolution of the interest differential turns on the recent depreciation rather than expected future depreciation (4.12) while the expected depreciation turns on the current interest differential (4.13), which suggests the ordering outlined above. The alternative sub-ordering for the domestic and expected depreciation was tested and while the magnitudes change, the qualitative results do not. The variance decompositions were estimated for a fourth-order

VAR using RATS. The focus is on how the variance decomposition has evolved over time and three five-year sub-periods from 1980 to 1994 are examined. Table 4.4 reports the percentage of total variance of the domestic interest rate explained by the foreign rate, domestic rate and three-month-ahead change in the natural log of the exchange rate six, 12 and 24 months out.

The proportion of innovations to the domestic interest rate caused by the foreign interest rate has increased over time in Australia, Hong Kong, Indonesia, Japan, the Philippines, Singapore and Thailand, such that the foreign rate now accounts for a greater proportion of innovations than the domestic rate does itself in Australia, Hong Kong, Japan, the Philippines and Singapore. Home-currency depreciation has also been a source of innovations to the domestic interest rate in all countries, less so in Hong Kong, Japan, Korea and Singapore, but notably so in Australia, Indonesia and Malaysia. Overall, domestic factors appear to dominate in Korea, Malaysia, Taiwan and Thailand.

There is an important issue of interpretation in these results. Increased importance of foreign shocks in successive periods can be caused by (at least) two factors. In the first place, it may be that there are more or bigger shocks to foreign than to local rates. Or, alternatively, it could be that the shocks are the same but domestic markets are more open and so foreign shocks have a bigger relative impact than before. Only the latter should properly be regarded as 'increased integration'. Table 4.5 sets out the standard deviations and coefficients of variation of the US Treasury Bill rate and domestic rates during the sub-periods referred to in table 4.4. Variability has increased in the United States but it has also done so, often by a substantial amount, in most countries, but particularly in Australia, Hong Kong, Indonesia, Japan and Singapore. This suggests that, for these countries at least, the increased importance of foreign shocks is not caused by more variability in US rates but by more openness in their domestic financial systems.

Real interest rate parity

Uncovered interest parity, the absence of a currency-risk premium, the Fisher effect and relative PPP are preconditions for real interest rates to be equalised across countries and, given the existence of an UID for a number of countries in the region, equalisation is unlikely (see Piggott 1994 for evidence for G10 countries). This section presents evidence on whether real interest rates in east Asia tend to equalise over time and if not why not.

If the Fisher effect holds, the real interest rate differential may be decomposed as

Table 4.4. *Variance decomposition of the domestic interest rate,*
1980M4–1994M6

Country	Period	% of variance due to foreign rate (number of months)			% of variance due to domestic rate (number of months)			% of variance due to Δ *log spot exchange rate* (number of months)		
		6	12	24	6	12	24	6	12	24
Australia (*o*)	1980M4–1984M12	9	19	21	59	53	51	32	28	28
	1985M1–1989M12	17	2	32	81	74	67	2	2	1
	1990M1–1994M9	47	57	60	39	27	21	14	15	19
Hong Kong (*o*)	—	—	—	—	—	—	—	—	—	—
	1985M1–1989M12	34	56	59	62	40	37	4	4	4
	1990M1–1994M9	79	86	89	19	11	8	2	3	3
Indonesia (*o*)	—	—	—	—	—	—	—	—	—	—
	1985M1–1989M12	5	11	16	94	86	80	1	3	4
	1990M1–1994M5	9	22	25	61	49	45	31	29	30
Japan (*o*)	1980M1–1984M12	30	35	37	65	61	59	5	4	4
	1985M1–1989M12	6	22	33	91	74	62	3	4	5
	1990M1–1994M7	23	57	81	70	40	17	7	3	2
Korea (*r*)	1980M4–1984M12	5	16	20	93	81	76	2	3	4
	1985M1–1989M12	12	30	30	85	60	43	3	10	27
	1990M1–1994M9	7	8	10	92	91	89	1	1	1
Malaysia (*o*)	1981M5–1984M12	31	37	35	57	47	49	12	16	16
	1985M1–1989M12	5	10	13	71	52	50	24	38	37
	1990M1–1994M7	8	14	24	91	83	72	1	3	4
Philippines (*r*)	1980M5–1984M12	5	4	12	81	68	64	14	28	24
	1985M1–1989M12	7	31	50	88	62	44	5	7	6
	1990M1–1994M2	17	42	52	76	53	44	7	5	4
Singapore (*o*)	1980M5–1984M12	52	45	43	42	49	51	6	6	6
	1985M1–1989M12	43	54	54	50	38	36	7	8	10
	1990M1–1994M9	50	63	69	48	35	28	2	2	3
Taiwan (*r*)	1981M3–1984M12	29	28	27	68	67	67	3	5	6
	1985M1–1989M12	17	42	48	72	50	43	11	8	9
	1990M1–1994M3	11	9	9	83	67	65	6	24	26
Thailand (*r*)	1980M5–1984M12	75	54	11	20	13	30	5	33	59
	1985M1–1989M12	10	29	40	89	65	54	1	6	6
	1990M1–1994M6	14	26	38	76	62	52	10	12	10

Notes:
   o = open capital account; *r* = restrictions on capital account.
   — = not available.

Table 4.5. *Relative variability in foreign and domestic interest rates,*
1980M4–1994M6

Country	Period	Standard deviation	Coefficient of variation
United States (*o*)	1980M4–1984M12	2.49	0.23
	1985M1–1989M12	1.05	0.15
	1990M1–1994M9	1.70	0.36
Australia (*o*)	1980M4–1984M12	12.12	0.18
	1985M1–1989M12	14.51	0.17
	1990M1–1994M9	8.21	0.44
Hong Kong (*o*)	—	—	—
	1985M1–1989M12	2.05	0.29
	1990M1–1994M9	2.02	0.37
Indonesia (*o*)	—	—	—
	1985M1–1989M12	2.50	0.19
	1990M1–1994M5	3.93	0.32
Japan (*o*)	1980M1–1984M12	2.15	0.28
	1985M1–1989M12	1.00	0.20
	1990M1–1994M7	2.29	0.47
Korea (*r*)	1980M4–1984M12	4.30	0.27
	1985M1–1989M12	1.78	0.17
	1990M1–1994M9	2.29	0.16
Malaysia (*o*)	1981M5–1984M12	—	—
	1985M1–1989M12	1.00	0.25
	1990M1–1994M7	1.47	0.23
Philippines (*r*)	1980M5–1984M12	7.91	0.49
	1985M1–1989M12	6.79	0.39
	1990M1–1994M2	4.92	0.27
Singapore (*o*)	1980M5–1984M12	2.19	0.24
	1985M1–1989M12	0.89	0.19
	1990M1–1994M9	1.65	0.41
Taiwan (*r*)	1981M3–1984M12	4.29	0.40
	1985M1–1989M12	1.98	0.41
	1990M1–1994M3	1.91	0.26
Thailand (*r*)	1980M5–1984M12	3.68	0.32
	1985M1–1989M12	3.03	0.33
	1990M1–1994M6	3.16	0.36

Notes:
o = open capital account; *r* = restrictions on capital account.
— = not available.

Table 4.6. *Decomposition of the real interest differential*

Country	Period	Real interest differential	Uncovered interest differential	PPP
Australia (o)	1980Q1–1994Q4	−0.58* (0.16)	−0.49 (0.68)	0.09 (0.67)
Hong Kong (o)	1984Q4–1994Q4	1.03* (0.13)	0.05 (0.07)	−0.98* (0.15)
Indonesia (o)	1986Q3–1994Q2	−0.70* (0.29)	−0.81* (0.20)	−0.11 (0.26)
Japan (o)	1980Q1–1994Q3	0.11 (0.11)	−0.94 (0.87)	−1.05 (0.85)
Korea (r)	1980Q1–1994Q4	−0.62* (0.18)	−0.65* (0.27)	−0.03 (0.29)
Malaysia (o)	1981Q1–1994Q3	0.05 (0.14)	0.48 (0.34)	0.43 (0.32)
Philippines (r)	1985Q5–1994Q2	−1.73* (0.35)	−1.97* (0.62)	−0.24 (0.57)
Singapore (o)	1980Q1–1994Q4	0.26* (0.10)	−0.04 (0.31)	−0.30 (0.33)
Taiwan (r)	1980Q4–1994Q1	−0.24 (0.18)	−0.49 (0.36)	−0.25 (0.43)
Thailand (r)	1980Q1–1994Q3	−0.47* (0.20)	−0.93* (0.23)	−0.46* (0.18)

Notes:
* = statistical significance at the 5 per cent level.
o = open capital account; r = restrictions on capital account.

$$r^*_{t,k} - r_{t,k} = i^*_{t,k} - p^{e*}_{t,t+k} - i_{t,k} + p^e_{t,t+k}. \tag{4.21}$$

Adding and subtracting the expected depreciation of the spot rate over the k-period on the right-hand side of (4.21), the real interest differential becomes

$$r^*_{t,k} - r_{t,k} = [i^*_{t,k} + \Delta s^e_{t,t+k} - i_{t,k}] - [p^{e*}_{t,t+k} + \Delta s^e_{t,t+k} - p^e_{t,t+k}] \tag{4.22}$$

where the first bracketed term is the UID and the second is relative PPP. Given the Fisher effect, real interest rates converge only if both uncovered interest parity and relative PPP hold. Expectations are assumed to be formed rationally in the Muthian sense, and so the real interest differential is measurable as

$$r^*_{t,k} - r_{t,k} = [i^*_{t,k} + \Delta s_{t,t+k} - i_{t,k} - \xi_{t+k}] \\ - [p^*_{t,t+k} + \Delta s_{t,t+k} - p_{t,t+k} - \xi_{t+k} - \zeta_{t+k}] \tag{4.23}$$

where ξ is a white-noise depreciation forecast error and ζ is a white-noise inflation forecast error.

Table 4.6 follows (4.23) and decomposes the mean real interest differential into the mean uncovered interest differential and mean purchasing power differential for countries in the region from 1980 to 1994 (using consumer price indexes). It differs from tables 4.1 and 4.2 in that the estimations are based on quarterly rather than monthly observations (since price data are generally only quarterly).

Only in Japan, Malaysia and Taiwan do real interest rates not diverge systematically from real US rates. In Taiwan's case, the mean is relatively large but so are the standard errors, while the mean is relatively small for Japan and Malaysia. In all three countries, numerically large nominal interest differentials are offset by numerically large inflation differentials. Real interest rates in Hong Kong diverge from US real rates over time owing to the failure of PPP, which is not unexpected since nominal rates in Hong Kong closely follow US rates but consumer price inflation is substantially above that of the United States (owing to high productivity in the traded goods sector and a secular shift in expenditure towards the services sector). Real interest rates are not equalised in Australia or Singapore, and it appears to be caused by UID in the case of Australia and a purchasing power differential in the case of Singapore.[22] Real interest rates in Indonesia, Korea, the Philippines and Thailand have systematically diverged from US rates, caused unambiguously by the failure of uncovered interest parity. PPP also fails in Indonesia and Thailand but the failure of uncovered interest parity accounts for most of the real interest differential. Given that the analysis is in terms of averages calculated using quarterly data over an 8–15-year period, the effect of expectation errors is minimised.

This analysis has two implications for research related to the east Asian economies assessed in the book. The first is for applied analysis. Capital controls and exchange risk premia are a recurring source of the wedge between local and foreign interest rates. But this is not always the case, with Hong Kong and Singapore being notable examples. The wedge in these cases arises because of the failure of PPP. The upshot is that empirical modelling based on the assumption that the real interest wedge simply reflects capital controls may be misleading. A major source of the wedge, however, *is* due to capital controls and so it is more than appropriate to motivate theoretical work by claiming that capital controls are a major cause of non-zero real interest differentials.

Conclusion

Money and foreign exchange markets in the region have grown and become more open as governments have deregulated markets and as market players have expanded operations and technology. As Chinn and Frankel (1992) have pointed out, covered interest differentials narrowed considerably over the 1980s, and this chapter shows that differentials are generally even smaller in the 1990s. This would appear to be due to efficiency gains in technology and to the internationalisation of banking.

---

[22] While the rejection of the null that the real interest differential in Australia is zero seems to be caused by the failure of uncovered interest parity, the tests on quarterly and monthly data do not support this conclusion.

However, CIDs are not *uniformly* minimised: the monetary authorities in Malaysia, Taiwan and Thailand have at times imposed exchange controls in order to influence foreign exchange market outcomes and, apart from Taiwan, the effects of these controls are not clearly identified by the generalised analytic techniques popular in the literature. Informal controls such as exist in Singapore do not appear to isolate the local market. While parity is technically also rejected for Australia, Hong Kong, Japan and Singapore, the rejection is not economically significant. The test could not be applied to Indonesia, Korea and the Philippines owing to a lack of data.

The standard view in the literature is that uncovered interest parity contains little or no information about financial openness. This chapter has argued that this is premature. In the first place, information about controls and risk premia may be gleaned by examining *average* UIDs. The mean differential over the past decade or so is negative and significant for Indonesia, Korea, the Philippines, Taiwan and Thailand, for example – probably owing to controls on capital inflow for Korea and Taiwan, a combination of controls and exchange risk premia for the Philippines and Thailand and an exchange risk premium for Indonesia but is not different from zero for Australia, Hong Kong, Japan, Malaysia and Singapore. An interpretation consistent with this result is that while expectation errors may have a substantial impact on estimating parity in the short run, they are not systematic and net out over the longer run.

In the second place, the standard test of uncovered interest parity (regressing the depreciation over period t to $t+k$ on a constant and the interest differential on k-period instruments) applied to countries in the region yields some unusual results. A rise in the domestic rate relative to the foreign rate is associated with a subsequent appreciation of the exchange rate in countries with open and developed financial markets but either a depreciation in countries with exchange controls or no change in the exchange rate in countries with exchange risk premia. The anomaly that parity is more likely to hold in repressed economies but not liberalised economies was shown to be consistent with McCallum's (1994) model of the interaction of uncovered interest parity and a monetary policy reaction function. Indeed, if McCallum's (1994) model is correct, then standard tests of uncovered interest parity may reveal a lot more about financial integration than usually thought and in a rather unexpected way: the more closed the capital account or the riskier the country, the more likely is the slope coefficient to be positive and significant. As shown in the empirical work of this chapter, the oft-derided perverse negative slope coefficient may appear really to be an indication of financial openness and low risk. An interpretation consistent with this result is that uncovered interest parity is not necessarily of itself a flawed device for exposition of argument or simulation modelling.

In the third place, the uncovered parity condition can be rewritten with the domestic rate on the left-hand side and the foreign rate and expected depreciation on the right-hand side. Given non-stationarity of interest rates, the relationship between interest rates can be examined within a cointegration framework. Domestic rates are positively correlated with the US rate in all countries except Malaysia and cointegrated with US rates over all or most of the past 15 years for most countries. Only rates in Hong Kong were shown to be equal to the US rate over the full period, but rates in Australia, Singapore and Thailand have more closely approximated US rates over time. The decomposition of variance from vector autoregressions over time showed that innovations to the domestic rate due to the foreign interest rate have increased over time in Australia, Hong Kong, Indonesia, Japan, the Philippines, Singapore and Thailand. Moreover, the foreign rate now accounts for a greater proportion of innovations than the domestic rate itself in Australia, Hong Kong, Japan, the Philippines and Singapore. Capital controls do not isolate domestic rates completely from foreign rate developments but Korea, Malaysia and Taiwan still appear to be relatively isolated. Overall, the evidence favours the view that markets have become increasingly integrated and assets increasingly substitutable as controls have been eased.

A number of papers have also tested whether there is a greater tendency for real interest rates to be equalised, and interpreted these results as increased financial integration. This inference is generally invalid unless real interest rates are conditioned for exchange rate and inflation expectation errors, risk premia, imperfect pass-through of changes in inflation expectations to nominal interest rates, and real exchange rate dynamics. Mean real interest rate differentials relative to the United States were estimated and found to be insignificantly different from 0 only for Japan, Malaysia and Taiwan (for which the standard errors were large). The mean real interest rate differential was decomposed for countries in the region and the main cause of systematic wedges between domestic and foreign real interest rates was shown to be the failure of uncovered interest parity for Indonesia, Korea, the Philippines and Thailand, and of relative PPP for Hong Kong and Singapore. This implies that the standard theoretical modelling device (used in chapter 6) of assuming that a narrowing of real interest differentials indicates greater financial integration may be a valid first approximation for most countries in this survey.

The policy implications from this analysis are four-fold. First, exchange controls can be effective in the short run, as the experience of Taiwan,

Malaysia and (perhaps) Thailand suggests. The important caveat is, however, whether the trigger for the controls is a flow of short-term 'hot' money or fundamental macroeconomic imbalance. As the failure to avert a ringgit depreciation in 1986 in the face of deteriorating macroeconomic fundamentals in Malaysia demonstrates,[23] interventions may be ineffective if they are used by the authorities to avoid structural adjustment. In this case, deferring necessary adjustment may itself carry additional costs. Even if the controls are effective (in the face of 'hot-money' flows), there are downsides to their use. In the first place, they occur at the cost of frustrating foreign exchange transactions and generating greater uncertainty and risk for market participants. Speculators may be the target of controls but it is difficult, if not impossible, to distinguish the 'hot' from the underlying 'regular' transactions. Moreover, as selective interventions become routine, markets may start to price in a risk premium and investor confidence may be undermined. As discussed in chapter 1, the evidence suggests that controls are not effective in the medium to long term. The experience of Singapore indicates that softer controls, such as moral suasion, do not have an effect over time (if they are inconsistent with the incentives of market players).

Second, countries in the region with capital controls generally have higher real interest rates than countries with free markets. As domestic financial markets are liberalised, policies which maintain this wedge may imply an unnecessarily higher cost of capital and impediment to growth. (This is not necessarily the case if the controls are associated with less volatility in the exchange rate and a lower exchange risk premium in interest rates.)

Third, the deepening of international financial linkages in the countries surveyed in this chapter highlights the need for more market-based monetary management tools and procedures and for more market-consistent domestic macroeconomic policy. If markets are more open and susceptible to external influences, a new discipline is forced on policy. This in turn can have far-reaching and unforeseen consequences for the structure of the economy and the operation of goods and labour markets.

Fourth, there is an increasing focus within the APEC forum on identifying and measuring impediments to trade in services in the Asia Pacific region. For example, the Pacific Economic Cooperation Council (PECC) issued a preliminary report (November 1995) identifying legal restrictions in trade and investment in goods and services in APEC member countries. This information will subsequently be used in implementing APEC's liber-

---

[23] See Beng (1989: 9) and Bank Negara Malaysia *Annual Reports* for details.

alisation programme. What is more relevant to such discussions is not the existence of legal restrictions as such, but whether the restrictions matter – that is, do they affect the outcome in markets? In the case of the financial markets examined in this chapter, the conclusion would be that there are restrictions in markets in some countries in east Asia, particularly Korea and Taiwan, and that these restrictions generate an outcome different to that which a free market would produce.

5

Domestic financial integration: a precondition for international financial integration

It is hardly surprising that economists who are interested in analysing international financial integration focus primarily on the relationship between interest rates on internationally traded financial instruments such as money market instruments and government and corporate bonds. This is, after all, a major part of international financial integration. But it is not the whole story. The macroeconomic impact of international financial integration also depends on the extent of *domestic* financial integration – that is, the integration of domestic institutional interest rates such as deposit and loan interest rates with domestic money market rates – which itself turns on the regulatory and competitive structure of domestic financial markets. This is particularly important in assessing the international financial integration of east Asian economies, since domestic financial markets in these countries are in very different states of development. This chapter focuses on the changing relationship between the money market interest rate and deposit and lending interest rates in the economies of Australia, Hong Kong, Indonesia, Korea, Japan, Malaysia, the Philippines, Singapore, Taiwan and Thailand. The analysis centres on the integration of retail with wholesale markets – or, alternatively stated, with the relationship of non-traded with traded financial instruments.

The first section motivates the analysis of domestic integration by examining the relative depth of money markets and institutional markets in each country. The next section provides a brief summary of institutional arrangements and changes in each country, and notes that substantial liberalisation, greater competitiveness and occasional deterioration in asset quality are three characteristics of banking systems in the region. A set of simple pricing rules is then derived for deposits and loans in a regulated market and in a free market in order to provide an analytical framework to assess the interactions between money market and institutional interest rates. The rules highlight the importance of competition, financial liberalisation and the permanency of money market interest rate shocks in analysing the changing relationship between money market and institutional interest rates. As such, it captures the salient features of banking systems in the east Asian and western Pacific region. Term-structure effects are also shown to be relevant since the effect of a change in the money market rate on institutional rates depends on the permanence of changes to the money market rate. Correlation coefficients and an error-correction model for money and institutional interest rates are presented to reveal how the relationship between them has changed over time. A discussion of the results and country developments is also provided. Finally, the discussion is summarised and three policy implications set out in the conclusion.

The money market and institutional markets

As discussed in chapter 4 and elsewhere (Chinn and Frankel 1994a, 1994b; Glick and Moreno 1994), markets in traded wholesale financial assets in east Asia are generally well integrated with world markets in the sense that arbitrage trade can be, and is, conducted between them, and that foreign interest rate shocks have a direct and often substantial effect on domestic money market rates. In short, money market centres in the region are integrated internationally.

These tests are narrow since they apply to only a quite limited range of assets traded wholesale financial assets. While interest rates on traded assets affect the macroeconomy directly via the exchange rate, their broader effect on consumer and producer choice – and hence national income – depends on how they affect intermediated interest rates. As shown in table 5.1, domestic deposit and bank loan markets are often considerably larger than domestic money markets in east Asian economies.[1] At least until the 1990s, most economies in the region could

---

[1] The money market is defined as the market for traded financial instruments with a maturity of less than one year. The particular instruments which are included varies by country and this chapter follows the definitions outlined by Emery (1991), where relevant. The Australian money market includes bank placements with authorised money market dealers, bank bills (BBs), treasury notes (TNs), negotiable certificates of deposit (NCDs) and promissory notes (PNs). The Hong Kong market includes interbank loans, commercial paper (CPs) and floating rate notes (FRNs), NCDs, bankers' acceptances (BAs) and bills of exchange (BEs). The Indonesian market includes interbank loans, NCDs, CPs, repurchase agreements (RAs), SBIs (sertifikat bank indonesia or Bank Indonesia certificates) and SBPUs (surat berharga pasar uang or money market securities). The Japanese market includes call loans and bills, NCDs, CPs, gensaki or bond repurchases (BRs), financial bills (FBs) and Treasury Bills (TBs). The Korean market includes monetary stabilisation bonds (MSBs), CPs, RAs, NCDs, and TBs (interbank data not available). The Malaysian market includes NCDs, TBs, interbank loans, BAs, and discounts (RPs not available). The Philippine market includes interbank loans, TBs, PNs, CPs and RAs. The Singaporean market includes interbank loans, commercial bills (CBs), TBs and NCDs. The Taiwan market includes TBs, NCDs, CPs and BAs (interbank data not available). The Thai market includes interbank loans, TBs

Table 5.1. *Deposit, loan and money markets in east Asia 1993*

Country	Deposits[a]/GDP	Loans[b]/GDP	Money market/GDP
Australia	0.56	0.69	0.27
Indonesia	0.37	0.44	—
Hong Kong	1.05	1.20	0.71
Japan	1.02	1.19	0.22
Korea	0.38	0.58	0.19
Malaysia	0.77	0.75	0.30[c]
Philippines	0.36	0.27	0.98[c]
Singapore	0.82	0.89	0.40[c]
Taiwan	0.90	0.83	0.15[c]
Thailand	0.69	0.73	0.02[c]
Unweighted average	*0.69*	*0.76*	*0.36*
Canada	0.57	0.60	0.10
USA	0.49	0.61	0.59

Notes:
  [a] = Deposits include demand, savings and time deposits placed with banks (IMF code 24 and 25).
  [b] = Loans are bank credit to the private sector (IMF code 22).
  [c] = 1989 data.
  — = not available.
Source: IMF, *IFS Statistics*; central bank *Statistical Bulletins*; Emery (1991).

generally be characterised as heavily reliant on bank deposits for the domestic mobilisation of funds and on bank credit for external finance. Access to private capital through the stock market or corporate bond issuance has also generally been restricted though, again, this constraint eased somewhat in the 1990s.

   When covered and uncovered interest parity tests were being developed, they were regarded as relevant to policy precisely because the money market rates used were regarded as being closely linked to other rates in the financial system, such that the tests could be used to draw general conclusions about financial integration. Prachowny (1970), for example, tested covered interest parity by using deposit and loan rates. When Marston (1993) tested parity relationships for the G7 countries, he first used prime rates and then used euro rates to demonstrate the effect of capital controls. The interest parity tests can still be applied to the east Asian economies, of course, but the additional step must be taken to assess

and BRs (CBs, CPs and BEs data not available). The Canadian market includes TBs, BAs, CPs and sales finance and consumer loan company paper (interbank data not available). The US market includes interbank loans, TBs, CDs, mutual fund shares, money market fund shares and security repurchase agreements.

whether the integration of money markets does indeed signal broader, more fundamental financial integration.

Recent developments in bank deposit and loan markets

The institutional arrangements and history of markets in the region vary widely by country, but the common thread in the past decade has been a clear shift towards lifting controls on deposit and lending interest rates, on increasing the competitiveness of the domestic banking sector, and on improving supervision of the banking sector, largely in response to serious deteriorations in asset quality. Appendix 5.1 (p. 204) provides a chronology of relevant major banking reforms in each country for the past two decades. The account provided here is very brief, and the reader is referred to Fischer (1993), Fischer and Reisen (1993), Haggard, Lee and Maxfield (1993), Andersen (1993) and central bank annual reports for more detail.

As shown in appendix 5.1, all countries in the sample have now instituted major liberalisation of deposit and lending rates, though the speed of reform has varied substantially by country. Singapore instituted reform in 1975, Australia in the early 1980s, Indonesia in 1983, Japan in 1985–94, Malaysia in 1987 (deposits) and 1991 (loans), Taiwan in 1989, Korea in 1991–4, Thailand in 1992 and Hong Kong in 1994 and 1995.

The formal liberalisation of rates does not necessarily mean that monetary authorities have surrendered other, non-market-based forms of control over institutional rates. The authorities at times use moral suasion (to attempt) to influence the setting of rates by banks, especially when they consider competition in the domestic banking system to be imperfect (as in Thailand, Indonesia, Japan and, to a lesser extent, Australia) or when they provide direct liquidity to banks (as in Indonesia and Japan). Moreover, the shift to a market-based system for the determination of interest rates has not necessarily meant that direct credit rationing and preferential financing have been discontinued (consider Indonesia, Korea, the Philippines and, to a lesser extent, Japan). Historically, public ownership of banks has also been important in Indonesia and, particularly, Taiwan in allowing the authorities to influence the rate outcome.

Generally speaking, monetary authorities have also tried to improve competition within the domestic sector, mainly through easing controls on bank branching (as in Indonesia and, more recently, the Philippines) and on foreign bank entry (as in Australia, Indonesia, the Philippines, Taiwan and Thailand), and through encouraging competition from smaller banks (as in Australia and, more recently, Indonesia) and non-bank financial intermediaries (NFBIs) (as in Korea and Thailand). These policies are not always successful. In Thailand, for example, NBFIs did not compete with banks since they were themselves largely controlled by them. Capital divestiture, initiated in the 1980s, proceeded only slowly and, while it did dilute shareholdings, it failed to break the control of the 16 Chinese families over the domestic banking system (Chaiyasoot 1993). While concentration ratios are generally a flawed measure of competition, since they do not take account of the contestability of markets, such ratios can be informative when branching and foreign bank entry are restricted. In most countries, a small number of large banks have typically dominated the banking sector – as, for example, in Australia, Indonesia, Japan and Thailand. While the number of banks is larger in the Philippines, Hutchcroft (1993) reports that both national and private banks have engaged in express collusive behaviour. Privatisation has been touted as a key policy reform in some countries (Korea and Taiwan), though the process has sometimes been painstakingly slow (as in Taiwan) or only relatively superficial (as in Korea, where major banks were privatised in the early 1980s but their presidents and directors continued to be appointed by government).

At times, however, the monetary authorities have been ambivalent in pursuing competition. While banks are free to set institutional interest rates in Singapore, the authorities largely exclude foreign institutions from the domestic banking market and continue to enforce tight controls on bank branching and automation (APEG 1995). Hong Kong, on the other hand, encourages foreign institutions but sanctioned a cartel to reduce competitive pressure in domestic bank markets until 1994. In Japan, the Ministry of Finance unsuccessfully attempted to use administrative guidance in early 1995 to prevent regional credit banks from offering competitive deposit rates (in the form of interest lotteries). Bank Indonesia initially opposed the 1983 financial reform package (MacIntyre 1993), but adopted a pro-competition stance in the late 1980s which resulted in a substantial expansion of private banking and increase in competition. The Indonesian, Malaysian and Philippine authorities also at times used measures to reduce 'undue' or destabilising competition.

As in various European countries, problems with banks' asset quality have also been a recurring phenomenon in east Asia. In the 1990s, banks in Australia, Indonesia and Japan experienced serious difficulties with non-performing loans and bad debts, which led to major reform of banking supervision.[2] Thailand suffered a series of financial failures from 1983 to

---

[2] In Indonesia, for example, problem and non-performing loans at the state banks rose from 6 to 21 per cent of outstanding credits between December 1990 and October 1993 (Euromoney, *Indonesia Supplement*, July–August 1994: 20).

1986 owing to poor supervision and management practices (mainly lending to executives and associates), which led to major, successful reform (Doner and Unger 1993). The Philippines has experienced four major crises of confidence in its financial institutions since the 1960s, reportedly caused by weak supervision and corruption; the central bank was substantially restructured in June 1993, partly in response to this. Bad debts have also caused periodic major problems in banking in Korea, where the government has bailed out institutions (Choi 1993). Taiwan's banking sector, on the other hand, has largely been free of bad debt problems due to the high risk aversion of its commercial bankers (since as we saw above bankers face civil liabilities if they make loans which fail, Cheng 1993).

Deposit and loan pricing rules under fiat and market regimes

In order to identify how the relationship between the money market interest rate and institutional interest rates may have changed over time, it is necessary to have a benchmark model of the determination of institutional interest rates. This section outlines simple pricing rules for deposit rates and loan rates under both a fiat regime and a market regime, and so provides a perspective on the conditions under which changes in money market rates lead to changes in institutional rates. There is an extensive literature on banks and the pricing of their assets and liabilities – see, for example, Klein (1971), Monti (1972), Baltensperger (1980), Takeda (1985), Cottarelli and Kourelis (1994) and Borio and Fritz (1995). The model outlined in this chapter, however, is constructed in a way which is reflective of the main characteristics of banking in the region, and which focuses on both deposit and loan markets.

Fiat deposit and loan rate rules

When the deposit market is determined by the authorities, the deposit interest rate, d, is given by fiat:

$$d_t = \bar{d}.$$ (Rule (1a))

When the loan market is determined by the authorities, the loan rate, l, is given by fiat:

$$l_t = \bar{l}.$$ (Rule (1b))

The particular rule used by the authorities to set rates is not specified, since it will vary by country and by time, and it may or may not conform to the market rule outlined below.

Market deposit and loan rate rules

In this sub-section, a model of institutional rate determination is constructed, the retail interest rate rules are stated, predictions of the rules for regression analysis outlined and, finally, the model and rules critically assessed. The deposit and loan rates are assumed to be determined by a profit-maximising bank with a simplified balance sheet comprising reserves (R) and loans (L) on the asset side, and money market borrowings (M), deposits (D) and equity (E) on the liabilities side. It is assumed initially that these instruments are of the same maturity, n. Reserves are proportional to deposits, $R = rD$, where r is the reserves ratio, and it is assumed that reserves do not pay interest. Accordingly, the balance sheet constraint for the bank is

$$L_t = E_t + M_t + (1 - r)D_t. \tag{5.1}$$

Expected total profit is expected total revenue (TR) less expected total cost (TC) which are respectively,

$$TR_t = l_{n,t}p_tL_t \tag{5.2}$$

$$TC_t = (q_t + {_c})L_t + e_{n,t}E_t + m_{n,t}M_t + (d_{n,t} + r + z)Dt \tag{5.3}$$

where $l_{n,t}$, $e_{n,t}$, $m_{n,t}$ and $d_{n,t}$ are the rates of return at time t on the n-period instruments L, E, M and D, respectively, p is the probability of payment of loan interest, q is the probability of default on the loan principal, c is the administrative cost of loans and z is the administrative cost of deposits. It is assumed that the administrative costs on loans and deposits are constant and those on equity and money market borrowings are zero (equivalently, deposits are costlier to administer than equity and money market borrowings). Following Lowe (1995), the probabilities of interest payment and loan default are included since banks face asset risk in the sense that they must pay out deposits and deposit interest at par but are not guaranteed to receive loan principal and loan interest payments at par.

Banks may enjoy monopsony power in the determination of deposit interest rates, implying $d = d(D)$ and $d'(D) > 0$, since banks must increase the deposit rate to attract depositors, or monopoly power in the determination of loan rates, implying $l = l(L)$ and $l'(L) < 0$, since banks must reduce the loan rate to attract borrowers. Following the literature (Baltensperger 1980), it is assumed, however, that banks are price-takers in the money market.

The deposit rate is determined through profit-maximising liabilities management by the bank. The Lagrangean may be written as

$$\mathfrak{L} = (l_{n,t}p_t - q_t - c)L_t - e_{n,t}E_t - m_{n,t}M_t - (d_{n,t}(D_t) + r + z)D_t$$
$$+ \lambda[L_t - E_t - M_t - (1-r)D_t]. \tag{5.4}$$

Banks hold a proportion of their loans as equity for prudential purposes, and this is assumed to be a requirement imposed on them. Accordingly, banks maximise the Lagrangean with respect to M and D. The first-order conditions imply

$$d_{n,t} = (1-r)m_{n,t} - r - z - d'(D_t)D_t. \tag{5.5}$$

Since banks only have price-fixing power in the deposit market, they take the money market rate as given. From (5.5), the deposit rate rises as the money market rate rises but falls as the reserve ratio, administrative costs and monopsony power of banks increase.

This specification assumes that money market instruments and deposits are of the same maturity, but in practice this need not be so. The term structure is assumed to be defined in discrete time by the unbiased expectations hypothesis (Hicks 1946) and so the interest rate on the n-period money market instrument at time t, $m_{n,t}$, is

$$1 + m_{n,t} = \left(\prod_{i=0}^{n-1}(1 + m_{1,t+i})\right)^{\frac{1}{n}} \tag{5.6}$$

where m_1 is the interest rate on a one-period money market instrument. Adding 1 to both sides of (5.5) and substituting (5.6) for m_n, (5.5) may be rewritten as

$$(1 + d_{n,t}) = (1-r)\left(\prod_{i=0}^{n-1}(1 + m_{1,t+i})\right)^{\frac{1}{n}} - z - d'(D)Dt. \tag{5.7}$$

Given that $d'(D) > 0$, this may be rewritten as

$$(1 + d_{n,t}) \le (1-r)\left(\prod_{i=0}^{n-1}(1 + m_{1,t+i})\right)^{\frac{1}{n}} - z. \tag{5.8}$$

If banks do not enjoy monopsony power in the deposit market then (5.8) holds as an equality.

This derivation assumes that depositors do not enjoy the same access to the money market as they do to the retail deposit market, for if they did and deposit rates were less than money market rates, they would place all their funds in the money market. The rejection of this arbitrage mechanism (and the consequent equalisation of money market and retail deposit rates) is made on the ground that most deposits fall below the minimum amount required for transacting in the wholesale market, thereby excluding depositors from the wholesale market and restricting them to the retail market.

To the extent that arbitrage occurs (perhaps through NBFIs), the deposit rate will tend to equal the money market rate and the cost of reserves will be passed directly into the loan rate.

Now consider the loan rate. The loan rate is determined by profit maximisation – that is marginal revenue equal to marginal cost. Taking the total differential of equations (5.2) and (5.3), letting ΔL and L equal 1, and setting the change in E, M and D equal to their share in L, $\alpha_1 = E/L$ (which is determined exogenously to banks), $\alpha_2 = M/L$ and $\alpha_3 = (1-r)D/L$, then

$$\Delta TR_t = pl_{n,t} 1 pl'(L_t) \tag{5.9}$$

$$\Delta TC_t = q + c + \alpha_1 e_{n,t} + \alpha_2 m_{n,t} + \alpha_3 (d_{n,t} + r + z). \tag{5.10}$$

Equating these and solving for the loan rate, yields

$$l_{n,t} = \frac{1}{p}[q + c + \alpha_1 e_{n,t} + \alpha_2 m_{n,t} + \alpha_3 (d_{n,t} + r + z) - pl'(L_t)]. \tag{5.11}$$

Substituting (5.6) for the money market rate and (5.7) for the deposit rate (and assuming that the deposit market is competitive), the loan rate is given as

$$l_{n,t} = \frac{1}{p}\left[q + c + \alpha_1 e_{n,t} - \alpha_2 + (\alpha_2 + (1-r)\alpha_3)\left(\prod_{i=0}^{n-1}(1+m_{1,t+i})\right)^{\frac{1}{n}} - \alpha_3(1-r) \right.$$
$$\left. - pl'(L_t) \right], \tag{5.12}$$

where l is increasing in the probability of loan default, loan administration costs, the cost of equity, the cost of money market funds, the reserve ratio and market power and is decreasing in the probability of payment of loan interest. This may be rewritten as

$$l_{n,t} \geq \frac{1}{p}\left[q + c + \alpha_1 e_{n,t} - \alpha_2 + (\alpha_2 + (1-r)\alpha_3)\left(\prod_{i=0}^{n-1}(1+m_{1,t+i})\right)^{\frac{1}{n}} - \alpha_3(1-r) \right], \tag{5.13}$$

which holds as an equality when banks do not have monopoly power in the loan market.

The deposit and loan rate rules may now be stated. Under the assumption of perfect foresight, the profit-maximising bank sets the deposit rate in relation to its other, exogenously determined funding costs – specifically the cost of money market funds – according to the deposit pricing rule,

$$(1+d_{n,t}) \leq (1-r)\left(\prod_{i=0}^{n-1}(1+m_{1,t+i})\right)^{\frac{1}{n}} - z \tag{Rule (2a)}$$

which is (5.8). The rule predicts that the deposit rate is less than or (at most) equal to the money market rate, and that the deposit rate is increasing in the money market rates expected to prevail over the deposit period and decreasing in both reserve requirements and net deposit administration costs. If the market for deposits is perfectly competitive, then rule (2a) holds as an equality; otherwise banks can suppress deposit rates below the implied term-structure equivalent rate.

When loans are priced in the market, the profit-maximising bank sets the loan rate in relation to its funding and administration costs, the riskiness of its assets and its market power according to the pricing rule:

$$l_{n,t} \geq \frac{1}{p}\left[q + c + \alpha_1 e_{n,t} - \alpha_2 + (\alpha_2 + (1-r)\alpha_3)\left(\prod_{i=0}^{n-1}(1+m_{1,t+i})\right)^{\frac{1}{n}} - \alpha_3(1-r) \right]$$

Rule (2b)

which is (5.13). The rule predicts that the loan rate is greater than or (at least) equal to the money market rate, and that the loan rate increases when the cost of equity or money market borrowing increases, when the probability of loan default increases or the probability of interest payment falls and when deposit reserve ratios increase. If markets are perfectly competitive, then rule (2b) holds as an equality; otherwise banks can use market power to extract a higher loan rate than implied by funding and administration costs.

The rules indicate that institutional rates are functions of several variables, most of which are not observable or available – at least not on a monthly or even quarterly basis and usually not for a reasonable length of time.[3] Accordingly, like Cottarelli and Kourelis (1994) and Borio and Fritz (1995), the analysis is restricted to regressing the institutional rate on the money market rate with the other factors appearing in the constant or error term.[4] The rules are useful in that they yield a number of predictions about the constant and slope coefficients.

[3] One possible alternative is to use proxies for the missing variables. The effect of the risk of default on loan rates, for example, may be identified if economic growth is included (since risk of default is expected to be inverse to economic growth). This was tried without success for the Australian loan equation for all sub-samples by using the deviation from linear trend of the Melbourne Institute's index of manufacturing production. One problem with using these sorts of variables is that monthly observations of real variables tend to be highly volatile. Another is that a deterioration in economic conditions will reduce the demand for loans at any given interest rate, which may offset the putative rise in the loan rate owing to the higher risk premium.

[4] If this approach is to yield consistent estimates, then the money rates must be uncorrelated with the unmodelled variables that appear in the error term. This may not necessarily be the case if, for example, the risk of default is positively correlated with the money market rate. However, tests showed that the error term is not correlated with either the level or change in the money market rate.

Consider the constant term. When the deposit rate is the dependent variable, the constant term is expected to be weakly negative since, by rule (2a), it is the negative of deposit administration costs. When the loan rate is the dependent variable, the model predicts that the constant will be weakly positive since it comprises loan administration costs, probabilities of default on loan principal and interest and the cost of equity (or, more strictly speaking, the incremental cost of equity relative to borrowing in the money market). As these factors change, so will the constant term. Given that some banking systems in the region have at times experienced serious problems with non-performing or bad loans, one would anticipate that the constant term in the loan rate equation will vary over time.

The slope coefficient, on the other hand, is principally affected by regulation (that is, whether there is a regime shift from rule (1) to rule (2)), by the degree of competition in the banking sector and by the nature of shocks to the term structure. As regulation, competition and the permanency of term-structure shocks change, so will the slope coefficient. Given that banking systems in the region have been increasingly deregulated and competition has improved over time, one would anticipate that the slope coefficient would increase over time. The inclusion of the term structure implies a smoothing process according to which the effect of shocks to money market rates on deposit and loan rates will depend on their expected permanency. A rise in the slope coefficient may, therefore, merely reflect changes in the permanency and timing of shocks to money market interest rates, perhaps caused by improvements in monetary management techniques or cyclical effects. To minimise this, the maturity of money, deposit and loan rates across countries should be as similar as possible.

The attraction of the rules is not just their simplicity but also their realism. In the first place, anecdotal evidence supports the claim that banks in fact use these sorts of rules in setting retail rates. Banks tend to set deposit rates with direct reference to money market rates, and they set loan rates on the basis of funding and administration costs and the riskiness of borrowers. In Japan, for example, banks price term-deposit rates and the short-term prime rate off the CD rate (Bank of Japan 1994). In general, banks make as much use as possible of their market power in retail markets. The rules capture key recent developments in deposit and loan markets in east Asia – regulatory regime shifts, increased competitiveness in the banking sector and occasional but significant changes in asset quality.

On the other hand, the model has some obvious shortcomings. First, it assumes that financial institutions are price-takers in the money market, but there are instances where this is violated. In Japan, for example, institutions which rely on call loans to fill a funds shortage sometimes borrow funds at above-market prices to allow institutions with a funds surplus to obtain extra profit.[5] Even in the negotiable certificate of deposit (NCD) market, banks will sometimes limit issuance in order to push up rates to strengthen their bargaining position with borrowers (since the short-term prime rate is priced off the NCD interest rate) (chapter 4). Similarly, in Thailand the number of players in the market is relatively small and prices at times have been subject to manipulation. While there are such examples of price-making in markets at various times, the approximation of perfect competition is not unreasonable. In Japan, for example, interbank rates generally closely follow open market developments, and CD rates very closely follow euroyen rates which are less subject to price-fixing (see chapter 3). Banks have occasional but not systematic price-setting power in money markets, and this is certainly considerably less than the power they may have in institutional markets.

Secondly, the model assumes profit maximisation, but this is not always the case in practice. At various times banks in Australia, Indonesia and Japan, among other countries, have sought to maximise the size of their balance sheets rather than profits, and this is more likely to occur when central bank credit depends on the size of a bank's operations (Takeda 1985). Banks are also less likely to be profit-maximisers when they are publicly owned (Cottarelli and Kourelis (1994). All else given, greater focus on balance sheet size implies higher deposit rates (Monti 1972) and lower loan rates, while less focus on profit-maximisation implies slower adjustment of institutional rates (Cottarelli and Kourelis 1994). The effect on the price-setting rules depends on the extent to which the bank can ignore profit-maximisation, but it is arguable that a policy of focusing on balance sheet size *at the expense* of profits is not sustainable over time, particularly in world markets which are increasingly integrated.

Thirdly, the model is perhaps too simple. The intertemporal dimension is modelled in the term structure but not in the profit-maximisation of the bank. If the bank is an intertemporal optimiser and possesses market power, then its strategic price rules may be considerably more complex and interesting. The model also does not explicitly consider the effect of developments in bond markets on the formation of institutional rates (Fry 1995) and does not attempt to explain how the process of regulation breaks down. It simply seeks to show that as the competitive market mechanism becomes dominant, institutional rates should be more responsive to money market rates. Another simplification is the modelling of the

---

[5] Based on an interview in Tokyo (27 February 1995).

probability of default. If the probability of default is a function of the level or variance of the money market rate or the loan rate, of regime shifts, or of learning, then changes in asset quality may not appear just in the constant term but also in the slope coefficient. The model also does not take account of equilibrium risk-sharing or implicit contracting between the bank and its customer (Fried and Howitt 1980) according to which banks may price institutional rates such that they are less variable than they would be in spot markets in return for a higher average loan rate or lower average deposit rate. One way to do this in the model is to include utility functions of depositors and borrowers which are concave in income and costs, respectively. Slope coefficients would also be a function of risk preference, and the results may indicate whether people had a preference for smoothing interest income over borrowing costs. Further modifications could include modelling the informal or curb loan market, modelling the different riskiness of borrowers in formal and informal markets, and modelling information asymmetries (as in Ahn 1994). While these modifications would enrich the theoretical model and are worthy of pursuit, they are second-order considerations in terms of the issues in this chapter.

Correlations, error correction and the adjustment of institutional interest rates

This section presents correlation coefficients and an error-correction model (ECM) of monthly domestic deposit and loan rates for Australia, Hong Kong, Indonesia, Japan, Korea, Malaysia, the Philippines, Singapore, Taiwan and Thailand for the four five-year periods from 1975 to 1994.[6] Results for Canada and the United States are included for comparison with well developed and liberalised financial markets. The deposit, loan and money market interest rates for each country are defined, sourced and graphed in appendix 5.2 (p. 218). The results are interpreted below.

The empirical analysis focuses on the evolution of the relationship between interest rates on traded and non-traded instruments, and this is shown by conducting the tests over four sub-periods, 1975M1–1979M12, 1980M1–1984M12, 1985M1–1989M12 and 1990M1–1994M12. These sub-samples are arbitrary but are of sufficient length (60 observations) to provide reasonable estimating power and show how systems have evolved over different periods of time. Moreover, they are generally of sufficient length to capture all or most of an economic cycle, thereby minimising cyclical effects on the speed of adjustment. When a major structural

[6] In some cases, data were not available for the full period, and so actual sub-periods may contain fewer observations. See appendix 5.4 (p. 000) for details.

change occurs at around the start or end of a sub-period, the sample length is modified. When a change occurs around the middle of a sub-period, the results for alternative sub-samples are reported in footnotes. The change in the relationship between rates both over periods of time and over regimes is accordingly identified.

Given the observations made above about possible term-structure effects, money, deposit and loan rates were selected with as common a maturity length as possible, and this information is summarised in columns (2)–(4) of table 5.2. Maturity-matching is more difficult with loan rates, and they are generally defined as short-term prime rates (variable rates on a loan of less than one-year to a bank's best customers). The remainder of table 5.2 sets out the correlation coefficients of the first difference of *domestic* deposit and loan rates against *domestic* money market rates.

The correlation coefficients provide an insight into the instantaneous or impact effect of changes in money rates on institutional markets, but they do not consider dynamics and how long it takes changes in wholesale rates to be reflected in institutional rates. One way to view this would be to examine sub-samples of the cross-correlation function or the distributed lag structure between money market rates and institutional rates, with the length of the lag structure indicating the speed at which changes in one set of rates affect the other, as in Cottarelli and Kourelis (1994). On the other hand, if there is an underlying equilibrium relationship between money market and institutional interest rates, then it is natural to estimate adjustment in that context.[7] The possibility of such a relationship is suggested by the result that nominal interest rates appear to be integrated of order one, according to the augmented Dickey–Fuller (ADF) test (using critical values drawn from MacKinnon 1991), since the null hypothesis of a unit root is accepted for the variables in levels but not for the variables in first differences. The methodology and test statistics are reported in appendix 5.3 (p. 226) for the complete 1975–94 sample and the four five-year sub-samples (tables A5.3.1–A5.3.11).[8]

The equilibrium relationship is conducted using a general-to-specific modelling procedure embedded in an ECM (Banerjee *et. al.* 1993).[9] The

[7] Cottarelli and Kourelis (1994) state that an ECM performs poorly, but this is because they impose the condition that in equilibrium the loan rate equals the money market rate.

[8] Money market rates generally possess one unit root. Depending on the country and regulatory regime, however, deposit or lending rates are sometimes I(0) processes as, for example, in Indonesia and Thailand in the 1980s) or I(2) processes as, for example, in Australia, Singapore and Taiwan from 1990 to 1994). A finding of second-order integration is difficult to accept.

[9] An ECM is a reparameterisation of a regression between variables measured in levels and can be applied regardless of the order of integration. This is potentially an issue here,

Table 5.2. *Correlations of deposit and lending rates with money market rate, first difference, monthly, 1975–94*

Country	Money	Deposit maturity	Loan	Deposit rates				Loan rates			
				1975–9	1980–4	1985–9	1990–4	1975–9	1980–4	1985–9	1990–4
Australia	3m	3mn	prime	—	0.62*	0.12	0.70*	—	0.14	0.70*	0.40*
Indonesia	av.	3–6m	prime	—	−0.03	−0.13	0.18	—	—	0.15	0.05
Hong Kong	3m	3m	prime	—	—	0.53*	0.65*	—	—	0.51*	0.65*
Japan	ont.	3m	prime	0.48*	0.58*	0.49*	0.55*	0.33*	0.70*	0.44*	0.64*
Korea	av.	3m	<1 yr	−0.11	−0.34*	0.00	0.14	—	−0.23	−0.03	0.13
Malaysia	ont.	3m	prime	−0.18	0.15	0.37*	0.67*	−0.12	0.23	0.13	0.27*
Philippines	3m	2–3m	av.	−0.06	0.67*	0.38*	0.39*	0.29*	0.33*	0.23	0.60*
Singapore	3m	3m	min	0.24	0.65*	0.35*	0.30*	0.44*	0.64*	0.26*	0.27*
Taiwan	3m	3m	av.	—	0.21	0.46*	0.35*	—	0.25	0.70*	0.12
Thailand	av.	3–6m	max	0.00	0.17	0.17	0.03	0.00	0.13	0.08	−0.01
Average	—	—	—	*0.06*	*0.36*	*0.27*	*0.40*	*0.19*	*0.28*	*0.27*	*0.31*
Canada	ont.	3m	prime	0.62*	0.36*	0.31*	0.30*	0.37*	0.43*	0.62*	0.45*
USA	ont.	3m	prime	—	0.82*	0.73*	0.75*	0.65*	0.80*	0.50*	0.79*

Notes:

* = statistical significance at the 5 per cent level. — = not available.

av. = average.

ont. = overnight.

analysis is bivariate, since the focus is the adjustment of an institutional rate (i) to a money market interest rate (m). The series, m and i, are integrated of order 1 and are assumed to be n-order autoregressive distributed lag processes. This chapter focuses on the response of the rate on a non-traded financial instrument to changes in that of the traded financial instrument, and the analysis is restricted to single-equation estimation with the retail interest rate as the dependent variable.[10]

An additional issue is whether both the deposit and lending rate should enter the estimating equation for each institutional interest rate – that is, whether the equation should include three rather than two variables. If banks set deposit and lending rates according to rules (2a) and (2b), respectively, then the deposit–loan rate spread is superfluous: the loan rate does not enter the deposit rate equation and, while the deposit rate enters the loan rate equation, it is substituted out and replaced by the money market rate. In short, when institutional rates are market-determined, there is no particular relationship between deposit and loan rates. On the other hand, when deposit and loan rates are determined by fiat, the authorities *may* use a rule by which they set these rates in relation to each other, and so both institutional rates *may* be relevant. Since the issue being examined is the changing relationship between money and institutional rates, and not the particular rule used to set institutional interest

despite the finding that the series are I(1). First, the tests used to determine the order of integration have low power, and so the time series may in fact be stationary but strongly autoregressive. Moreover, the variables examined in this chapter are interest rates, and it is not clear that they behave like other I(1) series. While interest rates are not bounded from above and do attain extreme positive values at times, they are bounded from below at zero and there is a tendency for shocks to die out and for rates to revert to *around* their previous level, which is not typical of integrated series. Finally, the full sample period is 20 years and the four sub-sample periods are five years each, but one would not necessarily expect a data series to possess the same time series properties over these two very different period lengths or between any two of the sub-sample periods. In fact, the series do tend to exhibit similar behaviour across periods, but even when this is not the case, the ECM is still valid, though the statistical interpretation is different.

[10] In order for such estimation to be efficient and unbiased, the interest rate on the traded instrument must be weakly exogenous for the parameters of concern – the adjustment factor and the cointegrating vector. This is assumed to be the case on the basis of general observation of wholesale and retail financial markets: banks set rates on retail instruments in relation to rates in the wholesale markets and not vice versa and that innovations to the system of short-term interest rates tend to come from monetary policy interventions or international financial flows, and these usually have their initial influence in wholesale rather than retail markets. By starting with the conditional model rather than a systems approach such as that outlined by Johansen (1988), the method used here does not strictly conform to the general-to-specific modelling procedure (Urbain 1992). There are, however, statistical indicators that the assumption of weak exogeneity is appropriate: in the single-equation estimations, the adjustment coefficient is generally stable in each period as nuisance parameters are deleted (Ericsson (1992). Overall, the gain in using a simpler modelling procedure does not appear to occur at the cost of a serious loss of precision and efficiency.

rates, the deposit–loan spread is not generally included in the estimating equation. This issue is revisited in more detail in the discussion below since declining statistical significance of the spread may be an indication of a regime shift.

The adjustment process is estimated in the single conditional error-correction equation,

$$\Delta i_t = \mu - \beta_1 i_{t-1} + \beta_2 m_{t-1} + \sum_{j=1}^{n-1} \pi_j \Delta i_{t-j} + \sum_{j=0}^{n-1} \theta_j \Delta m_{t-j} \text{ for } i = d,l. \tag{5.14}$$

The adjustment coefficient of the institutional rate to itself is β_1 and to the money market rate is β_2. If they are statistically significant, then there exists a long-run relationship between i and m of the form

$$i = \mu/\beta_1 + \beta_2/\beta_1 m,$$

where μ/β_1 is the long-run constant and is positive (negative) if μ is positive (negative). The pricing rules suggest that the constant is weakly negative for the deposit rate and weakly positive for the loan rate.

The cointegrating vector normalised on the money market interest rate is calculated from the ECM as

$$(-1, \beta_2/\beta_1).$$

The pricing rules suggest that

$$\beta_2/\beta_1 \leq 1$$

for both the deposit rate and the loan rate, and that it is strictly equal to one only if rates are fully market-determined, markets are perfectly competitive, shocks to money market rates are permanent and occur at the start of the maturity period and there is no reserve requirement. These are stringent conditions and one would generally expect the coefficient to be less than 1. Greater liberalisation, competition and the permanency of shocks to money market rates tend to increase the coefficient. The value of the coefficient is an empirical issue and so the long-run relationship is unrestricted. The result will also depend on whether the money and institutional rates are of the same maturity. It is easier to match the maturities of money market rates (typically three-month interbank rates) with deposit rates (typically three-month fixed deposit rates) than with lending rates (typically short-term prime rates), and so one may expect the coefficient to be closer to 1 in the case of deposit rates since the term-structure effects are more precisely netted out.

The ECM in (5.14) is estimated for deposit and loan rates relative to money market rates for the countries listed in table 5.2 using monthly data for the full 20-year period (where possible) and the four five-year sub-periods. Equation (5.14) may contain nuisance parameters in the form of insignificant dynamics terms, and these can be eliminated by sequential reduction using the standard general-to-specific methodology. Six lags were included in the autoregressive distributed lag model. The results are presented in appendix 5.4 (p. 231) for the most acceptable parsimonious model for each country.

The estimations over the full sample period are generally poorly specified, but specifications over sub-samples are better and goodness of fit improves over time. Given that institutional rates over much of the period were inflexible and subject to sharp discrete movements in most countries, the errors are usually non-normally distributed and hetero-scedastic. Sharp discrete movements in institutional rates are a character-istic of controlled-rate systems (and give rise to non-normality), and as markets are liberalised, these movements become smoother (which gives rise to non-constancy in the variance of the equation). There also tends to be less volatility in money market rates, which may be caused by improve-ments in domestic monetary management techniques (for example, the changes in operating procedures in Hong Kong in 1988 and in Australia in 1989) or less weight put on bilateral exchange rate targeting. Whatever the case, an examination of the residuals indicates that reduced money rate volatility is a relatively minor source of non-normality. Broadly speaking, not only changes in the adjustment mechanism but also the improvement in the diagnostic performance of the estimations indicate increased domes-tic integration.

The specifications generally reduce to a simple model whereby the change in the institutional rate is a function of the disequilibrium between institutional and market rates and the current change in the money market rate.[11] The dynamic lag specification tends to be more complex for loan rates than for deposit rates, which implies relatively greater price sluggish-ness in the loan market (discussed below). It is unusual in these estima-tions for lags of the dependent variable to be significant: lagged dependent variables are significant only for Indonesian deposit rates, which suggests

---

[11] The inclusion of the contemporaneous change in the money market rate is controver-sial, since it is permissible only if the money market rate is weakly exogenous to the institutional rate, but it does not appear to disturb the results. For example, when the general-to-specific modelling procedure is applied to the Australian loan rate exclud-ing the contemporaneous change in the money market rate, a dynamics term appears in the estimation only from 1980M1 to 1984M12 (the first lag of the change in the money rate), and the adjustment process is largely unchanged. Adjustment of the deposit rate, however, is moderately faster, since the speed of adjustment coefficient generally increases.

that in this case the autoregressive behaviour dominates the error-correction process.[12] As anticipated, in general, the slope coefficient is less than 1, and the constant term is weakly negative in deposit-rate equations and weakly positive in loan-rate equations.

Tables 5.3 and 5.4 present a summary of relevant results on the speed of adjustment for deposit and lending rates, respectively. The structure of the table is identical in both cases. The rows list the results for each country. Column (1) nominates the respective country, while columns (2)–(5) list the adjustment coefficient of the institutional rate to itself (β_1) in the top row and to the money market rate (β_2) in the bottom row for each of the four sub-periods (1975–9, 1980–4, 1985–9, 1990–4). The cointegrating vector is β_2/β_1. Columns (6)–(8) list the cumulative adjustment of the respective institutional rate to a 1 percentage-point change in the money market rate after one, four and 12 months for each of the sub-periods after taking account of short-run dynamics. The figure in parentheses in these columns is the percentage of adjustment completed one, four and 12 months after a change in the money market rate. The formula is provided in appendix 5.5 (p. 243).

A discussion on domestic integration

Even a glance at the graphs of domestic money, deposit and lending interest rates set out in appendix 5.2 shows that rates in Australia, Canada, Japan, Malaysia, the Philippines, Singapore, Taiwan and the United States are closely linked to each other. Rates in Indonesia and Thailand, on the other hand, were not well linked for most of the period but have become more so in the 1990s, especially in Thailand. Posted institutional rates in Korea are barely linked with money market interest rates,[13] but curb loan rates do tend to follow money market developments. This pattern is reflected in the correlations between money and institutional rates, the nature of the equilibrium relationships between rates and the speed of adjustment of institutional rates to changes in money market rates.

The average correlation between both deposit and loan rates and money

---

[12] The Indonesian rates are weighted averages for all deposit banks – the private banks and the more sluggish state banks. Rates from private banks were also used for the 1990M1–1994M12 sub-sample, but with little effect. One problem with Indonesian rates may be that the reference rate for institutional rate determination is not the Jakarta interbank rate but LIBOR *plus* the swap premium (Cole, Scott and Wellons 1995b: 13).

[13] The Korean institutional interest rates analysed in this chapter have been liberalised, but other rates are yet to be deregulated. The published figures do not report actual market rates.

market rates across both time and the east Asian region is substantially below 1, indicating that shocks, foreign or otherwise, which affect domestic money rates are not immediately transmitted in full to the rates on non-traded domestic financial assets. This can be explained by the static nature of correlation analysis, the existence of interest rate ceilings or controls, imperfect competition in the banking sector, by shocks which affect only part rather than the whole of the term structure, or by implicit contracts between financial intermediaries and their customers to smooth retail deposit and loan rates either over the cycle or during periods of volatility in money markets.

On the other hand, correlation coefficients, error correction and the time taken to complete adjustment differ substantially by country and over time. *By country*, correlations are higher and the adjustment to equilibrium is relatively fast in Australia, Canada, Japan, Malaysia (deposit rates only), the Philippines and the United States. Adjustment is slower in Hong Kong, where deposit and loan rates are set by an officially sanctioned bank cartel (HKBA), and in Singapore, where branching and foreign competition are tightly controlled. Interestingly, the result that the speed of adjustment of Japanese institutional rates is similar to that of other non-cartelised banking systems suggests that its 'main bank' system does not generate abnormal behaviour in institutional interest rates. While cross-country comparisons are difficult to make, since the maturity profile of the instruments differs across countries, correlations tend to be negative or 0 and adjustment negligible when countries set retail rates in a way which does not conform with market rates. In Korea, for example, the correlation between changes in money and deposit rates was significantly negative in the early 1980s, and not different from 0 otherwise. Correlations for Thai and Indonesian rates are also not different from 0.

By period, correlations and the speed of adjustment to equilibrium have increased for Australia,[14] Canada, Indonesia, Japan, Malaysia and the Philippines. In Malaysia in the first half of the 1980s, for example, a third

[14] Note that the adjustment of the deposit rate to the bill rate slows down in the 1985M1–1989M12 sub-period. As official interest rates rose during 1985 and 1986, savings banks (whose assets chiefly comprised housing loans) became constrained by the 13.5 per cent ceiling on loans for owner-occupied housing. They responded to tighter margins by rationing housing credit and, taking advantage of price-making power in the deposit market, by limiting the rise in deposit rates, thereby driving a wedge between deposit and bill rates. The impasse was broken by providing special subsidies to savings banks and the liberalisation of interest rates on new loans for owner-occupied housing in April 1986, after which the wedge between deposit and bill rates narrowed. When the regression excludes this period, and is run from 1987M1 to 1989M12, β_1 is 0.48 and β_2 is 0.47, implying that 48 per cent of adjustment is completed after one month, 93 per cent after four months, and 100 per cent after 12 months. This is considerably faster than the 1980M1–1984M12 period but not as fast as the 1990M1–1994M12 period.

Table 5.3. *Adjustment of domestic deposit interest rates to domestic money market interest rate changes, 1975–94*

Country (1)		β_1 (adj. to deposit rate) / β_2 (adj. to money rate)				Cumulative adjustment of deposit rate to a 1 percentage-point rise in the money market rate after one, four and 12 months											
		1975–9 (2)	1980–4 (3)	1985–9 (4)	1990–4 (5)	1975–9			1980–4			1985–9			1990–4		
						1 (6)	4 (7)	12 (8)	1 (6)	4 (7)	12 (8)	1 (6)	4 (7)	12 (8)	1 (6)	4 (7)	12 (8)
Australia	β_1	—	0.29	0.15	0.51	—	—	—	0.30 (50%)	0.49 (82%)	0.59 (99%)	0.15 (15%)	0.49 (49%)	0.87 (86%)	0.62 (70%)	0.85 (97%)	0.88 (100%)
	β_2	—	0.18	0.15	0.45												
Hong Kong	β_1	—	—	0.21	0.23	—	—	—	—	—	—	0.65 (84%)	0.71 (92%)	0.76 (99%)	0.57 (63%)	0.75 (83%)	0.88 (98%)
	β_2	—	—	0.17	0.21												
Indonesia	β_1	—	n/c	0.03	0.05	—	—	—	0 (0%)	0 (0%)	0 (0%)	0 (0%)	0 (0%)	0 (0%)	n/e	n/e	n/e
	β_2	—	n/c	0.03	0.10												
Japan	β_1	0.24	0.63	n/c	0.47	0.36 (66%)	0.47 (85%)	0.54 (98%)	0.27 (63%)	0.41 (98%)	0.42 (100%)	0.31 (n/a)	0.31 (n/a)	0.31 (n/a)	0.54 (91%)	0.59 (99%)	0.59 (100%)
	β_2	0.13	0.27	n/c	0.28												
Malaysia	β_1	n/c	0.37	0.18	0.48	0 (0%)	0 (0%)	0 (0%)	0.28 (37%)	0.64 (84%)	0.76 (100%)	0.14 (18%)	0.41 (55%)	0.69 (91%)	0.78 (74%)	1.02 (96%)	1.06 (100%)
	β_2	n/c	0.28	0.14	0.50												
Philippines	β_1	n/c	0.49	0.54	0.45	—	—	—	0.48 (78%)	0.60 (97%)	0.62 (100%)	0.40 (71%)	0.55 (97%)	0.56 (100%)	0.54 (58%)	0.86 (93%)	0.93 (100%)
	β_2	n/c	0.30	0.31	0.41												
Singapore	β_1	n/c	0.60	0.11	0.21	0 (0%)	0 (0%)	0 (0%)	0.73 (79%)	0.91 (99%)	0.93 (100%)	0.20 (21%)	0.42 (43%)	0.74 (77%)	0.23 (32%)	0.49 (67%)	0.69 (95%)
	β_2	n/c	0.55	0.10	0.15												

	(1)	(2)	(3)	(4)	(5)	(6)	(7)	(8)
Taiwan	—	0.11	0.17	0.08	—	0.19 (32%)	0.39 (64%)	0.56 (93%)
	—	0.19	0.16	0.04	—	0.43 (41%)	0.69 (65%)	0.97 (91%)
						0.13 (26%)	0.22 (42%)	0.36 (70%)
Thailand	n/c	n/c	0.21	0.18		0 (0%)	0 (0%)	0 (0%)
	n/c	n/c	0.11	0.18		0.11 (21%)	0.32 (61%)	0.49 (94%)
						0.18 (21%)	0.52 (60%)	0.81 (94%)
Canada	n/c	0.46	1.01	0.23	n/a	0.20 (n/a)	0.20 (n/a)	0.20 (n/a)
	n/c	0.44	0.94	0.23	n/a	0.77 (82%)	0.92 (97%)	0.95 (100%)
						0.93 (100%)	0.93 (100%)	0.94 (100%)
USA	—	0.71	0.33	0.36		0.97 (99%)	0.99 (100%)	0.99 (100%)
	—	0.70	0.31	0.35		0.96 (100%)	0.96 (100%)	0.96 (100%)
						0.93 (96%)	0.96 (99%)	0.97 (100%)

Notes:

n/c = no cointegration.

n/a = not applicable.

n/e = not estimated.

— = not available.

The figures in parentheses in columns (6)–(8) in tables 5.3 and 5.4 are the percentage of total adjustment expected in the first, fourth and twelfth month after a change in the money market rate.

Table 5.4. *Adjustment of domestic loan interest rates to domestic money market interest rate changes, 1975–94*

Country (1)	β_1 (adj. to loan rate) / β_2 (adj. to money rate) 1975–9 (2)	1980–4 (3)	1985–9 (4)	1990–4 (5)	Cumulative adjustment of loan rate to a 1 percentage-point rise in the money market rate after one, four and 12 months — 1975–9 / 1 (6)	4 (7)	12 (8)	1980–4 / 1 (6)	4 (7)	12 (8)	1985–9 / 1 (6)	4 (7)	12 (8)	1990–4 / 1 (6)	4 (7)	12 (8)
Australia	—	0.17	0.45	0.53	—	—	—	0.38 (53%)	0.52 (72%)	0.68 (94%)	0.68 (67%)	0.96 (95%)	1.02 (100%)	0.49 (56%)	0.84 (96%)	0.87 (100%)
	—	0.12	0.46	0.49												
Hong Kong	—	—	0.45	0.20	—	—	—	—	—	—	0.62 (70%)	0.84 (95%)	0.89 (100%)	0.52 (61%)	0.67 (80%)	0.81 (97%)
	—	—	0.40	0.17												
Indonesia	—	—	n/c	0.12	—	—	—	—	—	—	0 (0%)	0 (0%)	0 (0%)	0.12 (10%)	0.43 (33%)	0.90 (70%)
	—	—	n/c	0.10												
Japan	n/c	0.34	0.30	0.69	0.25 (n/a)	0.25 (n/a)	0.25 (n/a)	0.55 (100%)	0.55 (100%)	0.55 (100%)	0.43 (66%)	0.57 (88%)	0.65 (99%)	0.82 (94%)	0.87 (100%)	0.87 (100%)
	n/c	0.19	0.19	0.60												
Malaysia	n/c	n/c	0.11	0.17	0 (0%)	0 (0%)	0 (0%)	0 (0%)	0 (0%)	0 (0%)	0.06 (11%)	0.21 (37%)	0.43 (75%)	0.13 (17%)	0.41 (52%)	0.71 (89%)
	n/c	n/c	0.06	0.13												
Philippines	n/c	0.23	0.63	0.54	0 (0%)	0 (0%)	0 (0%)	0.23 (23%)	0.64 (65%)	0.94 (96%)	0.58 (70%)	0.82 (98%)	0.83 (100%)	0.69 (80%)	0.84 (98%)	0.86 (100%)
	n/c	0.23	0.52	0.46												
Singapore	n/c	0.36	0.12	0.18	0 (0%)	0 (0%)	0 (0%)	0.55 (58%)	0.85 (89%)	0.95 (100%)	0.14 (26%)	0.28 (50%)	0.45 (83%)	0.12 (18%)	0.36 (55%)	0.60 (91%)
	n/c	0.35	0.07	0.12												

Taiwan	n/c	0.02	0.09	n/c	0	0	0.32	0.60	0.80	0.30	0.46	0.71	n/e	n/e	n/e
	n/c	0.23	0.11	n/c	(0%)	(0%)	(39%)	(72%)	(96%)	(34%)	(52%)	(80%)	n/e	n/e	n/e
Thailand	n/c	0.39	0.18	0.14	0	0	0.06	0.12	0.14	0.06	0.21	0.42	0.13	0.36	0.64
	n/c	0.06	0.06	0.10	(0%)	(0%)	(39%)	(86%)	(100%)	(12%)	(40%)	(78%)	(18%)	(46%)	(83%)
Canada	n/c	n/c	0.28	0.59	1.11	1.11	0.19	0.19	0.19	0.57	0.79	0.91	0.80	0.94	0.95
	n/c	n/c	0.26	0.56	n/a	n/a	n/a	n/a	n/a	(62%)	(86%)	(99%)	(84%)	(99%)	(100%)
USA	n/c	0.61	0.44	0.15	1.13	1.13	0.87	1.07	1.08	0.78	1.01	1.06	0.78	0.79	0.81
	n/c	0.66	0.47	0.13	n/a	n/a	(81%)	(99%)	(100%)	(73%)	(95%)	(100%)	(96%)	(97%)	(99%)

Notes:

n/c = no cointegration.
n/a = not applicable.
n/e = not estimated.
— = not available.
The figures in parentheses in columns (6)–(8) in tables 5.3 and 5.4 are the percentage of total adjustment expected in the first, fourth and twelfth month after a change in the money market rate.

of the expected adjustment of the deposit rate to a rise in the money market rate had taken place by the end of the first month after the rise but, by a decade later, this had risen to three-quarters of the expected adjustment. Moreover, while there were no equilibrium relationships between rates in Indonesia and Thailand during the 1970s or 1980s, they emerged in the 1990s. All this points to substantial and increasing integration of domestic financial markets. In Singapore and Taiwan, on the other hand, equilibrium adjustment appears to have slowed, and the adjustment of the loan rate has slowed in the United States. In the case of Singapore, this is partly due to the insulation of domestic institutional rates from money market rates through 1988, 1989 and 1990. Excluding this period, the co-movement of rates rises slightly.[15] The deterioration in the case of Taiwan may be due to an increase in the volatility of money market rates in the 1990s,[16] while the slowdown in the adjustment of the US prime rate may reflect the decreasing importance of that rate for pricing bank loans. Nonetheless, there has been a notable increase in the co-movement of institutional rates with money market rates in most east Asian economies over the past decade, largely attributable to deregulation and a greater focus on competition in the banking sector.

It is worth noting that regulation and control *per se* are impediments to domestic rate integration only if they are not market-conforming. Japan and Taiwan are cases in point. While deposit rate liberalisation started in Japan in 1985 and was completed only in 1994, the rate was based on the CD rate, and so moved fairly closely with interbank rates. But the margin between the deposit rate and CD rate narrowed only *after* deregulation, suggesting that the aim of regulation was to subsidise the cost of bank funds. Taiwan's deposit rates also seem to have been set with money market developments in mind. The story is less clear with loan rates. In Japan's case, until 1989 the short-term prime rate was set with respect to the ODR, *below* the money market rate, which is in violation of a market model of loan rate determination. This rate was formally liberalised in January 1989, but informal practices ensured that it initially remained relatively inflexible: banks met considerable borrower resistance in trying to implement a market-based lending rate when the rate was first liberalised

---

[15] Estimating over 1985M1–1987M12, β_1 is 0.24 and β_2 is 0.19, and for 1991M1–1994M9, β_1 is 0.28 and β_2 is 0.23, which are marginally above the coefficients estimated when the period is included.

[16] The money market rate used in this case is the average of call rates across all maturities, which is dominated by very short-call transactions. Since the term structure of money and institutional rates is not well matched, an increase in short-lived shocks to the money market rate will depress the adjustment coefficients. Other money market interest rate data, such as the one–90-day NCD secondary market rate, exhibit a similar pattern.

and were forced to forgo the requirement that borrowers place compensatory balances with them (so that the effective cost of borrowing rate was less affected). At the same time, risk of default increased markedly in 1992 as the economy deteriorated and the number of bankruptcies jumped, and the loan–call rate spread widened. The speed of adjustment also increased in the 1990s, especially when compared to the second half of the 1980s. One further reason why the deposit rate may have conformed more to the market than the loan rate is that Japan, like some other east Asian countries, consistently sought to maintain positive real rates of interest on financial assets in order to promote saving, while at the same time trying to subsidise industry with cheap credit.

More generally, there is an apparent difference between the adjustment process of deposit rates and loan rates. Correlations tend to be higher, the adjustment process simpler and the adjustment to equilibrium faster in deposit than in loan markets. This is most apparent in Indonesia, Malaysia and Thailand, but it also occurs in other countries. The fact that it occurs generally is consistent with a number of hypotheses:[17] first, the maturity matching with money market rates is more precise with deposit rates than with lending rates; secondly, the smoothing of rates under implicit contracts is more important in the loan than the deposit market, since borrowers are more concerned with fixing costs than depositors are with fixing income; thirdly, it is easier and cheaper for a depositor to change accounts or banks than it is for a borrower, which means that arbitrage between deposit rates will be faster than for lending rates for any given change in market rates (see Lowe and Rohling 1992).

The fact that the difference is most pronounced in Indonesia, Malaysia and Thailand suggests that it is difficult to enforce controls when substitutes to the controlled instruments can be readily created. In south-east Asian countries, there have usually been close substitutes for domestic currency-denominated deposits, either in the form of foreign currency (US dollar) deposits at local banks or access to offshore foreign currency deposits, for example in Singapore. If the authorities hold deposit rates below the 'market' rate, they risk hollowing out the banking sector and

---

[17] In any sub-sample, the adjustment of deposit rates will be faster than that of loan rates if the deposit market is liberalised ahead of the loan market, as occurred in Malaysia (October 1978 compared to February 1991) and Thailand (March 1990 compared to June 1992). The 1990M1–1994M12 sub-sample for the loan rate is re-estimated for Malaysia and Thailand with the starting date being the date the loan rate was liberalised. The coefficients are almost identical for Thailand but change substantially for Malaysia. In this case, β_1 is 0.28 (up from 0.17) and β_2 is 0.19 (up from 0.13). These coefficients are still significantly lower than the corresponding values for the deposit rate (0.48 and 0.50), and so the different speed of adjustment is not simply due to the timing of liberalisation.

increasing the volatility and size of capital flows and exchange rate fluctuations. Substitutability is typically greater for deposits than loans, given the additional contracting costs and information asymmetries in the loan market, and this implies a lower adjustment coefficient on loan rates. However, this is not sustainable in a stable banking system. One would also expect that the ability of the authorities to insulate the domestic market would have declined over the past decade as capital inflows to south-east Asia have increased (so the range of foreign substitutes for loans has increased) and as domestic capital markets have grown apace (so the range of domestic substitutes for both deposits and loans has expanded).

As discussed above, banks in most countries in the region have experienced periodic deterioration in the quality of their assets. The loan-pricing rule for a free market predicts that this forces the loan-rate up, and the positive constant in the loan-rate equation should rise, which is what actually occurs. The constant term in the Philippine loan equation is positive, relatively large and statistically significant in all sub-periods, as expected. The constant term increases substantially in the Japanese, Canadian and Australian loan rate equations in the 1990M1–1994M12 sub-period, coincident with a substantial rise in business risk and non-performing loans (Okina and Sakuraba 1994; Lowe 1995). Indonesia has also experienced severe problems with non-performing loans, but the constant term for 1990M1–1994M12, while positive, is not significant, and this may indicate that the pricing of risk and the recovery of the banking system is being effected through non-market mechanisms (such as central bank bailouts). The constant term in the Thai loan equation is very large, positive and significant in the 1980M1–1984M12 sub-period, reflecting the series of banking crises from 1983 to 1986. The constant subsequently falls over successive periods, following substantial and effective reform of bank supervision, though it is still statistically significant. The constant is positive, significant and mostly stable in Singapore and the United States over the sub-periods.[18] The constant is positive but insignificant in Malaysia in 1990M1–1994M12, apparently reflecting sound banking practices and effective supervision in that country.

There are two additional issues to be considered. The first is whether foreign rates should be included in the institutional-rate estimating equation. Consider the loan rate. The simple bank balance sheet from which the rules for institutional rates are derived ignores foreign liabilities, which

---

[18] In the case of the United States, however, the adjustment coefficient declines over subperiods, which may be due to risk or the declining significance of the prime rate as an indicator lending rate.

can be important sources of funds when the capital account is open. This is unlikely, however, to be important in practice, if banks cover foreign currency borrowing in the forward exchange market, and so the cost of foreign funds will be the same as the money market rate when covered interest parity holds.[19] In regard to the deposit rate, on the other hand, it is reasonable to think of the foreign interest rate as a determinant of the domestic deposit rate when foreign-currency deposits are close substitutes for home-currency denominated deposits, as in Indonesia and Malaysia. The foreign interest rate is not significant in deposit-rate equations.[20]

The second issue is the relevance of the other institutional rate in the determination of institutional rates, discussed above. If institutional rates are determined by fiat, then the money market rate and both institutional rates may contain information about the process for each of the institutional rates, whereas if they are market-determined, only the money market rate and the particular institutional rate under consideration should contain information about its process. Using data for Thailand and Australia, regressions which included the money market rate and both institutional rates were conducted for each country for the sub-sample periods, 1985M1–1989M12 and 1990M1–1994M12. The countries and periods were selected on the grounds that institutional rates were liberalised in both periods in Australia, but only the second period in Thailand, and so implicitly provide a test of the model (the prediction that the loan–deposit spread is not relevant in a free market).[21] Estimation proceeded as follows. The lagged level and lagged first difference of the other institutional interest rate were added to the preferred equation estimated using (5.14), which effectively nests the hypothesis that the regulatory regime makes a difference to the determination of institutional interest rates. Table 5.5 reports the chi-square (2) statistic for *excluding* the other institutional rate.

The results are relatively straightforward. For Australia, it is unambigu-

---

[19] This is generally a reasonable assumption for most of these markets (see chapter 3 and Chinn and Frankel 1994a).

[20] For example, three-month SIBOR and its first difference are individually and jointly statistically insignificant (chi-square (2) = 0.21) when added to the 1990M1–1994M7 Indonesian deposit-rate equation.

[21] This test was also applied to the other east Asian and western Pacific economies from 1990M1 to 1994M12. As for Australia and Thailand, the other institutional rate was not significant for Japan, Malaysia and the Philippines, but was for Hong Kong, Indonesia, Singapore and Taiwan. While rates are determined by market participants rather than governments in the latter set of countries, these markets are also the more closed or cartelised in the region. For Hong Kong and Singapore, where cartels are dominant, the interbank rate becomes statistically insignificant in the loan-rate equation once the deposit rate is included, but is significant in the deposit-rate equation along with the loan rate.

Table 5.5. *Chi-square (2) test for the exclusion of the other institutional rate, 1985M1–1994M12*

	Australia		Thailand	
	Deposit equation	Loan equation	Deposit equation	Loan equation
1985M1–1999M12	2.48 (0.289)	1.99 (0.370)	5.31# (0.070)	1.52 (0.468)
1990M1–1994M12	0.03 (0.984)	2.47 (0.291)	3.04 (0.219)	19.00* (0.000)

Notes:
= statistical significance at the 10 per cent level; * = statistical significance at the 5 per cent level.
Marginal significance in parentheses.

ous that, in both periods, including the deposit rate in the loan-rate equation provides no additional information and vice versa. For Thailand, the loan rate (in this case, the lagged level) did provide information about the deposit rate before deregulation, but not afterwards. On the other hand, the deposit rate provides information about the loan rate in the 1990s, though in this case the first lag of the differenced deposit rate provides information, and not the lagged level, which indicates that the information concerns dynamics and not fundamentals. Moreover, the loan rate was liberalised only in mid-1992 and so the results are the average of two regimes.[22] Overall, the evidence suggests that the rules are reasonable first approximations of institutional-rate determination. Australian institutional rates are market-determined, as expected, and Thai deposit rates have been market-determined this decade, though the evidence is less clear for Thai loan rates. The impact of money market rates on institutional interest rates has increased.

Conclusion

This chapter addressed the integration of *domestic* financial markets – an issue unexamined in the literature of international financial integration – by exploring the relationship between money market interest rates and deposit and loan interest rates. Rules for setting interest rates on deposits and loans were derived, and these were shown to conform to banking practice and capture recent key developments in the banking sectors of east Asian economies – progressive deregulation and liberalisation,

---

[22] When the first lags of the differenced money and loan rates are included in this equation, the lag of the differenced deposit rate remains significant but the coefficient (0.28) is offset by the other dynamics on the loan rate (− 0.20) and on the interbank rate (− 0.05).

increasing competitiveness and episodic deterioration in the quality of loan assets.

The modelling shows that the integration of domestic institutional financial markets has increased substantially over the past decade, due to pervasive liberalisation and, more recently, growing competitiveness. The adjustment of domestic institutional rates to changes in money market rates has increased, often significantly, and by the first half of the 1990s the speed and pattern of adjustment of institutional rates in most of the developing/newly developed economies of east Asia had become similar to that in economies with developed financial systems. There is also a difference between the adjustment of deposit and loan rates, with the former adjusting more rapidly. This may be explained by differences in the maturity, substitutability and transactions costs associated with loans and deposits. The riskiness of private borrowers and the poor health of the banking system were shown to have a significant, deleterious effect on the level of loan rates in the region.

There are three policy implications that flow from this analysis. First, when monetary policy is implemented by indirect monetary management techniques, its effectiveness is significantly enhanced when institutional interest rates are liberalised: the transmission from the money market to institutional markets is considerably more rapid when the latter markets are deregulated. Regulation can be market-conforming, and the gains from deregulation are obviously smaller in this case, but most regulations have been non-conforming. All the economies examined had substantially liberalised institutional interest rates by the mid-1990s, although this does not preclude the authorities from using non-market influence over rates. Secondly, competition in banking is crucial, both to securing greater rewards for savers and lower costs for borrowers and to ensuring that innovations in money market interest rates are transmitted to institutional rates. There is still considerable progress to be made in this area, particularly in dissolving cartels and oligopolistic behaviour in Korea, Taiwan and some economies in south-east Asia. Thirdly, sound bank management and effective prudential supervision are necessary conditions to securing a lower level of loan interest rates, given funding costs. There is again still a considerable way to go in this regard for most economies.

6

Financial integration and capital formation, foreign debt and the real exchange rate

A further question to be addressed is the effect of financial integration on macroeconomic structure, particularly on domestic capital formation, the current account and the real exchange rate. This question is topical because the policy debate in a number of east Asian economies, including Korea (Dornbusch and Park 1994; Kim 1994); Park 1994), Malaysia, Taiwan and Thailand (Nijathaworn and Dejthamrong 1994) is concerned that the nominal and real exchange rate will appreciate and hence international competitiveness be eroded when the capital account is fully liberalised. Should this factor be a concern for policy?

A view from the literature

The traditional Mundell–Fleming model neither links financial flows to the formation of capital (Makin 1994: 63) nor explores the evolution of the real exchange rate in the process of financial opening, and so is not a useful device with which to analyse the effects of liberalisation on economic structure. Surprisingly, these matters have received little attention so far in dynamic, intertemporal optimising models.[1] The predictions from two-period, two-country and two-good models are generally straightforward. Van Wijnbergen (1990) argues that the elimination of capital controls reduces the current interest rate and so is equivalent to reducing a tax on current consumption. He predicts that it boosts demand for the home good and induces a real appreciation in the current period, but reduces demand for the home good and induces a real depreciation in the next period. Edwards (1989) reaches similar conclusions.

Kahn and Zahler (1983) were the first to assess capital account liberalisation in a dynamic general equilibrium model. They assumed a small economy with exogenous traded goods prices, a fixed exchange rate and

[1] See Khan and Zahler (1983), Bacchetta (1992); Dornbusch and Park (1994) for remarks to this effect. Edwards (1989) makes a similar comment about two-period general equilibrium models.

liberalised domestic financial markets. Capital flows are a function, β, of the difference between the domestic rate and the foreign rate, adjusted for a risk premium and the expected depreciation of the exchange rate. Financial repression is modelled as $\beta = 0$ and financial integration as $\beta = 1$. The model is bulky (37 equations, of which 17 are behavioural) and is solved by simulation. The removal of capital controls creates a capital inflow and an excess supply of money which initially stimulates aggregate demand but then ignites price pressures and worsens the current account. The domestic interest rate eventually equals the world rate and the economy moves to an equilibrium in which a surplus on the trade account is required to generate the income to finance the higher external debt. The real exchange rate, defined as the ratio of traded to non-traded prices, initially appreciates as non-traded prices rise but must depreciate in the long run since the price of non-tradeables must fall to ensure an improvement in the trade balance.

While the model is dated by its reliance on a pure money transmission mechanism, the assumption that the capital stock is exogenous through the process of financial opening is its key weakness. The assumption of fixed capital is also a feature which until only recently persisted in the literature. Obstfeld (1986b), for example, set out an elegant model of a small open economy with infinitely lived consumers and sticky wage and price adjustment in order to examine the effects of financial liberalisation on the real exchange rate and net external asset position. Assuming that in the repressed state the domestic interest rate is set by the local authorities and is above the world rate, financial integration increases absorption, the real exchange rate initially appreciates, the current account shifts into deficit and net external assets fall. In the long run, this is sustainable only if the steady-state real exchange rate depreciates, so that trade in goods and services increases to finance the now larger income deficit. In models where liberalisation induces initial current account deficits, the balance of payments and transversality conditions require the real exchange rate to depreciate in the long run (Mussa 1984, 1986).

Bacchetta (1992) appears to be the first paper to address the effect of financial integration on domestic capital formation in a dynamic framework. He models financial repression by assuming that the cost of investment funds exceeds the world interest rate but that the return on savings is below the world interest rate. The domestic distortion is the wedge between borrowing and lending rates and the external distortion is the wedge between the domestic rates and the world rate. Assuming that investment is decreasing in both the cost of funds and capital stock (implications of the standard neo-classical model), financial integration lowers the hurdle rate for investment, induces capital inflow and domestic saving and boosts the capital stock. Viaene (1992) presents a similar model and reaches similar conclusions. Makin (1994: chapters 4 and 5) analyses a two-country world: when local expected rates of return exceed the foreign interest rate, financial integration equalises the domestic and foreign interest rates, and induces an immediate stock adjustment embodied in an increase in the home country's capital stock, foreign debt and net national wealth which leaves both countries better off in the long run.

Makin adds the caveat that financial integration may not generate net wealth if there are large inefficiencies in financial markets. Checchi (1992) constructs a model which shows that financial liberalisation can reduce the capital stock when public-sector borrowing crowds out private investment or when the gains from overseas investment exceed local expected returns. Makin's model predicts that in this case the reduction in output is more than compensated by an increase in income from abroad and so does not reduce national welfare. Hughes (1987) and McCulloch (1994) argue that the capital inflow 'package' matters, with direct investment likely to generate more human capital than portfolio capital, at least in the earlier stages of development. The increase in the capital stock will also depend on the structure of firms and financing patterns. If firms finance investment out of retained earnings, which is typical of small firms (McCulloch 1994), then capital liberalisation may have little effect on capital formation if financing patterns do not change.

The papers which unify the analysis on the real exchange rate, net indebtedness and endogenous capital formation are scant. Dornbusch and Park (1994) present a model in which financial integration induces capital inflow in response to a positive differential between the domestic and foreign real interest rates, and thus boosts the real price of capital, the stock market, investment and the physical capital stock. Labour also benefits since the real product wage increases. They define the 'real exchange rate' as the real product wage and so a rise in domestic wages means an appreciation of the real exchange rate. This raises the marginal cost of investment and induces an offsetting fall in investment.[2] Households also increase their demand for the home good which will induce a further real exchange rate appreciation. Dornbusch and Park (1994: 11) posit that the net result of liberalisation is that net investment increases, the real exchange rate appreciates and consumption and the trade deficit both rise.

---

[2] This definition assumes that the non-traded good is produced using only labour and that traded good prices are constant and normalised at unity. The increase in the real product wage depresses investment since investment uses labour and so depends on the cost of labour.

They do not examine the transversality conditions of the model which would require the real exchange rate to depreciate in the long run, and so their analysis is incomplete.

The prediction that capital account liberalisation is associated with an appreciation of the real exchange rate is based on particular types of models. Fears of an appreciation also tend to focus on the short-term effect of financial liberalisation. Models like those of Obstfeld (1986b), Edwards (1989) and van Wijnbergen (1990), reviewed above, are simplified and stylised, generally assuming, for example, that the capital stock is fixed. They do not take account of the long-run effects of opening the capital account on the formation of physical capital. This may be valid for assessing some short-term, dynamic properties of models, but it is not valid for broader analysis based on changing fundamentals. If there have been constraints on access to foreign funds, then usually those constraints are binding. Easing the constraint should affect physical capital formation and, therefore, the supply of the home good. If so, then the equilibrium relative price of the home good – the real exchange rate – also changes. The net effect would be expected to depend on the relative change in supply and demand for the home good which occurs as a result of liberalisation. In fact, it is not clear whether the real exchange rate depreciates or appreciates as a result. This chapter explores the predictions of an extended, but still simplified, model which suggests a more complex and rich set of outcomes for the real exchange rate. The assumption that the physical capital stock remains unchanged as a result of financial integration is not innocuous.

There are a number of definitions of the real exchange rate, and which definition is selected depends on the analytical exercise being undertaken (Dwyer and Lowe 1993). A home-good/foreign-good model is used here and the real exchange rate is defined as the foreign good price relative to the home-good price. One other popular definition of the real exchange rate is the ratio of traded to non-traded prices. This is not used here since this dichotomy is relatively arbitrary: what is traded and non-traded varies over countries and over time. In a sense, more is known about the general price level than its constituent parts. Some studies also indicate that the traded/non-traded good distinction does not matter in practice (Engel 1995). The focus of this chapter, then, reverts to the definition of the real exchange rate as the ratio of the price of the foreign relative to that of the home good.

The chapter comprises two sections. The first outlines a simple model of an open economy in order to derive steady-state conditions for the physical capital stock, foreign debt and real exchange rate. The focus is on the steady-state properties of the model. In models of this complexity, analytical dynamic solutions are not tractable (or obtainable) and, in terms of numerical analysis, a range of dynamic responses can be generated by specifying different parameter values and different starting values. Focusing on the steady-state properties highlights the fundamental properties of the model; if the analysis were to focus also on the dynamics, the model would have to be more complicated. The dynamics of interest parity, for example, make sense only when there are two financial assets and so it would be necessary to specify corporate or government bond markets (and the latter means modelling government). But comparing steady states across capital account regimes with one financial asset makes sense, and reduces the complexity of the model. The second section examines the effect of financial repression on these macroeconomic variables in order to identify the effects of financial integration on their values in the steady state. The conclusion summarises the results.

The real exchange rate, foreign debt and capital in a financially integrated economy

This section examines the steady-state properties of an economy with open and integrated financial markets. The foundation for the analysis is the standard Ramsey model – described, for example, in Blanchard and Fischer (1989) and Barro and Sala-i-Martin (1995) – extended to two goods, a home good and a foreign good. The model comprises two countries, the home country and the foreign country, where variables and parameters of the foreign country are superscripted with an asterisk. The representation of production and consumption is relatively straightforward.

Production

The home good is produced by a combination of capital and labour: $Y = F(K,L)$. For fixed labour, output per unit of labour is a function of the effective capital stock, $y = f(k)$. The population is assumed to be constant. If production technology is Cobb–Douglas with constant returns to scale, then $y = k^a$ where α is the capital share. Installation costs are assumed to be convex, $w(j)$, where j is investment net of installation costs and $w(0) = 0$, $w'(0) = 0$, $w' > 0$ and $w'' > 0$. If, for example,

$$w(j) = \frac{\phi}{2} \cdot \frac{j^2}{k},$$

then

$$w'(j) = \frac{\phi j}{k} \text{ and } w''(j) = \frac{\phi}{k}.$$

Gross investment is

$$i = j\left(1 + \frac{\phi}{2} \cdot \frac{j}{k}\right).$$

The capital stock evolves at the rate, $k = j - \delta k$, where δ, is the depreciation rate.

In terms of the home good, the firm maximises the value function,

$$V_s = \int_t^\infty [f(k_s) - i_s] e^{-r(s-t)} ds \tag{6.1}$$

with respect to net investment, j, and subject to $\dot{k} = j - \delta k$. This implies two first-order conditions

$$jt = \frac{(q_t - 1)k_t}{\phi} \tag{6.2}$$

and

$$\dot{q}_t = (r_t + \delta)q_t + \frac{\phi}{2}\left(\frac{j_t}{k_t}\right)^2 - f'(k_t). \tag{6.3}$$

In the steady state, net investment, j, is δk and the shadow price of investment, q, is $1 + \phi\delta$. Gross investment is a function of the capital stock,

$$i_t = \gamma k_t \tag{6.4}$$

Solving (6.3) implies that steady-state capital is a function of the real interest rate and structural parameters,

$$k_t = \left[\frac{r_t(1 + \phi\delta)}{\alpha} + \frac{\delta(2 + 3\phi\delta)}{2\alpha}\right]^{\frac{1}{\alpha-1}}. \tag{6.5}$$

If the home economy is financially integrated, then $r = r^*$ and the capital stock depends on the foreign real rate. In the steady state, an increase in the real interest rate reduces the capital stock:

$$\frac{dk}{dr} = \frac{1 + \phi\delta}{\alpha(\alpha - 1)}\left[\frac{r(1 + \phi\delta)}{\alpha} + \frac{\delta(2 + 3\phi\delta)}{2\alpha}\right]^{\frac{2-\alpha}{\alpha-1}} = <0 \text{ since } \alpha < 1. \tag{6.6}$$

Consumption

The representative consumer in each country is assumed to be infinitely lived. Consumption falls over two goods, the home good, H, and an imported good, M. Expenditure in terms of the home good is $z_t^{1-\beta}C_t = H_t + z_t M_t$, where β is the share of the home good in home expenditure and z is the real exchange rate and is defined as the relative price of the foreign good $z_t = p^*/p$ (where p is the price of the home good and p^* is the price of the foreign good). A rise in z is a depreciation of the real exchange rate. These variables are defined on a *per capita* basis, denoted by lower-case letters,

$$z_t^{1-\beta}c_t = h_t + z_t m_t. \tag{6.7}$$

The budget constraint evolves as

$$b = z_t^{1-\beta}c_t + r_t b_t - y_t, \tag{6.8}$$

where b is the *per capita* stock of foreign liabilities, r is the real interest rate and y is income in terms of the home good. Preferences are assumed to be isoelastic,

$$u(c) = \ln(h^\beta m^{1-\beta}). \tag{6.9}$$

Cobb–Douglas preferences imply that the ratio of consumption on each good is constant,

$$\frac{z_t m_t}{h_t} = \frac{1-\beta}{\beta} \tag{6.10}$$

The marginal rate of substitution between the two goods for the foreign country is, analogously,

$$\frac{m_t^*}{z_t h_t^*} = \frac{1-\beta^*}{\beta^*} \tag{6.11}$$

As shown in appendix 6.1 (p. 244), total consumption, c, is determined in the steady state as

$$c_t = \theta z_t^{\beta-1}(q_t k_t + W_t - b_t) \tag{6.12}$$

where q is the price of capital relative to the home good and W is human wealth,

$$W_t = \int_t^\infty w_s e^{-r(s-t)}ds.$$

In the steady state,

$$W = \frac{(1-\alpha)k^{\alpha}}{r},$$

and this expression is used from now on since the steady-state properties of the model are the focus of analysis. Foreign consumption is given analogously as

$$c_t^* = \theta^* z_t^{1-\beta^*}(q_t^* k_t^* + W_t^* + b_t/z_t). \tag{6.13}$$

Note that the net foreign liabilities term is positive in the foreign-consumption equation, with

$$b_t^* = -\frac{b_t}{z_t},$$

because of the adding-up constraint for foreign liabilities and assets: the home country's net foreign liabilities are the foreign country's net foreign assets.

Imports for the home country are determined from the national accounts identity,

$$z_t m = z_t^{1-\beta} c_t + i_t + x_t - y_t, \tag{6.14}$$

where c, i and y are defined as above. An expression for exports, x, which are foreign imports of the home good valued in terms of the home good, is obtained using the expression for the foreign marginal rate of substitution between the two goods, (6.11),

$$x_t = (1 - \beta^*) c_t^* z_t^{\beta^*-1}. \tag{6.15}$$

Substituting for these terms in (6.15), home imports in terms of the home good are

$$z_t m_t = (rq + \gamma)k_t - \alpha k_t^{\alpha} + (1-\beta^*)(r_t^* q_t^* k_t^* + (1-\alpha)k_t^{*\alpha}) + (r_t^*/z_t - r_t)b_t. \tag{6.16}$$

Consumption of the home good is determined by the adding-up constraint for consumption,

$$h_t = c_t z_t^{1-\beta} - z_t m_t, \tag{6.17}$$

which implies, given (6.16),

$$h_t = (k_t^{\alpha} - \gamma k_t) - (1-\beta^*)(r_t^* q_t^* k_t^* + (1-\alpha)k_t^{*\alpha}) - r_t^* b_t/z_t. \tag{6.18}$$

As the real exchange rate appreciates (z falls), consumption of imports rises while that of home goods falls. Home good consumption rises with net output (the first expression in parentheses on the right-hand side), but falls as foreign demand increases.

External balance

External liabilities increase as interest payments accrue and as imports exceed exports,

$$\dot{bt} = r_t b_t + z_t m_t - x_t. \tag{6.19}$$

The home country's marginal rate of substitution, (6.10), and the identity that the home good equals output *less* gross investment and exports, imply that imports can be written in terms of net output and exports,

$$z_t m_t = \frac{1 - \beta}{\beta}(y_t - i_t - x_t). \tag{6.20}$$

Substituting for y, i and x yields the expression for foreign debt,

$$b_t = \frac{z_t[(1 - \beta^*)(r_t^* q_t^* k_t^* + (1 - \alpha)k_t^{*\alpha}) - (1 - \beta)(k_t^\alpha - \gamma k_t)]}{\beta z_t r_t - r_t^*(1 - \beta)}. \tag{6.21}$$

One country's debt is the other country's asset and so steady-state debt reflects the interaction of the two countries' preferences and endowments. Foreign debt in the steady state depends on three factors: the relative size and gross wealth of the countries, as indicated by the size of the two countries' respective capital stocks; the relative openness of the countries, as indicated by preference for the home good in the consumption bundle; and the relative price of the countries' goods, as indicated by the real exchange rate.

From (6.21), the home country's net foreign debt is higher, the smaller is its capital stock or the higher is the capital stock of the other country. An increase in the capital stock reduces debt,

$$\frac{db}{dk} = \frac{-(1 - \beta)(\alpha k_f^{\alpha-1} - \gamma)z_t}{\beta_t r z_t - (1 - \beta^*)r_t^*} < 0, \tag{6.22}$$

but the size of the effect depends on the size of the capital stock. The larger the capital stock, the smaller is the reduction in debt. Consider the intuition behind this set of results. A country with a relatively large capital stock, and hence gross wealth, will tend to be a lender rather than a borrower in world capital markets. This conforms to an expectation that wealthier and more developed countries have less need to borrow than poorer and less developed countries. Countries require debt to form capital and generate income, and so reduce their reliance on debt as capital increases and approaches the desired steady-state level. At low levels of capital stock, the output gains from an increase in capital are large and so the decline is comparatively bigger than at high capital levels.

Preferences and prices also matter. A shift in foreign preferences towards the home good (a fall in β^*), implies an increase in debt while a shift in home preferences to the home good implies a reduction in foreign debt. This makes sense. As demand for the home good increases in the foreign country, that country is more willing to lend its wealth to the home country. Similarly, as demand for the home good increases in the home country, exports fall and net borrowing increases. Now consider relative prices. The partial derivative of debt with respect to the real exchange rate is

$$\frac{db_t}{dz_t} = \frac{-r_t^*(1-\beta)[(1-\beta^*)(r_t^*q_t^*k_t^* + (1-\alpha)k_t^{*\alpha}) - (1-\beta)(k_t^\alpha - \gamma k_t)]}{(\beta z_t r_t - r_t^*(1-\beta)^2}. \tag{6.23}$$

If the home country is relatively small, then the term in the square brackets is positive and the numerator negative. A depreciation of the real exchange rate (a rise in z) induces a fall in the steady-state level of debt.

The real exchange rate

The model is closed by the expression for the real exchange rate. The steady-state real exchange rate is determined by the remaining unused equation in the system, the national accounts equation for the foreign country,

$$y_t^* z_t^{\beta^*-1} c_t^* + i_t^* + x_t^* - m_t^*/z \tag{6.24}$$

where, letting $\theta^* = r^*$,

$$y_t^* = k_t^{*a^*}$$

$$c_t^* = z_t^{1-\beta^*}(r_t^*q_t^*k_t^* + (1-\alpha)k_t^{*\alpha^*} + r_t^*b_t/z_t)$$

$$i_t^* = \gamma^* k_t^*$$

$$x_t^* = m_t = \frac{1}{z_t}\left[(r_t q_t + \gamma)k_t - \alpha k_t^\alpha + \left(\frac{r_t^*}{z_t} - r_t\right)b_t + (1-\beta^*)(r_t^*q_t^*k_t^* + (1-\alpha)k_t^{*\alpha^*})\right]$$

$$m_t^* = x_t = (1-\beta^*)(r_t^*q_t^*k_t^* + (1-\alpha)k_t^{*\alpha^*} + {}_t^*b_t/z_t).$$

In a two-country model it is possible to define the equilibrium value of the real exchange rate by looking at just one country because of Walras' law. Substituting for this set of equations into (6.24), the real exchange rate is a quadratic,

$$0 = z_t^2[(1-\beta^*(1-\alpha))k_t^{*\alpha^*} - (\gamma^* + \beta^* r_t^* q_t^*)k_t^*] - z_t[(\beta r - r_t)b_t$$
$$+ (r_t q_t + \gamma)k_t - \alpha k_t^\alpha + (1-\beta^*)(r_t^* q_t^* k_t^* + (1-\alpha)k_t^{*\alpha^*})] - r_t^* b, \tag{6.25}$$

or, in summary form,

$$0 = z_t^2 a_0 + z a_1 + a_2,\tag{6.26}$$

where the *a*s take on the obvious values from (6.27). There are two solutions for the real exchange rate,

$$z_1, z_2 = \frac{-a_1 + / - \sqrt{a_1^2 - 4a_0 a_2}}{2a_0}\tag{6.27}$$

or, in detail,

$$z_1, z_2 = \frac{(\beta^* r_t^* - r_t)b_t + (r_t q_t + \gamma)k_t - \alpha k_t^q + (1 - \beta^*)(r_t^* q_t^* k_t^* + (1 - \alpha^*)k_t^{*\alpha^*})}{2((1 - \beta^*(1 - \alpha^*))k_t^{*\alpha^*} - (\gamma^* + \beta_t^* r_t^* q_t^*)k_t^*)} + / -$$

$$\frac{\sqrt{[(\beta^* r_t^* - r_t)b_t + (r_t q_t + \gamma)k_t - \alpha k_t^q + (1 - \beta^*)(r_t^* q_t^* k_t^* + (1 - \alpha^*)k_t^{*\alpha^*})]^2 + 4 r_t^* b_t((1 - \beta^*(1 - \alpha^*))k_t^{*\alpha^*} - (\gamma^* + \beta_t^* r_t^* q_t^*)k_t^*))}}{2((1 - \beta^*(1 - \alpha^*))k_t^{*\alpha^*} - (\gamma^* + \beta_t^* r_t^* q_t^*)k_t^*).}$$

$$\tag{6.28}$$

The stable solution is z_1 since this ensures that a rise in *b* induces a rise in *z* – that is, a real depreciation. From (6.23), a real depreciation induces a fall in the steady-state debt, which, if z_2 were the solution, would lead to a further depreciation and dynamic instability. With z_1 the solution, a depreciation reduces the debt which in turn induces an appreciation. The system is stable. The real exchange rate is a function of r, r^*, k, k^*, b and preference and production parameters in both countries. Equation (6.28) implies that the real exchange rate depreciates (z rises) as the foreign debt increases, as home capital increases and as foreign capital decreases. The partial derivatives of z_1 with respect to capital and debt and capital are, respectively,

$$\frac{dz_1}{dk} = \frac{(r_t q_t + \gamma) - \alpha^2 k_t^{\alpha - 1}}{2((1 - \beta^*(1 - \alpha^*))k_t^{*\alpha^*} - (\gamma^* + \beta_t^* r_t^* q_t^*)k_t^*)}.\tag{6.29}$$

$$\frac{dz_1}{db} = \frac{[(4 + \beta^*)r_t^* - r_t][(1 - \beta^*(1 - \alpha^*))k_t^{*\alpha^*} - (\gamma^* + \beta_t^* r_t^* q_t^*)k_t^*] - (r_t - \beta^* r_t^*)}{2((1 - \beta^*(1 - \alpha^*))k_t^{*\alpha^*} - (\gamma^* + \beta_t^* r_t^* q_t^*)k_t^*)}.\tag{6.30}$$

The sign for both these partial derivatives would seem to depend on the magnitude of key parameters. It is, perhaps, easier to show that the derivatives are expected to be positively signed by assigning values that tend to occur in the literature and solve the derivatives numerically. Table 6.1 sets out some relevant parameter values for the model with values that tend to appear in numerical simulations (for example, McKibbin and Sachs 1991; Barro and Sala-i-Martin 1995). Parameters are assumed to be identical in both countries (and so only one set is reported). The capital stock is a func-

Table 6.1. *Parameter values for numerical simulation*

r	ϕ	δ	α	β	γ	q	k	a_0	a_1	a_2	$z\,(b=0)$	$z\,(b=1)$	$z\,(k\times 2)$
0.05	2.00	0.10	0.30	0.80	0.11	1.20	1.92	0.23	2.25	0.00	0.85	1.00	2.04

tion of parameters and is estimated from (6.5). For simplicity, foreign debt is initially set to zero. The real exchange rate, z, is reported as well as the value for an increase in b, modelled as $b=1$, and an increase in k, modelled as a doubling of capital.

The values for z_2 are not reported but if $b=0$, z_2 is zero (by definition in (6.27)) and if $b>0$, then is negative. Obviously, a negative price is not allowed. From table 6.1, an increase in foreign debt or home physical capital *depreciates* the real exchange rate. It follows from (6.29) that the extent of the depreciation in the real exchange rate due to an increase in capital depends on the size of the capital stock to start with. The depreciation is larger the bigger the capital stock.

The effect of incomplete financial integration

In the literature, capital controls are modelled either as a limit (usually zero), on net foreign borrowing, or as a tax wedge in the real interest parity condition (Edwards 1989); van Wijnbergen 1990). In this section, consider capital controls as a tax wedge in the real interest parity condition,

$$r = (1 + \tau)r^* \tag{6.31}$$

where τ is the implied tax rate on foreign borrowing. When capital controls are in place, the home real rate of interest exceeds the foreign real rate. Assume further that before liberalisation, $\theta = r$ and $r^* = \theta^*$.

In this schema, what is the effect of reducing the tax wedge on the capital stock, foreign debt and the real exchange rate? Substituting (6.31) for r in the capital-stock equation, (6.5), yields

$$k = \left[\frac{r^*(1 + \tau)(1 + \phi\delta)}{\alpha} + \frac{\delta(2 + 3\phi\delta)}{2\alpha} \right]^{\frac{1}{\alpha - 1}}. \tag{6.32}$$

Differentiating with respect to r yields

$$\frac{dk}{d\tau} = \frac{r^*(1 + \phi\delta)}{\alpha(\alpha - 1)} \left[\frac{r^*(1 + \tau)(1 + \phi\delta)}{\alpha} + \frac{\delta(2 + 3\phi\delta)}{2\alpha} \right]^{\frac{2 - \alpha}{\alpha - 1}} < 0 \text{ since } \alpha < 1. \tag{6.33}$$

A reduction in capital controls reduces the local real interest rate and unambiguously increases the local capital stock.

Substituting (6.31) for the interest rate in the foreign debt equation, (6.21), yields

$$b_t \frac{z_t[(1-\beta^*)(r_t^* q_t^* k_t^* + (1-\alpha)k_t^{*\alpha^*}) - (1-\beta)(k_t^\alpha - \gamma k_t)]}{r_t^*(\beta z_t(1+\tau) + \beta - 1)}. \tag{6.34}$$

Taking the partial derivative with respect to yields

$$\frac{db_t}{d\tau} = \frac{-\beta r_t^* z_t^2[(1-\beta^*)(r_t^* q_t^* k_t^* + (1-\alpha)k_t^{*\alpha^*}) - (1-\beta)(k_t^\alpha - \gamma k_t)]}{r_t^*(\beta z_t(1+\tau) + \beta - 1)} < 0. \tag{6.35}$$

Given that the home country is relatively small (so foreign country wealth exceeds home-country income), an increase in capital taxes reduces the foreign debt. Financial integration, therefore, should lead to an increase in foreign debt if the disposition of the country is to be a net debtor rather than a net lender. This is hardly surprising since the effect of capital controls is to limit access to foreign markets, either as borrower or lender. The total effect is more complicated since there are also partial derivatives of the capital stock and the real exchange rate to consider in this framework. The partial derivative of debt with respect to the capital stock is, from (6.22), negative and the partial derivative of the capital stock with respect to the tax wedge is, from (6.33), also negative. The feedback effect of financial integration through the capital stock, therefore, offsets the direct effect. Financial integration boosts the domestic capital stock and this in turn implies that desired foreign debt falls. One would anticipate that the direct effect would dominate the indirect capital effect, but this need not necessarily be the case. There is also an indirect effect through the real exchange rate. As shown below, the direct effect of financial integration is to appreciate the real exchange rate (although this is offset by indirect effects). An appreciation increases the debt and so the second indirect effect also offsets the direct effect.

Consider, now, the effect of the capital tax on the real exchange rate. Substituting (6.31) for the interest rate in the real exchange rate equation, (6.28), yields

$$z_1, z_2 = \frac{(\beta^* - 1 - \tau)r_t^* b_t + ((1+\tau)(r_t^* q_t + \gamma)k_t - \alpha k_t^q + (1-\beta^*)(r_t^* q_t^* k_t^* + (1-\alpha^*)k_t^{*\alpha^*})}{2((1-\beta^*(1-\alpha^*))k_t^{*\alpha^*} - (\gamma^* + \beta_t^* r_t^* q_t^*)k_t^*)} + / -$$

$$\frac{\sqrt{[(\beta^* - 1 - \tau)r_t^* b_t + ((1+\tau)r_t^* q_t + \gamma)k_t - \alpha k_t^q + (1-\beta^*)(r_t^* q_t^* k_t^* + (1-\alpha^*)k_t^{*\alpha^*})]^2 + 4r_t^* b_t((1-\beta^*(1-\alpha^*))k_t^{*\alpha^*} - (\gamma^* + \beta r_t^* q_t^*)k_t^*))}}{2((1-\beta^*(1-\alpha^*))k_t^{*\alpha^*} - (\gamma^* + \beta_t^* r_t^* q_t^*)k_t^*).}$$

$$\tag{6.36}$$

Differentiating with respect to yields

$$\frac{dz_1}{d\tau} = \frac{r_t^*(k_t - b_t) [1 + (\beta^* - 1 - \tau)b_t + (r_t^*(1+\tau) + \gamma)k_t - \alpha k_t^q + (1-\beta^*)(r_t^* q_t^* k_t^* + (1-\alpha^*)k_t^{*\alpha^*})]}{2((1-\beta^*(1-\alpha^*))k_t^{*\alpha^*} - \gamma^* + \beta_t^* r_t^* q_t^*)k_t^*)} \tag{6.37}$$

Given that a country's capital exceeds its foreign debt $(k>b)$, the direct effect of an increase in the tax is to depreciate the real exchange rate. In other words, as financial integration proceeds, the real exchange rate appreciates. But there are also two indirect effects. Financial integration boosts capital formation (equation 6.33)) and increases foreign debt (equation (6.35)) and hence, from equations (6.29) and (6.30), respectively, depreciates the real exchange rate. The indirect effects offset the direct appreciation of the real exchange rate.

Conclusion

Tractable and elegant models of the open macroeconomy, such as those of Obstfeld (1986b), Edwards (1989) and van Wijnbergen (1990), predict that, when the capital account is opened, the real exchange rate initially appreciates but then depreciates in the long run. One limitation of these types of models is that they assume that the capital stock does not change as access to foreign funds changes. If capital controls impose a binding liquidity constraint – that is, they make the home interest rate differ from the world interest rate – then one would not expect the capital stock to be invariant to the degree of financial integration. By implication, the optimal debt and real exchange rate will not be the same as that for fixed capital. This chapter has highlighted the result that, even in the still relatively simple model outlined, the long-run effect of financial integration on basic macroeconomic structure is ambiguous. The model used predicts that the capital stock increases as financial integration proceeds: the cost of capital falls, new investment is stimulated and the capital stock rises. But the long-run effect on foreign debt and the real exchange rate is *not* clear since there is a mix of direct and indirect effects on foreign debt and the real exchange rate.

Foreign debt will tend to rise as the economy becomes more open if capital controls have been a constraint. However, this may be offset – partially or fully – by a decline in desired debt associated with a rise in the capital stock. The economy needs more capital to grow but, as it grows and assets increase, it needs relatively less foreign debt. There are also real exchange rate feedback effects. Financial integration appreciates the real exchange rate in the first instance which tends to increase the foreign debt. The net long-run effect of financial integration on foreign debt is ambiguous. Similarly for the real exchange rate. The direct effect of financial integration is to appreciate the real exchange rate. But this is offset by an increase in capital, which depreciates the real exchange rate, and an increase in foreign debt, which also depreciates the real exchange rate. The prediction for either foreign debt or the real exchange rate is simply not clear since a variety of mechanisms are working. Simple models tend to yield straightforward solutions, and policymakers like to have clear-cut answers. But the real world is more complicated. Endogenising the capital stock makes the analysis more difficult and complex, and it muddies the clear predictions from more simple models. This chapter has shown some of the complexities of the economy and some of the mechanisms by which financial integration affects macroeconomic structure.

It is axiomatic in this model that financial integration boosts the domestic capital stock and increases wealth. Accordingly, by assumption, financial integration will improve welfare since it increases consumption. The other, unexplored dimension of the welfare-improving properties of financial integration is that it better enables consumers to smooth their consumption over time. This issue is considered in more detail, and with reference to the data, in chapter 7.

7

Consumption and liquidity constraints: does financial integration matter?

A basic intuition is that when people are forward-looking, they try to reduce the variability of consumption over their life-time, and so expanding the means by which they can smooth consumption over time should reduce the dependency of their consumption on current income. There is a range of factors which facilitate so-called 'consumption smoothing', and it is difficult to identify domestic and international financial factors separately. This chapter assesses the effect of domestic and international financial integration on consumption in selected economies in the east Asian and western Pacific region. It outlines a simple model of consumer choice under liquidity constraints with changing real interest rates and demographics which motivates tests for a statistically significant effect on consumption of a range of variables which proxy financial and non-financial liquidity constraints. 'Consumption' is defined as expenditure on non-durables.

In the first section, a model is constructed of the consumption of households based on intertemporal optimisation with demographic change and subject to liquidity constraints. In the next section, this model is used to motivate the estimating equation, taking into consideration aggregation over time, aggregation over heterogeneous households, selection of proxies for the liquidity constraint, and various definitions of consumption and income. In the third section, econometric issues are discussed and the results for a basic model often used in the literature and for a more fully specified model are presented and discussed. Non-durable consumption is shown to be tied to income in all countries examined except Australia, where the innovation in non-durable consumption is unforecastable. Non-durable consumption appears liquidity-constrained in east Asian countries but the degree of the constraint and its source vary considerably between countries. The constraint is constant but relatively weak in Hong Kong and appears to be declining in Singapore, consistent with the extent and timing of domestic financial and capital account reform in these countries, but does not appear to have eased over time in Japan. Consumption in Korea, Taiwan and Thailand is also reliant on income, and in the latter two countries there is strong evidence that this is owing to an undeveloped and controlled financial system. Total private expenditure is shown to be dependent on income in Indonesia, Malaysia and the Philippines. The next section discusses whether it is possible to identify domestic and international financial effects separately. Two implications for welfare and policy are discussed. Finally, the conclusion summarises the results. The key findings of the chapter are that financial integration affects the real economy and that the liberalisation of *both* the domestic financial system and the capital account appear to be necessary for households to be able to smooth consumption over the life-cycle.

The Euler equation with liquidity constraints and demographic change

The literature on consumption smoothing is extensive and well summarised by Hall (1989), Deaton (1992), Muellbauer (1994) and Muellbauer and Lattimore (1994). The model presented here is based on Hall (1978) but includes demographic change, which is a major structural feature of east Asian economies (World Bank 1993: 38–40) and, following Muellbauer (1983) and Zeldes (1989), liquidity constraints, which is the factor commonly cited for the failure of the basic Hall model.

The representative household is assumed to maximise a concave expected utility function,

$$E_0\left[\sum_{t=0}^{T}(1+\theta+\zeta_t)^{-t}u(c_t)\right] \tag{7.1}$$

where E_0 is the subjective expectation at time 0 based on all available information, c_t is consumption, is the pure time discount and ζ_t is the time discount varying in the demographic change particular to the country,[1] assumed to be increasing in expected mortality and the birth of new cohorts,[2] (Masson 1992; Schmidt-Hebbel, Webb and Corsetti 1992). The

---

[1] Country-specific demographic variables are introduced by including a time-varying discount rate but they could have been introduced by including a separable country-specific argument in the utility function (Hayashi 1985). The formulation followed is judged to be the more natural since theory indicates that household age affects the discount factor. The alternative specification results in the same estimating equation, and so the argument is academic.

[2] This is based on the predictions of the life-cycle model that aged households work less and consume more out of savings than working households, and that households with dependents consume more when they have young dependents, reducing their life-time saving in the expectation of receiving benefits from their offspring (Schmidt-Hebbel, Webb and Corsetti 1992: 535). Another argument for why young households have a higher discount

household faces three constraints, the first being that its assets accumulate according to the rule,

$$A_{t+1} = (1+r_t)(A_t + y_t - c_t), \tag{7.2}$$

where A_{t+1} is end-period t net wealth, including financial wealth and real wealth such as housing and durables, y_t is labour income, r_t is the real interest rate (defined as the nominal rate less the expected inflation rate) and c_t is consumption. Secondly, given no bequest motive, the no-Ponzi game outcome requires that net assets are zero at the terminal date, T,

$$A_T = 0. \tag{7.3}$$

The no-Ponzi game requirement means that the present value of life-time expected consumption is tied to the present value of life-time expected income, and so consumption is always 'constrained' in the sense that income is limited and the bliss-point for consumption is never reached. This is not, however, the meaning of 'liquidity-constrained'. A liquidity constraint may exist for a number of reasons and hence may take a number of different forms. One form of the constraint, such as that out-lined by Zeldes (1989), is that household net assets *plus* saving must be non-negative each period,[3]

$$(A_t + y_t - c_t) \geq 0. \tag{7.4}$$

The expected utility function and constraints can then be expressed as a value function, written in recursive form, which describes the present dis-counted value of expected utility along the optimal path,

$$V_t(A_t) = \max\{u(c_t) + (1 + \theta + \zeta_t)^{-1} E_t V_{t+1}((1+r_t)(A_t + y_t - c_t)) \\ + \lambda_t(A_t + y_t - c_t)\}. \tag{7.5}$$

Maximising (7.5) with respect to c_t yields the first-order condition,

$$u'(c_t) = \frac{1+r_t}{1+\theta+\zeta_t} E_t V'_{t+1}(A_{t+1}) + \lambda_t \tag{7.6}$$

and the Kuhn–Tucker complementary slackness conditions, $\lambda_t (A_t + y_t - c_t)$ $= 0$ and $\lambda_t \geq 0$.

---

rate is that they typically have dependents and defer saving until the dependents have formed their own household. This seems to be more an argument for the existence of a liq-uidity constraint on young households than an explanation of why the time preferences of young households are different. Note also that the horizon is a long but finite time, T (Carroll and Summers 1989).

[3] Other specifications of the constraint may also generate a shadow price of borrowing and hence have an impact on consumption smoothing. This specification is not general, but the results it yields may be typical.

Maximising (7.5) with respect to A_t and evaluating the derivative at the optimal programme shows that the marginal utility of net wealth, $V'_t(A_t)$, equals the marginal utility of consumption, and so (7.6) can be re-written as

$$u'(c_t) = \frac{1 + r_t}{1 + \theta + \zeta_t} E_t u'(c_{t+1}) + \lambda_t. \tag{7.7}$$

This is a familiar result (Muellbauer 1983; Zeldes 1989; Chah, Ramey and Starr 1991). As summarised by Hall (1989), when the constraint that net worth is non-negative is binding, $\lambda_t > 0$, the household is denied access to its stream of future income and is forced to reduce current consumption in favour of future consumption to equate marginal utilities over time, much as it would if it faced a higher interest rate. Indeed, λ is the shadow price of borrowing, and so interpreting it as a rate is appropriate. The constraint does not mean that the household consumes all its current income. Rather, the liquidity-constrained household smooths consumption but, given a concave utility function, the more binding the constraint, the lower is current consumption, and the higher is future consumption. Hall's (1978) famous prediction that consumption follows a random walk does not follow in the presence of liquidity constraints (Hall 1989). Suppose, for example, that the utility function is quadratic, in the form $u_t = ac_t - bc_t^2$, demographics are unchanging, and the real rate is constant and equal to the rate of time preference. Equation (7.7) can then be written as $\Delta c_t = d\lambda_{t-1} + d\varepsilon_t$, where $d = 1/2b$ and ε_t is a white-noise term related to a revision to permanent income in period t unanticipated in period $t - 1$. Past information correlated with the shadow price is relevant in explaining the path of consumption over time.

Equation (7.7) can be re-arranged as

$$\frac{u'(c_{t+1})}{u'(c_t)} \frac{1 + r_t}{1 + \theta + \zeta_t} = 1 - \frac{\lambda_t}{u'(c_t)} - \varepsilon_{t+1} \tag{7.8}$$

where ε_{t+1} is an expectation error with zero mean and constant variance and is related to the unexpected change in permanent income. To obtain an estimating equation, the utility function must be specified. While the quadratic utility function is a convenient functional form and is commonly used in the literature, it implies that the Euler equation should be estimated in the first differences of consumption, but first differences tend to be I(1) – at least for a number of developing countries in this sample and to make error terms non-homoscedastic (Muellbauer 1983; Neusser 1992).[4] Growth rates, on the other hand, tend to be I(0) and esti-

---

[4] The quadratic utility function also implies *increasing* absolute risk aversion.

mation as such reduces heteroscedasticity. Accordingly, an isoelastic utility function,

$$u_t = \frac{1}{1-\alpha} c_t^{1-a},$$

which is also common in the literature, is used.[5] Using this functional form, linearising the equation by taking the natural logarithm, and noting that for small values of x, $\ln(1+x) \approx x$ (7.8) becomes

$$\Delta \ln c_t = \beta_0 + \beta_1 r_{t-1} - \beta_2 \zeta_{t-1} + \bar{\lambda}_{t-1} + \bar{\varepsilon}_t \qquad (7.9)$$

where $\beta_0 = -\dfrac{\theta}{\alpha} + \delta$, $\beta_1 = \dfrac{1}{\alpha}$, $\beta_2 = \dfrac{1}{\alpha}$, $\bar{\lambda}_{t-1} = \dfrac{\lambda_{t-1}}{\alpha c_{t-1}^{-\alpha}}$ and $\bar{\varepsilon}_t = \dfrac{\varepsilon_t}{\alpha}$

where δ is a drift term identifying a possible trend in consumption due to technological change (Bayoumi and Koujianou 1989) or long-run compositional changes in consumption when the dependent variable is an expenditure class.

Aggregation and the definition of variables

There are four issues (and a few transformations) to deal with before (7.9) can be used as an estimating equation: temporal aggregation, aggregation over households, defining the shadow price of borrowing (and assessing an alternative specification) and defining consumption and income.

---

[5] A major criticism of this utility function is that it ties the elasticity of substitution to be the inverse of the Arrow–Pratt coefficient of relative risk aversion, α. Other authors, such as Weil (1987), Epstein and Zin (1989, 1991), Giovannini and Weil (1989) and Attanasio and Weber (1989) separately identify risk aversion and intertemporal substitution by assuming Kreps–Porteus (1978) preferences (that is, they argue that the resolution of uncertainty about the outcome is relevant to welfare, and so reject the axiom of von Neumann–Morgernstern expected utility that the gambler is concerned with the compound probability, rather than the sequence, of a lottery, Giovannini and Weil 1989: 3–7). Attanasio and Weber (1989), for example, define a utility function for the representative individual with the certainty equivalent as its argument. In this case, the curvature of the utility function defines intertemporal substitution while the curvature of the certainty equivalent function defines risk aversion as related to portfolio structure. The separation literature developed due to the failure of consumption asset-pricing models, which are also derived from the Euler equation but are concerned with portfolio structure. This chapter abstracts from the issue of portfolio structure and so, like Hall (1989), follows the restricted model and interprets as a measure of intertemporal substitution rather than risk aversion related to portfolio composition. Deaton (1992: 20) argues that it is difficult to separate risk aversion from intertemporal substitutability: in an uncertain world, the substitution of future for current consumption increases exposure to risk, and so the two are not separable.

Aggregation over time

Annual data are used in the estimation because, (1) the demographic data and – for most countries – the expenditure and income data are available only on an annual basis and, (2) expenditure data, particularly those on a quarterly basis, are constructed using extrapolated data based on periodical and occasional surveys, and this introduces a degree of smoothing and measurement error in the series which can be minimised by using annual data. Moreover, seasonal adjustment, if made, induces further smoothing which can have non-trivial effects on the estimation results (Neusser 1992). Using annual rather than quarterly data does not necessarily mean a loss of power. It is difficult to reject the hypothesis that consumption follows a random walk, and Shiller and Perron (1985) show that the power of statistical tests for a random walk depends more on the span of the data than the number of observations, and that for a span of (say) 20 years, increasing the frequency of observations from annual to quarterly or monthly does not add power. Relatedly, Campos and Ericsson (1990: 15) show the importance of variation in data series in determining the power of a test.

The use of annual data, however, renders (7.9) unsuitable as the basis for an estimating equation because of temporal aggregation. When the consumption decision is made continuously or within a short period – such as a week, fortnight or month – then examining such decisions over a year implies that variables once-lagged are approximately current-dated variables. For example, if the household's non-durables' expenditure plan is tied to the profile of its income payments (which is, say, monthly) then the consumption decision is monthly and the real interest rate, demographic change and liquidity constraint in the previous month are relevant to the consumption decision in the current month. But on annual data, the interest rate etc. in the previous month are contemporaneous in eleven cases out of twelve and well approximated by the current-dated variable. At the limit, if consumption is made continuously in time, pre-dated variables are contemporaneous.

Demographic change and aggregation over households

If households were identical at each point in time and across time, aggregation would be relatively straightforward, but the analysis is complicated by the differences between the entering and exiting households in life-cycle models (Deaton 1992; Muellbauer and Lattimore 1994) and by the fact that households in the east Asian and western Pacific region are

Table 7.1. *Demographic change variables*

Variable	Definition
d0–19	First difference of ratio of population aged 0–19 years to total population
d65	First difference of ratio of population aged >64 years to total population
ddepend	First difference of ratio of population aged 0–19 and >64 years to total population

heterogeneous, with their demographic composition changing considerably in the past few decades as strong population growth eased, longevity increased and the share of the aged in the population increased. There is demographic change and it varies considerably between countries. Lahiri (1989), Takahashi and Kitamura (1993), Shintani (1994) and Lattimore (1994), to name only a few, have shown the empirical importance of this for saving or consumption decisions in various economies in the region and, accordingly, three differenced variables – $d0 - 19$, $d65$, and *ddepend* – which are defined in table 7.1 and plotted in levels in appendix 7.1 (p. 246), are included in the estimating equation in the form of a time-varying discount factor in the utility function in (7.1). First differences are used to capture demographic change.

One effect of demographic change is that the liquidity constraint will vary with the composition of the population. Suppose that there are three types of stylised households – young, middle-aged and aged. Young households have no assets, low current income (but higher expected income) and so are prime candidates to face liquidity constraints. Middle-aged households have some assets and relatively high current income, and so are unlikely to face liquidity constraints. Aged households have assets but little labour income. The aggregate liquidity constraint is a weighted average of the liquidity constraints of the three household types, and so a younger population will face a tighter constraint than (say) one with a middle-aged population. As the population ages over time, the constraint is downward-sloping. Demographic variables, therefore, contain information not just about how households *want* to smooth consumption over time (that is, information about discount rates) but also about whether they *can* do so (that is, information about liquidity constraints). These effects may work in opposite directions. For example, if the population is dominated by young households, then they may have higher discount rates, which implies higher current consumption, but because of liquidity constraints in the current period they are unable to bring this consumption forward, which offsets current consumption.

Identifying the shadow price

A non-zero shadow price of borrowing implies that the household is unable to bring permanent income forward, preventing it from smoothing consumption, rendering consumption uneven. The shadow price, however, is not observable. Various proxies, z, are selected, and the expected sign on the proxy depends on how it is related to this shadow price.

In the estimations, this specification is augmented by an error-correction term[6] which is included for a number of reasons. First, the Euler equation predicts that variables dated $t-1$ and earlier do not contain information about current consumption growth and should be statistically insignificant when included in the estimating equation, with the variables included in this case being the first lag of real *per capita* income and consumption. This argument is not particularly persuasive because aggregation across households has the effect that predictions based on an individual Euler equation do not generally follow through to the aggregate Euler equation when households are not infinitely-lived (Gali 1990, 1991; Clarida 1991; Deaton 1992: 37–43, 167–176; Muellbauer and Lattimore 1994: 272–3). On the other hand, even though labour income and consumption are not cointegrated at the individual household level, they will be at the *aggregate* level (Deaton 1992: 170). Moreover, if households are liquidity-constrained, then their consumption is forced to follow the path of their income, so that if income is a non-stationary process, consumption will also be non-stationary and cointegrated with income (Blinder and Deaton 1985), and including an unrestricted error-correction term is a further way of testing the existence of liquidity constraints (although given the problem of aggregation, interpretation is not unambiguous). Accordingly, the fully specified estimating equation used in this chapter is

$$\hat{c}_s = \beta_0 + \beta_1 r_s - \beta_2 \zeta_s + \beta_3 z_s + \beta_4 y_{s-1} - \beta_5 c_{s-1} + v_s. \tag{7.10}$$

This specification, however, is not typical of the literature. More usually and often on the basis of insights from modelling US data, it is assumed that real interest rates and demographics are constant and that there is not an error correction, and so the generalised equation reduces to

[6] While lags of the first difference of consumption and income are not included and the general-to-specific modelling strategy is not applied, this is not expected to have an effect on the results. In the first place, consumption and income appear to be random walks and so lagged first differences are unlikely to have explanatory power. Furthermore, given the likely correlation of the proxy variables with the error term and the need for twice-lagged instruments, as discussed below, it is unlikely that past differences will enter the equation.

$$\hat{c}_s = \gamma_0 + \gamma_1 z_s + v_s, \tag{7.11}$$

usually with income growth included as the proxy for the shadow price of the constraint. Equation (7.11) is also estimated but as a basic model with which to compare the results from the generalised model in (7.10).

Liquidity constraints (and hence a positive shadow price) may exist for a number of reasons. First, domestic financial markets may be repressed or insufficiently developed, or capital controls which impede access to international financial markets may exist. (As discussed below, separating the effects of domestic and international financial repression on consumption is not straightforward.) Second, when information about the borrower's credit risk is incomplete or asymmetric, the possibilities of moral hazard and adverse selection indicate that would-be borrowers may be denied access to capital markets (Stiglitz and Weiss 1981), at least until they have proven their reliability, which may be related to age and experience (Scheinkman and Weiss 1986). Third, lenders may prefer to extend credit secured by financial or real assets rather than on the basis of expected future labour income since lenders cannot indenture labour but can seize assets (Faruqee, Laxton and Symansky 1995), and so would-be borrowers without capital may find it more difficult to obtain funds than would-be borrowers with capital (see Cox and Jappelli 1993 for empirical evidence in the United States). If wealth is acquired over time or is increasing in human capital, then younger or unskilled people are more constrained than older or skilled people.

These reasons suggest a range of variables which may be used as a proxy for the shadow price. If financial repression is the source of the constraint, for example, financial variables – such as real credit growth, the spread between money market and deposit rates or between loan and deposit rates and financial depth – may be correlated with the liquidity constraint. Consider these in turn. Real credit growth is a constraint when there are controls on bank lending through window guidance, and is expected to be positively correlated with consumption since an expansion of credit reduces the constraint. As argued in chapter 5, interest rate spreads are a function of, among other things, interest rate regulation and the depth and development of the banking sector, and are expected to be negatively correlated with consumption. Financial depth, commonly proxied by the ratio of money: GDP, is expected to be positively correlated with consumption, since it implies greater access to financial markets.

Given that loan approval tends to depend on the ability of the prospective borrower to pay loan principal and interest out of *current* income, access to funds tends to be decreasing in the level of nominal interest rates

Table 7.2. *Proxies for the liquidity constraint*

Liquidity constraint	Expected effect on consumption
1. Real consumer credit growth	positive $(\beta_3 > 0)$
2. Money market–deposit spread	negative $(\beta_3 < 0)$
3. Loan–deposit spread	negative $(\beta_3 < 0)$
4. Financial depth (M/GDP)	positive $(\beta_3 > 0)$
5. Nominal interest rate	negative $(\beta_3 < 0)$
6. Population 20–29/Population 20–64	negative $(\beta_3 < 0)$
7. Real asset prices	positive $(\beta_3 > 0)$
8. Real *per capita* income growth	positive $(\beta_3 > 0)$

Note: M = money.

and nominal interest rates are expected to be negatively correlated with consumption (Wilcox 1989).[7] If establishing credibility or sufficiency of collateral are the issue, then the proportion of young people in the workforce (such as the proportion of the workforce aged between 20 and 29) may also proxy the shadow price and be negatively correlated with consumption.

If either financial repression or insufficiency of collateral is the source of the constraint, real asset prices and real income growth should be correlated with the liquidity constraint: an increase in real asset prices (such as real residential property prices and share prices) or real income eases the bind of the constraint, allows consumption to be brought forward, and current consumption rises. To the extent that constraints are binding and consumption cannot be brought forward, a rise in real income must increase current consumption, and so the excess sensitivity of consumption to income will occur generally when there is a constraint. The proxy variables outlined above and the expected effect of an increase in them on consumption growth are summarised in table 7.2.

The downside in this testing procedure is that since the proxies are not derived from first principles, their selection is relatively ad hoc, and the key test of validity is that they be signed as expected if statistically significant. On the upside, the testing procedure has some strong advantages. It is broader than the simple excess-sensitivity test and provides a way to discriminate explicitly, albeit crudely, between financial market

---

[7] The nominal, rather than the real, interest rate is the proxy for the shadow price of borrowing. In the early literature on the real effects of financial reform, the real interest rate was often used as a proxy for repression (with a low rate indicating repression) (Fry 1995: 45). In this model, the real interest rate enters the equation as the opportunity cost of consumption.

repression and other causes of liquidity constraints. The significance of real credit growth, interest rate spreads or financial depth, for example, implies that official controls or inadequate financial development generate the constraint, which can be remedied by liberalisation or implementing policies to develop financial markets. The significance of the nominal interest rate or share of young workers, on the other hand, points not to official controls or the underdevelopment of financial markets, but to a constraint which arises out of the operation of the labour and capital markets in general (although it is less clear what sort of policy should follow when this is the case). Nor does a judgement that there are liquidity constraints depend solely on the significance or otherwise of the unrestricted error correction.

The bifurcated population model

The use of income as a proxy for liquidity constraints in an equation such as (7.10) is similar to the specification initially presented by Hall (1978) and subsequently developed by Campbell and Mankiw (1987, 1989, 1991), which assumes that the population is bifurcated, with one group optimising consumption intertemporally and the other being myopic or liquidity constrained.[8] Total consumption growth is the weighted average of consumption growth of both groups,

$$\hat{c}_t = \mu \hat{c}_{1,t} + (1 - \mu)\hat{c}_{2,t} \tag{7.12}$$

where is the population share of the liquidity constrained, and the subscript 1 and 2 refer to the constrained segment and optimising segment of the population, respectively. Consumption by the first group is assumed to be proportional to their income (y), and so the growth in their consumption equals that in their income, which is assumed to be the same as the second group's,

$$\hat{c}_{1,t} = \bar{y}_t \tag{7.13}$$

The result for the optimisers is similar to that outlined in (7.9), except that there is no liquidity constraint,

$$\hat{c}_{2,t} = \beta_0 + \beta_1 r_{t-1} - \beta_2 \zeta_{t-1} + \bar{\varepsilon}_t. \tag{7.14}$$

---

[8] Applied to the United States, for example, these models suggest that the liquidity-constrained proportion ranges from about 20 per cent (Hall and Mishkin 1982; Mariger 1986) to 35–50 per cent (Campbell and Mankiw 1989, 1991). Hayashi (1985) suggests about 15 per cent for Japan. For other countries, see Bayoumi and Koujianou (1989) and Campbell and Mankiw (1991).

Substituting (7.13) and (7.14) into (7.12) and accounting for time aggregation yields an expression for total consumption growth,

$$\hat{c}_s = \gamma_0 + \gamma_1 r_s - \gamma_2 \zeta_s + \gamma_3 \hat{y}_s + v_s. \tag{7.15}$$

where $\gamma_0 = (1 - \mu)\beta_0$, $\gamma_1 = (1 - \mu)\beta_1$, $\gamma_3 = \mu$ and $v_t = (1 - \mu)\bar{\varepsilon}_s$.

When the real interest rate and demographics are constant, (7.15) is the same as (7.11), and this is the equation routinely tested in the literature. The bifurcated population model approximates the constrained optimisation model only when income growth is used as the proxy for the liquidity constraint in the former and when temporal aggregation induces current dating of the liquidity constraint. In this respect, the constrained optimisation model generalises the bifurcated model and, since it also explicitly allows for tests of the effects of financial constraints on consumption, is the preferred analytical framework.[9]

Defining consumption and income

It is well understood that consumption, which is the object of intertemporal optimisation, is not necessarily the same as expenditure, which is the object of statistical collection, and so time-series studies generally use data on sub-sets of consumption – either expenditure on non-durables[10] or (most commonly) on both non-durables and services[11] – or on the full set of consumption calculated as the sum of expenditure on non-durables and services and the estimated services flow from the stock of durables.[12] Other papers use total private expenditure as a proxy of consumption.[13]

In this chapter, results are reported for consumption measured as expen-

---

[9] An advantage of the bifurcated model, however, is that it allows for myopic or non-rational consumers.

[10] See, for example, Flavin (1981, 1985); Epstein and Zin (1991); Shintani (1993, 1994).

[11] See, for example, Hall (1978); Campbell and Mankiw (1987, 1991); Wilcox (1989); Jappelli and Pagano (1989); Bayoumi and Koujianou (1990); Campos and Ericsson (1990); Epstein and Zin (1991); Cushing (1992); Neusser (1992); Shintani (1993, 1994); Bayoumi and McDonald (1994a); Hendry (1994); Sekkat, Thys-Clement and van Regemorter (1994); Blundell-Wignall, Browne and Tarditi (1995).

[12] See, for example, Hayashi (1982) and McKibbin and Richards (1988). The estimation involves a substantial amount of judgement. McKibbin and Richards (1988), for example, calculate the flow of services on durables as the sum of the estimated depreciation rate on the estimated stock of durables and the estimated general net real rate of return on other assets. In practice, the results using this measure of consumption tend to be not all that different from those obtained using the national accounts measure of total private expenditure (for example, Debelle and Preston 1995), which is perhaps not surprising given relatively stable depreciation rates and real rates of return and the small share of durables expenditure in the total.

[13] See, for example, Haque and Montiel (1990); Vaidyanathan (1993), Canova and Ravn (1994); Blundell-Wignall, Browne and Tarditi (1995).

diture on non-durables, defined as food, beverages, tobacco and clothing – or, when this series is unavailable, total private expenditure. Expenditure on non-durables is coincident with consumption, at least on an annual basis, and so is consistent with the theoretical derivation, given that welfare is separable between non-durables, services and the services flow from durables[14] and asset accumulation includes the stock of durables. Using non-durable expenditure ensures, first, that consumption is additively separable, and so the marginal rate of substitution between consumption in non-contiguous time periods is irrelevant and, secondly, that difficulties associated with modelling adjustment costs do not arise (Deaton 1992). Expenditure on non-durables, as opposed to non-durables and services, is used as the base case for testing liquidity constraints since services expenditure may be contaminated by adjustment costs, time-series extrapolation or long-term welfare effects which render it non-additively separable even on an annual basis.[15] Disaggregated data on expenditure on non-durables are available for Australia, Hong Kong, Japan, Korea, Singapore, Taiwan and Thailand, but not for Indonesia, Malaysia and the Philippines.[16]

It is appropriate to ask what information non-durables expenditure contains about liquidity constraints. Common sense suggests that households do not generally use domestic and international credit markets to borrow for the purpose of buying a jar of vegemite or whatever, but do so to buy a car, household durables or a home, and so a better test of the evolution of liquidity constraints may be whether *durables expenditure* has become less sensitive to income (see Takahashi and Kitamura 1993). The microeconomics of durables *expenditure* is, however, different to that of durables *consumption* and has to be addressed explicitly.[17] Suffice it to say that the objection is an exaggeration. If individuals do not face liquidity constraints, then it should be most obvious in the case with the annual consumption of non-durable goods since issues of adjustment and time

---

[14] Bernanke (1985) supports separability between durables and non-durables for the United States. See also Hayashi (1985) that the lags of other expenditure groups do not generally enter the equations for individual expenditure groups in Japan.

[15] Caballero (1990: 735), for example, notes that imputed rent may generate positive error correlation in consumption equations. Chah, Ramey and Starr (1991) argue that non-durables and services should be treated separately because their prices are not cointegrated.

[16] Disaggregated expenditure data are not available for Indonesia since total private expenditure is derived as a residual in the national accounts. Disaggregated expenditure accounts for Malaysia do not appear to be published, while published disaggregated expenditure data for the Philippines are subject to major revisions and missing observations (for example, 1976) and hence are unreliable.

[17] Caballero and Engel (1993) present a model of (S,s) decision rules for durables' expenditure.

inseparability do not arise. Moreover, while expenditure on one item may be small, the bundle of total expenditure on non-durables is not (from an average 32 per cent in Japan to 58 per cent in Thailand) and credit markets, formal or informal, may facilitate these transactions. And, indeed, the existence of constraints on one class of expenditure, such as durables, would be expected to spread to other groups of expenditure since saving to finance the former type of expenditure occurs at the expense of the latter.

According to the theory, income should be defined as disposable labour income, but this definition is not generally available for the countries in this sample. The income variable for each country is defined in appendix 6.1, and varies from household disposable income (Australia, Japan and Thailand), factor income (Korea and Taiwan) to GDP (Hong Kong, Indonesia, Malaysia, the Philippines and Singapore). Growth in consumption and income for most of these countries is shown in figure 7.1.

Econometric estimation and results

The proxy variables are, like the liquidity constraint, current-dated variables, and are likely to be correlated with consumption innovation, rendering the estimated coefficients biased and inconsistent. This is notably so when current income is used as the proxy since innovations in current income are likely to be correlated with unforecastable innovations in permanent income which, liquidity constraints aside, are related to innovations in consumption in standard models (Muellbauer 1983; Blanchard and Fischer 1989). Accordingly, an instrumental variables procedure is used for the liquidity constraint proxies and the real interest rate. Lagged consumption and income are not instrumented since they are dated $t - 1$ and so are orthogonal to the error term dated t. The proxy for demographic change is also not instrumented.

The instrumental variables[18] are lagged two periods. In the case of income, the use of data for which the reporting interval exceeds the planning interval generates spurious correlation between the current consumption growth and the first lag of income growth, rendering first lags inadmissible as instruments (Deaton 1992: 96–8). Using the second lag has the additional benefit of excluding possible problems with measurement error or transitory income. Nelson (1987) and Attanasio and Weber (1989) report that the effect of temporal aggregation on the rejection of the rational expectations permanent income hypothesis (REPIH) is

[18] The instruments used vary with the country examined but are generally natural logs of *per capita* real income, *per capita* real consumption, real exports, real US GDP and the unemployment rate, in levels and in first differences.

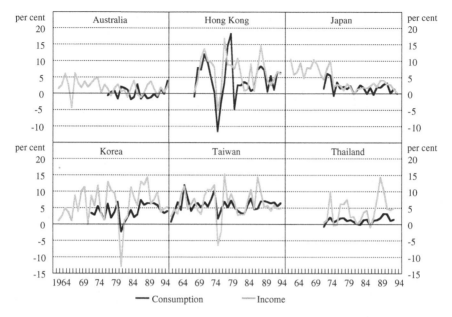

Fig. 7.1. Non-durable consumption and income growth, selected countries, 1964–1994

minimal, and its importance can be judged by comparing the results for OLS and IV estimation.

Results from the basic model equation – (7.11)

To introduce the material, the basic model, which regresses the growth of real *per capita* non-durables consumption on a constant and the growth of real *per capita* income, was estimated using instrumental variables. The results for the ten countries are reported in columns (2) and (3) of table 7.3, with the coefficient of determination in column (4). To form a view on the constancy of the regression coefficients, the equation was estimated for income growth with a multiplicative decade dummy (excluding the Philippines because of the short sample), shown in columns (5)–(7). Generally, the basic diagnostics were sound.[19]

---

[19] The equations were estimated using the instrumental variables option in Microfit 386, and the standard diagnostics are Sargan's test of misspecification, an LM test for first-order serial correlation, a Ramsey reset functional form test, Bera–Jarque normality test and the Ramsey reset heteroscedasticity test. The error term in the Japan equation was serially correlated and corrected using the Newey–West procedure with a Parzen window of two lags.

Table 7.3. *Growth in real per capita non-durable consumption, 1960–94*

	Data length (1)	Full-period constant (2)	Full-period income (3)	$\bar{R}^2$ (4)	1960s' income (5)	1970s' income (6)	1980/90s' income (7)	$\bar{R}^2$ (8)
Australia	1975–94	0.005 (0.005)	−0.24 (0.33)	−0.12	—	—	—	—
Hong Kong	1970–93	−0.007 (0.025)	0.74* (0.33)	0.274	—	0.61# (0.30)	0.77# (0.37)	0.229
Indonesia[a]	1970–93	0.005 (0.020)	0.88* (0.42)	0.151	—	0.73* (0.34)	0.32# (0.45)	0.203
Japan	1970–93	0.005 (0.004)	0.48* (0.13)	0.497	—	0.47* (0.120)	0.31 (0.21)	0.485
Korea	1970–94	0.027* (0.009)	0.20# (0.12)	0.482	—	0.22* (0.09)	0.34* (0.09)	0.544
Malaysia[a]	1970–93	0.017 (0.015)	0.47* (0.25)	0.469	—	0.39* (0.08)	0.61* (0.08)	0.802
Philippines[a]	1975–92	0.013* (0.003)	0.65* (0.11)	0.252	—	—	—	—
Singapore	1970–94	−0.015 (0.010)	0.57* (0.13)	0.288	—	0.51* (0.13)	0.34# (0.13)	0.399
Taiwan	1960–93	0.020* (0.009)	0.30* (0.13)	0.276	0.15 (0.14)	0.30* (0.09)	0.35* (0.12)	0.245
Thailand	1970–92	0.016# (0.008)	0.37* (0.15)	0.419	—	0.34* (0.16)	0.36* (0.12)	0.389

Notes:
[a] National accounts measure of total private consumption expenditure.
= statistical significance at the 10 per cent level; * = statistical significance at the 5 per cent level.
— = not available.

The results indicate a high degree of variation in the income dependence of non-durables consumption across countries and time. In Australia, non-durables expenditure growth has been independent of income growth, and this is not a problem of finding appropriate instruments since even using OLS the coefficient is insignificant (and in OLS it is minuscule). Non-durables consumption growth has been tied to income growth in Hong Kong, Japan, Korea, Singapore, Taiwan and Thailand, but has fallen (by more than one standard error) or become insignificant in the 1980s and 1990s in Japan and Singapore. The dependency of non-durables expenditure on income has remained unchanged (that is, within one standard error) in Hong Kong, Taiwan and Thailand but has increased in Korea. In Indonesia, Malaysia and the Philippines, total consumption expenditure growth depends on income and in the case of Malaysia, this is increasingly so over time.

These results largely accord with priors about the degree of financial repression and capital account openness in these economies, as outlined in chapter 4. For most of the period, Australian financial markets have been open and highly developed. Domestic financial repression was lower and access to international capital markets greater in Japan and Singapore in the 1980s than in the previous decade. Financial and exchange reform in Korea, Taiwan and Thailand is only recent, particularly in the case of Korea. Oddly, the coefficient on income growth in Hong Kong is consistently high.

Results from the fully specified model equation – (7.10)

The results and interpretation above are only tentative since relevant variables (such as the real interest rate and demographic change) and other variables which enable more specific identification of the form of the constraint have been excluded. Accordingly, a grid search procedure was applied to identify whether the real interest rate, demographic variables and the proxies for liquidity constraints other than current income growth were significant in economies for which non-durables expenditure data are available. The estimation procedure was as follows. An equation including current income growth, the first lags of consumption and income, the real interest rate and one of the three demographic variables was estimated, and insignificant regressors eliminated. This procedure was applied to the three definitions of the three demographic variables. Current income growth was then replaced by the other proxies for liquidity constraints and the procedure re-applied. If these proxies were statistically significant, current income growth was returned to the regression to

Table 7.4. *Summary of significance of liquidity constraints*

Constraint	Australia	Hong Kong	Japan	Korea	Singapore	Taiwan	Thailand
1. Credit growth	n	n	n	n	n	n	—
2. Money–dep. rates	n	n	n	—	n	—	—
3. Loan–dep. rates	n	n	n	n	n	#	#
4. M/GDP ratio	n	n	#	n	#	#	#
5. Nominal rate	n	#	n	#	#	#	#
6. Young workers	n	—	n	—	n	—	—
7. Real asset prices	n	—	#	—	#	—	—
8. Income growth	n	#	#	#	#	#	#
Error correction	n	n	#	#	#	#	#

Notes:
n = not significant.
# = statistical significance at at least the 10 per cent level.
— = data series not available.

test their relative explanatory power. Not all proxies were available for all countries and estimation periods vary with data availability. Tables A7.2.1–A7.2.7 in appendix 7.2 (p. 258) present the statistically significant results for Australia, Hong Kong, Japan, Korea, Singapore, Taiwan and Thailand.

The results vary substantially between countries. The coefficient on the real interest rate is positive and significant in Japan, Singapore and Thailand, indicating the importance of intertemporal wealth effects in consumption and suggesting that the basic Keynesian model is not adequate. Demographic variables are relevant in Japan, Taiwan and Thailand. In Japan, the change in the dependency ratio is significant and negative. In Thailand, the change in the proportion over 64 years is significant and negative. In Taiwan, however, the dependency ratio is significant and positive. A linear trend was included in these regressions to test whether demographic change is picking up a simple trend in the data but was not significant.

The significance or otherwise of the eight proxies for the shadow price listed in table 7.2 are summarised in table 7.4. In all countries except Australia and Hong Kong, an error correction between income and consumption was statistically significant. It was argued earlier that an error correction may be due, among other things, to aggregation over households or to liquidity constraints, but the result that the error correction is insignificant only for the two countries with among the most open and developed financial markets in the region suggests that it arises because of liquidity constraints rather than aggregation effects. Consistent with the results for the basic model outlined in table 7.3, current income growth was a significant determinant of consumption growth for all countries, and in all cases except real residential property prices in Japan, added the most explanatory power of all the proxies for liquidity constraints. This is not surprising since income growth is a catch-all variable.

Australia is an outlier in that neither current income growth nor any variable outlined in tables 7.1 or 7.2 could systematically explain the growth in non-durable consumption, and this supports the proposition that non-durables consumption in Australia is unconstrained and smoothed. In this case, however, the sample period is relatively short (1975–94), and when it is extended back to 1970 using the total private expenditure deflator in place of the non-durables deflator, the coefficients and equations are significant only when decade income growth dummies were included, and income growth is significant in the 1970s but not in the 1980/90s (see table A7.2.1), which is consistent with the results in table 7.3. The irrelevance of current income does not follow for broader definitions of consumption, although the interpretation is muddier when services and durables are included, since issues of data smoothing and stock adjustment arise. When consumption is defined as total private expenditure, income growth, the error correction, the proportion of the young working age population, and inflation are significant explanators. The coefficient on the share of young workers is negative, consistent with the view that the accumulation of reputation and collateral reduce constraints on smoothing. Rising inflation also depresses real consumption, presumably (in an intertemporal model) because it increases uncertainty in real income[20] and it suppresses the real interest rate when the nominal interest rate does not adjust instantaneously and completely, thereby generating a negative intertemporal substitution effect. The result that the basic Hall model is rejected for total expenditure is not surprising, given the lumpiness of durables' expenditure and the expectation that liquidity constraints operate most strongly with this type of expenditure. The insignificance of financial type proxies is consistent with the developed and open financial markets of Australia. Similar to Blundell-Wignall, Browne and Tarditi (1995) but unlike Debelle and Preston (1995) who use a long span of quarterly data, there is no evidence of a secular decline in the liquidity constraint on total expenditure.

---

[20] The model does not directly address the issue of uncertainty and precautionary saving but Blanchard and Fischer (1989: 288–91) present a model where consumption is decreasing in the real income uncertainty.

The evidence of liquidity constraints in east Asia is stronger, although the outcome varies substantially by country. Consider Hong Kong (table A7.2.2) and Singapore (table A7.2.5), two of the most financially developed economies in east Asia. In the case of Hong Kong, only current income growth enters the equation and the explanatory power is low. The coefficient on the nominal loan rate is significant and negative when income growth is excluded and an error correction included (although, again, the explanatory power is low). Hong Kong's financial markets are in general large and well developed but its domestic banking market was, until 1995, cartelised and domestic deposit and loan rates segmented somewhat from international and domestic money markets (chapter 5). The null hypothesis that the coefficient on income growth was unchanged in the 1980s–1990s from the 1970s is accepted. In Singapore, the evidence of a liquidity constraint over the whole period is more robust, with both the error correction and current income growth significant. Substituting other proxies of liquidity constraints for current income growth, financial deepening and the nominal interest rate are both significant and signed as expected (the former positive, the latter negative).[21] The significance of financial deepening implies that the constraint is declining over time as the depth of markets expands. Domestic markets were substantially liberalised in 1975 and capital controls removed in 1978, so one would expect a break in the regression between the 1970s and the 1980s–1990s. Indeed, the coefficient on both income growth and financial depth falls between decades. The results suggest that liquidity constraints have eased in Singapore over time, as a result of financial deregulation.

Japan (table A7.2.3) provides a different perspective on constraints and financial deregulation. Like Singapore, it initiated capital account reform in the middle of the sample period (1980) but it deregulated its bond, money and non-traded financial markets only slowly over the 1980s and 1990s, with the liberalisation of bank deposit rates, for example, extending from 1985 to 1994 (chapter 5 and de Brouwer 1996) and the Bank of Japan stopping window guidance only in 1991. The real interest rate, the change in the dependency ratio, the error correction and current-income growth are significant – a classic example of constrained intertemporal optimisation with demographic change. When current-income growth is excluded, financial depth and real residential land prices are also significant proxies of the liquidity constraint.[22]

[21] Real residential property prices were not significant but real residential property price inflation entered with a positive and significant coefficient in OLS regressions. A suitable set of instruments could not be found for IV estimation.

[22] The Nikkei 225 stock price index was also significant, but the equation was only marginally significant.

At first glance, the significance of financial depth suggests that in Japan, like Singapore, deregulation has enabled households to expand their consumption. There are two pieces of contrary evidence. First, when sub-sample decade dummies are included, the liquidity constraint, measured as income growth or real land prices, is significant in both periods and does not decline in the 1980s and 1990s relative to the 1970s. Secondly, real residential property prices are strongly significant and explain consumption growth 'better' than the money: GDP ratio, which is consistent with the claim that money in this case proxies only asset prices. As shown in appendix 7.1, money: GDP and real residential property prices follow the same trend and in the early 1970s and the late 1980s both rose and fell sharply. In the early 1970s, when domestic financial markets were closed, controlled and narrow, the monetary expansion fed directly into asset-price inflation. In the second half of the 1980s, when domestic financial markets were being deregulated, expansionary monetary policy also fed directly into asset-price inflation. In both episodes, policy was expansionary and asset prices rose, but only in the latter period were markets (being) deregulated, suggesting that deregulation has not *yet* had a separate identifiable effect on non-durable consumption. The tentative evidence in table 7.3 of declining constraints looks incorrect, and it is too early to identify an effect on consumption. Given that the capital account was liberalised at the start of the 1980s, however, the results are consistent with the interpretation that international financial openness is not sufficient for consumption smoothing when domestic markets remain undeveloped or controlled.

Korea, Taiwan and Thailand are examples of economies with regulated or repressed domestic and financial systems and controls on the capital account and, accordingly, are an interesting contrast to Australia, Hong Kong and Singapore. In the case of Korea (table A7.2.4), the error correction and current-income growth are the only significant explanatory variables.[23] The coefficients are stable over sub-periods, indicating no change in liquidity constraints. While these results are consistent with the casual observation that financial markets in Korea are among the least developed and liberalised in this sample set, Korea is also well known as a country which has regularly used controls on non-durable consumption imports to control demand and the current account (Hasan and Rao 1979: 271); Kim 1991: 47). The insignificance of financial variables suggests that it may be these trade controls that give rise to the constraint.

---

[23] The coefficient on the curb loan rate is significant and negative, but only in OLS and not IV estimation. The results across countries are rarely sensitive to the estimation procedure, which suggests that in this case the problem is finding suitable instruments for the curb loan rate.

The results for Taiwan (table A7.2.6) and Thailand (table A7.2.7) show stronger evidence that financial development affects consumption. For Taiwan, the change in the dependency ratio, the error correction, current-income growth and the margin between loan and deposit rates are jointly significant with the expected signs (except for the change in the dependency ratio). When current income growth is replaced with other proxies for the liquidity constraint, financial depth, the deposit rate and the loan rate enter significantly with the expected sign. For Thailand, aging, real interest rates, the error correction and current-income growth are significant and signed as expected. When current-income growth is replaced in the equation for Thailand, financial depth, deposit and loan rates, and the loan–deposit margin are significant with the expected sign. The significance of both the interest rate margin and financial depth point to financial repression or lack of development as causes of the liquidity constraint.[24] There is little evidence of falling liquidity constraints in either country: the coefficients on decade dummies for current income growth and other proxies for the constraint are not significantly different over time. This is not surprising since substantive reform in both countries is only relatively recent. While the capital account had been partially liberalised by the late 1980s in Taiwan, systematic controls on inflow still remain (Lee 1990: 160–1), covered interest parity did not hold from 1991 to 1994 (chapter 4) and additional foreign exchange controls have been implemented occasionally (for example, mid-1992). Substantive liberalisation of the Thai capital account only took place in May 1990 and April 1991 (chapter 4). Moreover, domestic interest rate liberalisation was implemented only in 1989 in Taiwan and in 1992 in Thailand (chapter 5).

There are two final comments to be made about the modelling procedure and results. First, while the proxies for the shadow price of the liquidity constraint are not derived from first principles, when they are statistically significant they are signed as expected, and this lends support to the model. For example, financial deepening (and real interest rates) are always positively correlated with consumption, and widening interest margins and nominal interest rates are always negatively correlated with consumption.

[24] It was argued above that the money: GDP ratio reflected wealth effects for Japan rather than financial deepening, and so it is necessary to answer the question here of why this may not also be the case for Taiwan and Thailand. Data for residential property prices for Taiwan and Thailand are not available and so the question cannot be answered conclusively but there is strong indirect evidence against it. First, the interest margin is also significant for these two countries, which is corroborating evidence of the effect of financial repression. Secondly, significance of the money: GDP ratio does not mean that asset prices are also significant and vice versa. In the case of Australia, real residential property prices are significant at the 10 per cent level but the money: GDP ratio is not.

Second, the results are probably not the outcome of data mining by which a grid search over a series of proxy variables has been used to select only those relationships which are significant (Lovell 1983). In the first place, all the proxy variables are relevant *a priori* to identifying the impact of the liquidity constraint on consumption, so degrees of freedom have not been 'wasted'. More to the point, statistically significant proxies tend to be bunched together for countries which have less developed, free and open financial markets rather than spread uniformly across all countries as would be the case if the results were purely random over a set of countries. It seems less plausible in this case, therefore, that the Type 1 error of rejecting the null hypothesis that the coefficient is zero when it is true is occurring to the detriment of correct inference. Whatever the case, the process is transparent since the chapter cites all the variables tested and the standard error of the significant variables. The marginal significance levels of the proxy variables is usually less than the standard 5 per cent level, often substantially so.

Domestic and international effects

The proxies for liquidity constraints in table 7.2 are defined in terms of domestic rather than international financial variables, for two reasons. The first is that a sufficient run of relevant time series, such as the covered interest differential (CID), which is a measure of exchange controls, is not available. The second is more fundamental, and is that it is difficult to sharply delineate between domestic and international effects, both in the mechanics – and, more fundamentally, the economic and political dynamics – of markets.

Consider some mechanics. A secular expansion in the money: GDP ratio is a proxy for financial development but this can reflect not just domestic but also a range of international influences, such as an expansion of domestic deposits due to the entry of competitive foreign banks, the monetisation of capital inflows under fixed exchange rates, or the balance sheet counterpart of the acquisition of foreign assets by domestic banks under an open capital account regime with floating exchange rates. The money: GDP ratio is a domestic variable and its expansion implies greater financial depth and scope for smoothing income, but the factors cited are international. Similarly, a domestic bank funds an expansion of its loan book by taking deposits or borrowing offshore, among other means, and so an expansion of domestic credit may have an international dimension. Domestic and international factors can both be relevant to the most simple of domestic financial transactions.

But more than mechanics, the economic and political dynamics of domestic and international markets are intertwined, as a few examples show. In Australia, there was a major consolidation and reform of banking services (for example, the introduction of ATMs and changes in hours) by domestic banks in the early 1980s, well ahead of the entry of foreign banks in 1985, but in anticipation of it some time in the future, and similar rationalisation has occurred in east Asia banking sectors. In Indonesia and Malaysia, easy access to offshore (mainly Singaporean) financial markets made control of deposit interest rates less effective and stimulated more rapid or effective liberalisation of deposit rates. Liberalisation of both domestic and international financial markets in Japan, Korea and Taiwan has been driven by, among other things, US pressure. There is no clear separation of domestic and foreign forces for reform.

The way that the domestic and international dichotomy has been drawn in this chapter to account for changes in the bind of liquidity constraints by the programme of liberalisation and deregulation followed. The capital account was liberalised in Singapore in 1978 and in Japan in 1980 and 1984, but their domestic financial systems were liberalised in 1975 and 1985–94, respectively. The evidence of declining constraints is stronger for Singapore than for Japan, which suggests that it is the confluence of domestic liberalisation and international openness that is important in facilitating households' intertemporal transfers on income. Domestic markets and the capital account were liberalised in Australia in the early 1980s, and liquidity constraints on non-durables expenditure cannot be identified from at least that time.

Bayoumi and McDonald (1994a) have presented a model to distinguish domestic from international effects. Their model is based on an earlier insight that the single-country permanent-income conditions for smoothing consumption over time can be expressed in terms of insurance in the form of smoothing consumption between countries at a point in time (Cochrane 1991; Obstfeld 1993, 1994; Canova and Ravn 1994). They define international financial integration as the equalisation of real interest rates and construct a model in which they interpret declining excess sensitivity of domestic consumption on domestic income as evidence of the development of *local* financial markets and a rising correlation with foreign consumption as evidence of the development of *international* financial markets. This reasoning seems flawed on two accounts. First, the derivation relies on real interest parity but this parity condition is stringent (Frankel 1993a), such that the real interest differential equals the expected depreciation of the real exchange rate only when there are no barriers to trade in financial assets, financial assets are perfect substitutes, the Fisher effect holds at all points in time and expectations are formed rationally. Even if all these conditions hold, real interest rates are identical, in general, only in the steady state when the real exchange rate is constant.[25] Hence, using real interest parity as the criterion for openness in applied work is not valid. Secondly, consumption is less sensitive to domestic income as the set of income-smoothing instruments expands, and this set includes both domestic and international instruments. A decline in excess sensitivity cannot necessarily be ascribed to increased domestic integration (even if that can be identified). Indeed, if the cause of the decline in excess sensitivity is because of international integration, then the decline in excess sensitivity is *tantamount* to greater consumption insurance.

Implications for welfare and policy

In terms of the neo-classical model outlined in this chapter, eliminating financial repression whatever the stage of development *must* improve household welfare, and so the policy implication would seem to be straightforward. Things are probably not that simple since the analysis is partial in that it ignores capital accumulation and growth. In Barro, Mankiw and Sala-i-Martin's (1995) neo-classical model of economic convergence, for example, financial openness is not the decisive factor in growth since the bulk of the capital stock is human capital and only real capital can be financed externally. Ideally, in this framework, a saving-deficit country would borrow on foreign markets to finance investment in real capital and would borrow on local markets to finance investment in human capital. In the earlier stages of development, the mobilisation of domestic saving may be necessary to finance real capital accumulation in order to build up the physical capital which secures acceptance of the country by foreign lenders, and so initially limiting access by households to domestic financial markets may be required. But once some productive capital is in place, maintenance of controls on household borrowing is difficult to justify because there *is* a welfare loss in preventing households from smoothing consumption, and because access to consumer credit augments the accumulation of human capital since households have access to funds for better education, better accommodation and higher living standards. The maintenance of controls on household credit in countries like Korea or Taiwan would seem difficult to justify from the welfare perspective.

The results suggest a loose hierarchy of countries in terms of constraint

---

[25] This argument does not apply to the application of the model of consumption insurance between provinces in Canada in Bayoumi and McDonald (1994b).

Table 7.5. *Saving, investment and the current account, 1980–94*

	Saving/GDP			Investment/GDP			Current Account/GDP		
	1980	1990	1994	1980	1990	1994	1980	1990	1994
Australia	24.2	18.2	20.3	25.4	21.3	21.5	−2.6	−5.1	−4.9
Hong Kong	31.7	33.6	33.0	35.9	28.5	29.2	−4.7	8.8	2.3
Singapore	37.5	45.2	48.8	46.3	36.8	43.6	−13.7	6.0	11.5
Japan	31.4	33.5	31.0	32.2	30.9	28.5	−1.0	1.2	2.7
Korea	24.3	36.4	34.5	31.7	37.0	33.8	−8.5	−0.9	−1.4
Thailand	26.4	32.3	34.0	20.1	38.3	39.6	−7.4	−8.3	−6.0
Taiwan	33.1	27.8	25.1	30.2	22.4	22.9	−1.7	6.6	2.4
Malaysia	32.9	32.3	32.4	30.4	36.1	37.0	−1.2	−2.1	−6.5
Philippines	24.2	18.2	18.5	30.6	22.5	25.0	−6.0	−6.1	−5.2
Indonesia	24.7	31.7	32.1	20.9	36.1	33.3	1.7	−5.9	−2.3

Source: APEC (1995).

– very roughly from least to highest, Australia, Hong Kong, Singapore, Japan, Korea, Thailand and Taiwan – and it is interesting to ask how this fits with the structure of their macroeconomies. Table 7.5 sets out the profile of saving, investment and current account balance for these countries over the 15 years 1980–94. It would seem that there is no correspondence between this hierarchy and current account balance, which is not surprising since the current account balance reflects not just private consumption decisions but also public consumption and private and public investment. It would also seem that there is no clear correspondence between this hierarchy and saving performance: the constraint is not less binding for countries with higher saving rates. Nor is it *generally* apparent that countries with forced saving occupy a clearly identifiable place in the hierarchy. It may be instructive, however, that for the three most financially open economies in the region, liquidity constraints appear more binding for Singapore, which does have such a system, than for Australia or Hong Kong.

Conclusion

The literature is ambivalent about the effect of financial integration on the macroeconomy (Fry 1995). This chapter has presented strong evidence that financial integration affects consumption. Non-durable consumption in Hong Kong, Japan, Korea, Singapore, Taiwan and Thailand can be modelled as the outcome of liquidity-constrained optimisation, while that in

Australia is liquidity-unconstrained, from at least the 1980s. The constraint is very weak in Hong Kong and is declining in Singapore, consistent with the extent and timing of domestic and international financial reforms in these economies. The constraint appears unchanged in Japan and Korea. For Taiwan and Thailand, there is strong evidence that domestic financial repression and control have stymied intertemporal optimisation of consumption. There has been major financial reform in these economies, but it is only recent (and piecemeal in the case of Taiwan). Since the tests are conducted on annual data, the effect of unwinding the constraint will take time to appear (but will be difficult to distil because of the financial shocks that have affected these economies). The experience of Australia and selected countries in east Asia suggests that liberalisation of the capital account combined with deregulation and expansion of the domestic financial sector is necessary for constraints on consumption smoothing to be eased. This is consistent with the argument in chapter 5 that the domestic macroeconomic effect of international integration of money market rates depends in large part on the linkages between domestic traded and non-traded financial markets. Financial integration *does* have real effects, in this case on the time profile of consumption, but the preconditions are that financial sector reform be genuine and cover both the external accounts and domestic markets.

8

Summary and policy considerations

Summarising the results

The focus in many current commentaries on financial integration in east Asia has been on the east Asian financial crisis. This is a major defining episode in the experience of these countries, but analysis of financial integration should not be excessively short-term or focused on these events. There are other dimensions and longer-term perspectives to the story. This book has provided some analysis of the financial crisis in east Asia, explaining what happened, and why in chapter 2. The crisis has shown that there can be significant macroeconomic and social costs when financial reform goes wrong – in this case, when there are fundamental imbalances in domestic financial systems which leave economies exposed and susceptible to adverse shocks. Even in this case, however, it is important to keep perspective, and focus on the broader microeconomic and macroeconomic advantages of financial openness.

The issue of financial integration in east Asia needs to be placed in a broader context. This book has attempted to do this by also addressing other questions concerning financial integration in east Asia. Are there differences between financially open and closed economies? Have economies in this region become more open financially? Does financial integration have real, structural macroeconomic effects? What happens to consumption? These questions have been addressed in two parts. The first, addressed in chapters 3, 4, 5 and 7, focused on the measurement of financial integration or openness. The second, covered in chapters 6 and 7, examined the effect of financial integration on the structure of the real economy. Consider these in turn.

In chapter 3, a wide-ranging survey was conducted of measures of financial openness and the results of the literature with respect to east Asia summarised. Based on legal restrictions, capital-flow data, consumption co-movements and interest rate relationships, the literature indicates that countries in the region became substantially more open in the 1980s. In chapter 4, the interest rate analysis was extended using data for the 1990s and analysing data for countries which had not previously been examined. The relationship between interest rates on domestic and foreign traded financial instruments became tighter over the 1990s. When local traded interest rates systematically deviate from overseas rates, it is generally due to restrictions on trade in financial assets (that is, capital controls), a country or exchange rate risk premium, or diverging rates of inflation. It was also argued that, contrary to what has now become the conventional view in the literature, uncovered interest parity can reveal considerable information about the degree of financial openness when modelled with a monetary policy reaction function, as in McCallum (1994). Moreover, uncovered interest differentials (UIDs) systematically differ from zero, even over periods of several years, for countries which employ capital controls, such as Korea and Taiwan, or for countries which are regarded as relatively 'risky', such as Indonesia, the Philippines and Thailand. The data also point to rising integration since foreign-sourced shocks to local interest rates are becoming more prevalent for most countries.

While there is a tendency in the literature to focus on movements and convergence in real interest rates, it was shown that there are three sources of a *persistent* wedge between local and foreign real interest rates: capital controls, country/exchange risk premia and the failure of relative PPP. Real interest rates can, of course, also differ at any point in time because of changes in the expected real exchange rate. At least one of these factors is present at some stage in the countries examined in the book, and it makes interpreting real interest rate movements quite difficult. It implies that greater integration *cannot* generally be inferred simply from a result that real interest rate differentials are becoming smaller over time. This inference is true in some but not all cases.

The analysis of international financial integration in chapter 4 was extended in chapter 5 by examining the integration of domestic non-traded financial interest rates with those on traded financial assets. Even if money markets in the east Asian region are open to world markets, the macroeconomic impact of integration turns in large part on *domestic* financial integration – that is, how closely interest rates on loans and deposits move with money market rates. A simple model was constructed to show that the relationship between traded and non-traded interest rates depends on the regulatory regime, competition in the banking sector and – in the case of bank loan interest rates – on the quality of banks' loans.

So what can be said about domestic and international financial openness in the countries examined? Australia has open international and local markets, and this openness has increased over time. Hong Kong, Japan and Singapore have open international markets and integration on this score seems to have increased in the 1990s, probably owing to advances in technology, 24-hour trading and increased internationalisation of banking. But the local bank-intermediated markets in these countries are somewhat segmented. Segmentation appears to have fallen in Japan in the 1990s but bank deposit and loan rates in Hong Kong and Singapore do not 'behave' as rates should if the banking system were open and competitive. This is probably related to local bank cartels and controls on banks. Indonesia is open but interest rates on traded financial assets are volatile and appear to bear exchange risk. Domestic institutional rates are not tied to the rates on traded assets. The Philippines has similar features in the relationship of local and international rates, but its domestic system is more integrated with the money market and is more open. Thai rates are increasingly affected by international developments, and bank-intermediated rates have become more closely tied to money market rates following banking reform in 1992. Malaysian interest rates are a bit of a puzzle: they are not tied to international rates, possibly because of occasional capital controls, but the system of domestic money and institutional rates is well integrated. Korea and Taiwan were the striking exceptions in terms of openness: on the standard tests, they did not appear to be well integrated at all. It was also shown that credit risk in the banking system – that is, the quality of bank loans – can have a big impact on the level of loan rates.

The other aspect examined in the book is whether financial integration matters. In other words, does increasing financial openness affect the real economy? In chapter 6, the Ramsey model was extended to two goods, and the long-run effect of financial integration on 'key' macroeconomic variables such as the physical capital stock, foreign debt and real exchange rate examined. In chapter 4, it was shown that capital controls are one key factor generating a non-zero interest differential for most countries examined in the book, and so financial integration is modelled in chapter 6 as reducing the wedge between local and foreign interest rates. In this stylised economy, financial integration boosts the capital stock but the effect on foreign debt and the real exchange rate is ambiguous. If capital controls have constrained access to financial markets and the accumulation of debt, then their removal would be expected to lead to an increase in foreign debt. But as the country builds up its capital stock and wealth, it requires less debt, and so the net effect is ambiguous. Similarly for the real exchange rate. The direct effect of financial integration is to appreciate the real exchange rate, but this is offset by an increase in capital and increase in foreign debt, both of which tend to depreciate the real exchange rate. The prediction for the foreign debt and real exchange rate is ambiguous since a variety of mechanisms are working. In a sense, this ambiguity does not matter since it is consumption in its broad sense, not endogenous variables like debt or exchange rates, which matters to the well-being of people.

One way to view the effect of financial integration on consumption, as done in chapter 7, is to think about financial openness as making it easier for people to 'smooth' their consumption over time, possibly over their life-time. Income flows tend to vary over months and years but people want to achieve a certain standard or level of consumption, to 'smooth' their consumption, as it were. The development of financial markets and easier access to these markets would be expected to facilitate this. This was examined for a number of east Asian countries by testing whether consumption patterns are related to measures of financial development (such as financial depth or interest rate margins), to other, more general, sources of constraints on borrowing, or to current income. A remarkably clear picture emerges. Consumption is smoothed in countries like Australia, Hong Kong and Singapore which have open capital accounts and relatively open domestic financial systems. But it is not in countries like Taiwan and Thailand and the reason that emerges from the empirical work is financial repression. Consumption in Japan and Korea has also been subject to liquidity constraint but the cause of the constraint is less clear (and, in the case of Korea, may be related to trade restrictions). The story that emerges is that openness in both the capital account and the domestic financial system is necessary for people to be able to smooth their consumption over time. Financial integration *does* matter to economic structure and to people's well-being. Based on the ranking of countries suggested by this test, there is no identifiable relationship between financial openness and current account imbalances, investment and savings. Financial openness does not mean that a country will be 'condemned' to current account imbalance, low saving or the like. There may be a negative relationship between compulsory saving and the ability of people to smooth their consumption over time: Singapore is ranked below Australia and Hong Kong in terms of financial openness and what distinguishes it from the other two countries is its long-standing and substantial compulsory savings scheme.

Another way to think about the effect of financial integration on consumption is through the effects of integration on capital formation and net wealth. In the model outlined in chapter 6, for example, people are better off as a result of financial integration since wealth is higher and the consumption bundle bigger. This is, however, axiomatic to the model and is an open empirical question.

To summarise, interest rates and consumption patterns in countries can reveal quite a lot about the openness of financial systems of countries in east Asia and the western Pacific and about how markets operate under different regulatory regimes. Some countries are more open than others. Australia, Hong Kong and Singapore consistently stand at the open end of the spectrum, while Korea and Taiwan consistently stand at the closed end. Japan is in the middle. Thailand looks more like a country with a closed financial system than an open one, but this has probably changed since substantial and genuine reform was introduced in the early 1990s. The Philippines has followed a similar path. The evidence for Indonesia and Malaysia is less clear since the data for some tests are not available, but there is some ambiguity about the degree of openness of these countries, especially in the case of Malaysia.

Some policy considerations

This section sets out some reflections on two sets of wide-ranging policy issues that the empirical and theoretical analyses of the book touch on. The first examines some implications of openness for the operation of policy. The second explores some issues related to the optimal policy response to changes in consumption and debt in east Asia. These are, of course, only a few of the policy issues that arise in the debate on finance, the macro-economy and economic development.

Financial integration and the operation of policy

In the first place, it is often difficult to assess how open or closed a country's financial system is. And, when there are restrictions on market access and the like, it is difficult to judge how important these restrictions are in affecting outcomes. The economist can observe certain forms of market behaviour and structure, and can use theory and knowledge about institutions to draw inferences about the degree of openness. If markets are open, they should exhibit certain forms or patterns of behaviour. Changes in foreign interest rates, for example, should become more important. Consumption profiles should change as people are able to use financial markets to smooth their consumption over time. But more than just telling the analyst whether markets are open or not, these sorts of tests also indicate whether controls are important that is, whether they change or affect the outcome. As discussed in chapter 4, this information is more relevant to policymakers than information on legal restrictions. If market access is restricted but the controlled or government-mandated outcome mimics the market outcome, then the argument for reform is weakened. But when outcomes are so strikingly different from market outcomes, as for Korea and Taiwan, then the argument for reform is strengthened. In this respect, the findings of the book support the work by PECC (1995) in identifying restrictions to trade and investment in the APEC group of countries and motivating further reform.

Another policy aspect that arises from the analysis of financial markets is the increasing importance of foreign interest rates in the formation of domestic rates and foreign influences on the local economy in general. This in turn may change the synchronisation of economic cycles between countries. Financial prices play a key role in the economy, since they affect marginal valuations and decisions and since they contain information about the future. As financial prices across countries converge, some shocks that were previously idiosyncratic should become common and the impulses they generate should be common to the local and foreign economies. The economy may respond to the same impulses but the generating mechanism of the impulses has changed with internationalisation. Financial integration, therefore, may imply greater integration of real economies.

At the same time, this should not be overstated. Foreign interest rates may be the source of more shocks to local interest rates, and more shocks may become common shocks, but this does not mean that domestic and foreign financial instruments are perfect substitutes and that foreign and domestic rates are identical. As ever, to the extent that the exchange rate is fixed, financial integration makes it more difficult for the local monetary authorities to set interest rates independently of the exchange anchor country. But to the extent that the exchange rate is flexible, local monetary policy has some power to set local rates independently of foreign rates.

In this context, the obvious upshot is that as financial systems become more open and integrated, the monetary authorities need to have effective market-based tools for setting policy. Events in Japan's money market in November 1988 are instructive in this respect (de Brouwer 1996). In July 1988, open market rates in Japan rose in anticipation of higher domestic inflation and higher US interest rates, but the Japanese authorities sought to contain the rise by holding down interbank interest rates. As a result, funds flowed to the euroyen market, the interbank market shrank and the interbank–open market rate spread widened dramatically. In November 1988, the Bank of Japan was forced to widen the maturity spectrum of interbank market bills and shift operations to new, shorter-dated instruments. When the authorities lack proper tools and techniques, they can lose influence over markets and lose the ability to implement policy changes. Openness without reform of the money markets and central bank operating procedures is likely to lead to crisis.

Similarly, as painfully shown by more recent events in the region, openness without proper prudential policy in place can generate a financial crisis and the loss of the benefits of openness. As shown in chapter 4, lending rates in countries with weak bank management or ineffective prudential policy tend to contain a risk premium and hence be higher than otherwise which, of itself, implies lower capital formation and growth. A key driving factor behind the financial crises in east Asia on 1997 and 1998 was the poor management systems in banks and attendant inadequate supervision and governance. Competition in the banking system is also important since it increases the return to saving, reduces the cost of borrowing and makes the operation of monetary policy more effective since it facilitates the transmission of policy changes in the money market to intermediated interest rates.

One criticism of openness is that it may imply a loss of independence, sovereignty and the right of self-determination. The argument goes that the internationalisation of finance robs governments of the power to set the policy they think is best; governments have to follow the dictates of 'foreign interests'. The counter-argument is that government need not have the same power, control and independence in an open economy as in autarky. In spite of the recent events in east Asia, there are demonstrable gains to be had from an open financial system and these gains are obtained at the 'cost' of greater *inter*dependence. It is an inevitable consequence of interdependence that other players have a say – when one person borrows from another, it is reasonable to expect the lender to charge interest and to set conditions on the use of funds by the borrower. If conditions and penalties for breach are not set, for example, the riskiness of the loan, and hence the interest rate payable, are higher. The same holds for sets of borrowers, the biggest of which is a country. Why would (and should) one set of borrowers grant one set of lenders licence to use funds any which way? Borrowing does place limits and discipline on borrowers and, therefore, on policy. But it is typically a consensual arrangement and it brings with it real and substantial benefits. In one sense, the discipline of markets can also itself be a benefit since it can penalise corruption or waste. The discipline imposed on borrowers typically includes such things as sustainable government budgets, inflation-focused monetary policy, accountability and the like. Such policies underpin sustainable income and employment growth and hence support rising living standards (Andersen and Gruen 1995; Barro 1996).

This is not uncontroversial since it is a common view that markets are fallible and can overshoot. It has been well documented in the literature that markets can get caught up in fads and that financial prices can diverge from the economic fundamentals which are thought to 'drive' the economic system. There is now also a large set of events, such as the October 1987 stock price fall, the collapse of the ERM in 1992, the 1994 Mexican crisis, the 1995 collapse of Barings and the 1997 east Asian financial crises, which lead some to think that markets are unstable and market participants unreliable. Greater openness, it is feared, will lead only to easier transmission of negative shocks and more destabilisation. These fears are certainly not without some foundation but, as was argued in chapter 2, closing or more tightly controlling markets is neither an effective nor a sound solution, at least in the longer term.

Closing or controlling markets is probably not *effective* since financial instruments are highly fungible and markets are able to avoid controls when they have a sufficiently strong incentive to do so. As discussed in chapter 2, controls on financial markets tend to be effective only in the short term, if at all, since markets can avoid them by creating substitutes or using avoidance mechanisms. Controls on foreign currency, for example, can be and are avoided by smuggling, corruption, or changing foreign trade invoices. This does not mean that capital controls cannot be used a short-term instrument to stabilise financial markets, only that the evidence is against them being effective for a sustained period of time.

Nor is closing or controlling markets likely to be the appropriate longer-term solution:

- While controls can be successful in dealing with short-run 'hot money', they are unlikely to work when they are inconsistent with economic fundamentals. Malaysia is a case in point. Short-term controls on capital inflow were put in place in 1994 in response to a rush of hot money. The inflow was subdued and the controls removed soon after: the controls were judged successful. Contrast this to the events of 1986 when controls were put in place against continued outflows in the face of speculation of ringitt devaluation. The devaluation was not prevented since it reflected a necessary relative price adjustment in response to a deterioration in the national and trade accounts due to a weakening in Malaysia's terms of trade. The controls only delayed adjustment, and delay may be costly if it exacerbates the underlying structural problem.
- Even if controls are effective in the short run, their continued use may undermine confidence in economic management. Such a break in confidence is likely to be discontinuous, in the sense that imposing controls may not disturb investor confidence for a while but, at some point in time, it may lead to a reversal of sentiment that will be difficult to correct.

- The events which are described as a 'market failure' may, in fact, not be the failure of markets but of policy itself; the market may simply have been doing its job. Two events can be interpreted in this light. Consider first the events in Europe in 1992. German reunification was tantamount to a major negative supply shock and positive demand shock for Germany. The only way to contain the sharp increase in demand for capital and incipient inflation was to raise local interest rates and revalue the deutschemark. Revaluation was not possible within the framework of fixed exchange rates in the European Monetary System (EMS) and so all countries in the system were bound to undergo rising interest rates at a time when demand in *their* economies was weak. For some countries, like the United Kingdom, Italy and Spain, this was not a credible policy and savers acted accordingly by restructuring their investment portfolios. Consider, also, the Mexican crisis of 1994. This occurred against a backdrop of rapid accumulation of US dollar-denominated liabilities without a build-up of foreign exchange reserves, marked deterioration in Mexico's fiscal position, political uncertainty and obfuscation by government (IMF 1995: 90–7). Masson and Agenor (1996) argue, moreover, that the devaluation itself revealed new information that the government's commitment to inflation and exchange rate stability had weakened.

The Mexican and east Asian financial crises do suggest, however, that there needs to be balance in both the structure and speed of capital flows (Truman 1996). In some cases, the inflows were to highly liquid, short-term instruments, and this meant that flows could be reversed easily and quickly. A balance of flows across direct and intermediated sectors and across short and long instruments is required for stability. These crises have also shifted the balance of views about the sequence of financial reform, with reform of the domestic financial system now required before reform of the capital account. The old view that there is no obvious difference between countries which have reformed in either sequence (Caprio, Atiyas and Hanson 1994) no longer holds.

Financial integration, consumption and debt

Chapters 6 and 7 of the book were concerned with assessing the effect of financial integration on the real economy and there are two implications for policy that are worthy of some discussion. The results of chapter 7 indicate that the gains from liberalisation, at least to consumers and probably also to firms (since they are also liquidity-constrained in financially repressed economies), come only when the domestic financial system is liberalised *and* the capital account is open. Countries such as Australia, Hong Kong and Singapore have open and relatively liberalised financial systems. Japan has an open capital account but a relatively repressed domestic financial system. Consumption profiles in Australia, Hong Kong and Singapore point to relatively unconstrained consumption smoothing but the consumption profile in Japan suggests liquidity constraints.

The second issue is whether consumption, debt and the real exchange rate really ought to be areas for concern. Like other examinations of the issue, the optimal control problem set out in chapter 6 treats foreign debt and hence the current account imbalance and the real exchange rate as endogenous variables. Foreign debt does not of itself affect people's well-being – and is, indeed, the means by which well-being is improved since it is one tool by which people are able to smooth their consumption over the life-cycle and over generations. Similarly, there is no 'ideal' real exchange rate since it is a relative price determined only by people's particular endowments and preferences. People's material living standards, embodied in their consumption levels, and not these economic variables, are the proper target of policy. In this respect, foreign debt and the real exchange rate are not appropriate targets: the model predicts rather that expanding the consumption possibilities set and expanding the means for people to smooth consumption over uneven income flows makes people better off.

Yet there are concerns that financial openness means allowing more consumption at the expense of lower savings, lower investment or higher current account deficits. Classical analysis predicts that higher consumption now implies lower saving, less investment and hence less output in the future. But in fact when economies grow so, too, does saving. Indeed, the prediction that expanding the opportunities for consumption reduces saving and investment is not supported by the data. The empirical work on liquidity constraints in chapter 7, for example, suggested a loose hierarchy of countries in terms of constraint. The ranking is – from least constrained to most constrained – Australia, Hong Kong, Singapore, Japan, Korea, Thailand and Taiwan. This hierarchy is not at all correlated with savings, investment or current account outcomes in these countries. Allowing people access to financial markets does not necessarily mean a deterioration in saving or investment – thrift and productivity are determined by other factors.

This does not mean that issues related to the sustainability of debt do not arise. The intertemporal model operates under the restriction that people must be able to service their debt, even in the longer run: the discounted value of consumption over time equals the discounted value of income over time, and so people and countries cannot simply borrow forever to finance consumption: Ponzi-games are ruled out. The burning issue is, as always, the sustainable level of debt. Reisen (1996: 158) has suggested that the 'standard' limit for foreign debt is 40 per cent of GDP, but there is nothing in these models which indicates that one number is better than any other. As derived in chapter 6, sustainability is ultimately tied to the ability of a country to generate trade surpluses to meet interest payments on the foreign debt.

Endpiece

The book has attempted to provide some new insights into the measurement of financial integration and economists' understanding of how financial integration affects the structure of the real economy. It has been argued that interest rates and consumption profiles contain much information about the openness, or otherwise, of financial markets in the east Asian countries examined. In respect of interest rate relationships, this information seems to emerge in quite an unexpected way. Domestic and international financial integration has proceeded apace in recent years in much of east Asia, and consumption patterns are changing as a result. The book indicates that financial integration is measurable and it *does* matter, even if theory suggests that the effects are not always unambiguously predictable.

Appendices

Appendix 3.1: Data and definitions of consumption correlations

The natural logarithm of domestic real *per capita* consumption (rc) is calculated as

$$rc_i = \frac{c_i}{cpi_i \cdot pop_i} \qquad (A3.1.1)$$

where the subscript refers to country i, and the time subscript is suppressed, and c, cpi and pop refer to private consumption from the National Accounts (in domestic currency) (code 96f, 96f.c), the consumer price index (1990=1) (code 64) and the mid-year population estimate (code 99z), respectively. The growth rate of domestic real *per capita* consumption is calculated as the difference of this logged term multiplied by 100.

For J countries in the world, the natural logarithm of the rest of world's real *per capita* consumption for country i is calculated as the geometric mean of the natural logarithm of real *per capita* consumption for the other countries in the sample,

$$\ln(rwc_i) = \frac{\sum_{j=1}^{J} \ln(rc_j)}{J}, \; i \notin J. \qquad (A3.1.2)$$

The ROW excludes Papua New Guinea since complete data are not available from the IFS until the mid-1970s. Korea is not part of ROW until 1967, when IFS data for it became available. These exclusions should have only a very slight impact on the correlations. The growth rate of ROW real *per capita* consumption is calculated as the difference of this logged term multiplied by 100.

Appendix 4.1: Definitions, sources and graphs of interest rate data

Inflation rates are quarterly and calculated using the consumer price index (code 64) published by the IMF *International Financial Statistics*. Sources of financial prices are set out below

Australia (figures A4.1.1–A4.1.3)

Domestic interest rate: alternatively, the last-week average of the three-month Australian Treasury Note auction rate, Reserve Bank of Australia, and the three-month Australian eurodollar rate quoted in the Swiss market at 10 a.m. on the last working day of the month, Bank for International Settlements, unpublished series.

Foreign interest rate: alternatively, the three-month secondary market US Treasury Bill rate, Nikkei database, and the three-month US eurodollar rate quoted in the Swiss market at 10 a.m. on the last working day of the month, Bank for International Settlements, unpublished series.

Forward discount and spot rate depreciation: the forward discount calculated alternatively from the mid-rate of the spot and three-month-forward exchange rate at 4 p.m. on the last Friday of the month, Reserve Bank of Australia, unpublished series, and the three-month forward discount on the Australian dollar quoted in London at midday on the last (Swiss) working day of the month, Bank for International Settlements, unpublished series, and the end-month spot rate at 4 p.m. on the last day of the month, Reserve Bank of Australia, *Bulletin*.

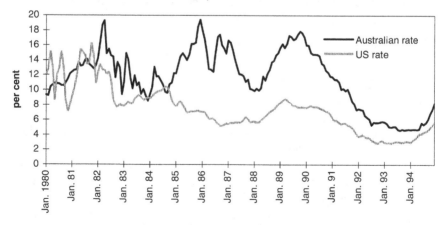

Fig. A4.1.1. Australia and the United States, three-month interest rates, January 1980–January 1994

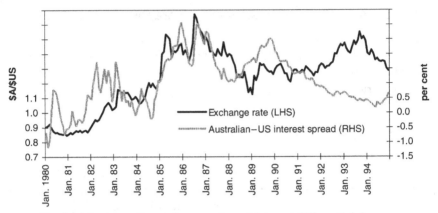

Fig. A4.1.2. Australia, exchange rate and interest differential, January
1980–January 1994

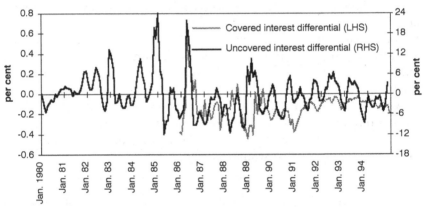

Fig. A4.1.3. Australia, covered and uncovered interest differential, January
1980–January 1994

Hong Kong (figures A4.1.4–A4.1.6)

Domestic interest rate: the end-period three-month Hong Kong dollar interbank offer rate, *Hong Kong Monthly Digest of Statistics*.

Foreign interest rate: the three-month interbank offer US dollar interest rate
in the Singapore market (SIBOR) on the last Friday of the month, Monetary
Authority of Singapore, *Statistical Bulletin*.

Forward discount and spot rate depreciation: calculated from the mid-rate of the
end-month spot and three-month-forward Hong Kong dollar/US dollar
exchange rate, Barclays Bank International, published by Datastream.

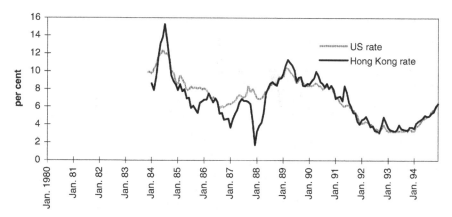

Fig. A4.1.4. Hong Kong and the United States, three-month interest rates, January 1980–January 1994

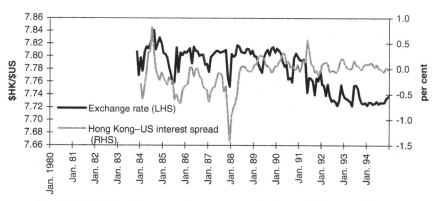

Fig. A4.1.5. Hong Kong, exchange rate and interest differential, January 1980–January 1994

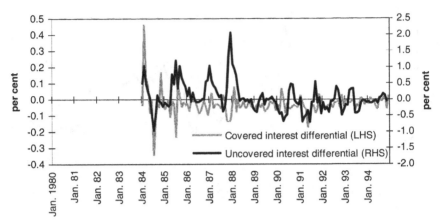

Fig. A4.1.6. Hong Kong, covered and uncovered interest differential,
January 1980–January 1994

Indonesia (figures A4.1.7–A4.1.9)

Domestic interest rate: the monthly weighted average of all maturities of
interbank market rates, Bank Indonesia, *Indonesian Financial Statistics*.
Foreign interest rate: the three-month interbank offer US dollar interest rate
in the Singapore market (SIBOR) on the last Friday of the month, Monetary
Authority of Singapore, *Statistical Bulletin*.
Spot rate depreciation: calculated from the mid-rate of the end-month spot
rupiah/US dollar exchange rate, IMF, *International Financial Statistics*.

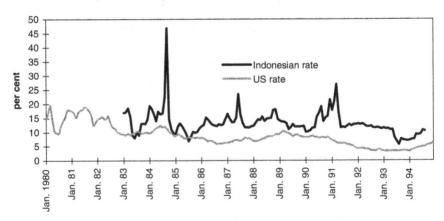

Fig. A4.1.7. Indonesia and the United States, money market interest rates,
January 1980–January 1994

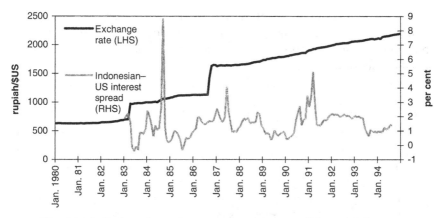

Fig. A4.1.8. Indonesia, exchange rate and interest differential, January 1980–January 1994

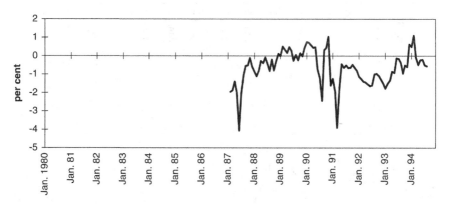

Fig. A4.1.9. Indonesia, uncovered interest differential, January 1980–January 1994

Japan (figures A4.1.10–A4.1.12)

Domestic interest rate: alternatively, three-month euroyen rate quoted in the Swiss market at 10 a.m. on the last working day of the month, Bank for International Settlements, unpublished series, and three-month gensaki and three-month secondary market certificate of deposit interest rates, Nikkei database.

Foreign interest rate: three-month US eurodollar rate quoted in the Swiss market at 10 a.m. on the last working day of the month, Bank for International Settlements, unpublished series.

Forward discount and spot rate depreciation: three-month-forward discount on the yen quoted in London at midday on the last (Swiss) working day of the month, Bank for International Settlements, unpublished series, and the end-month spot rate (about 8 a.m. Swiss time), Bank of Japan, *Economic Statistics Monthly*.

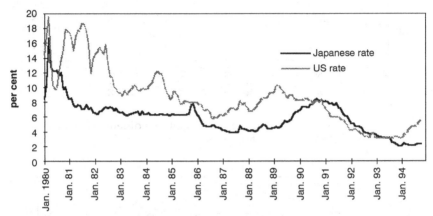

Fig. A4.1.10. Japan and the United States, three-month interest rates, January 1980–January 1994

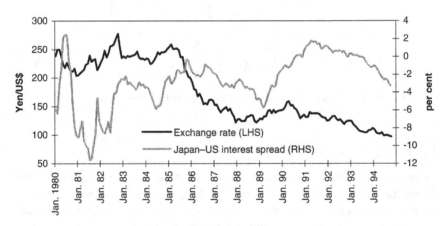

Fig. A4.1.11. Japan, exchange rate and interest differential, January 1980–January 1994

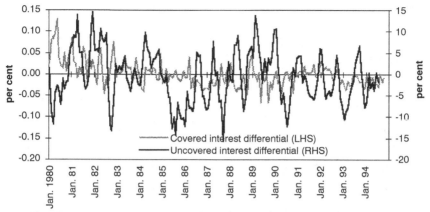

Fig. A4.1.12. Japan, covered and uncovered interest differential, January
1980–January 1994

Korea (figures A4.1.13–A4.1.15)

Domestic interest rate: the average daily rate on call money, weighed by
volume of transactions, Bank of Korea *Monthly Statistical Bulletin*.
Foreign interest rate: three-month interbank offer US dollar interest rate in
the Singapore market (SIBOR) on the last Friday of the month, Monetary
Authority of Singapore, *Statistical Bulletin*.
Spot rate depreciation: calculated from the mid-rate of the end-month spot
won/US dollar exchange rate, IMF, *International Financial Statistics*.

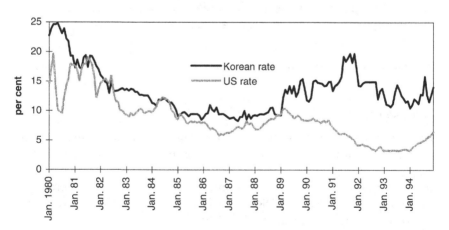

Fig. A4.1.13. Korea and the United States, money market interest rates,
January 1980–January 1994

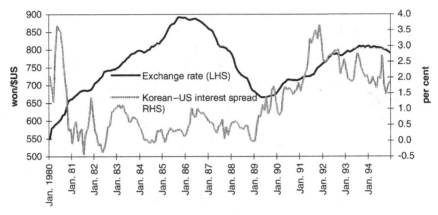

Fig. A4.1.14. Korea, exchange rate and interest differential, January
1980–January 1994

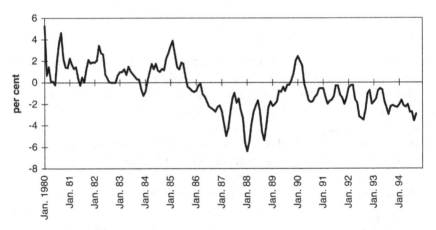

Fig. A4.1.15. Korea, uncovered interest differential, January 1980–January
1994

Malaysia (figures A4.1.16–A4.1.18)

Domestic interest rate: the three-month Kuala Lumpur interbank rate
(KLIBOR) on the last Friday of the month, Bank Negara Malaysia,
Quarterly Bulletin.

Foreign interest rate: the three-month interbank offer US dollar interest rate
in the Singapore market (SIBOR) on the last Friday of the month, Monetary
Authority of Singapore, *Statistical Bulletin*.

Forward discount and spot rate depreciation: calculated from the mid-rate of
the end-month spot and three-month-forward ringgit/US dollar exchange
rate, Barclays Bank International, published by Datastream.

Fig. A4.1.16. Malaysia and the United States, three-month interest rates,
January 1980–January 1994

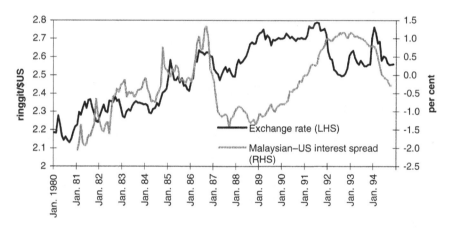

Fig. A4.1.17. Malaysia, exchange rate and interest differential, Malaysia,
covered and uncovered interest differential, January
1980–January 1994

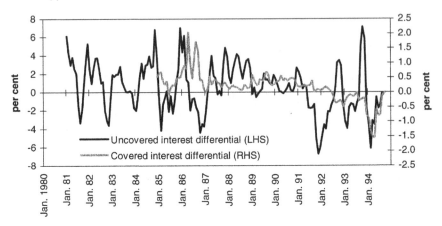

Fig. A4.1.18. Malaysia, covered and uncovered interest differential,
January 1980–January 1994

The Philippines (figures A4.1.19–A4.1.21)

Domestic interest rate: the end-month 91-day Treasury Bill rate, IMF
International Financial Statistics.
Foreign interest rate: the end-month three-month secondary market US
Treasury Bill rate, Nikkei database.
Spot rate depreciation: calculated from the mid-rate of the end-month spot
peso/US dollar exchange rate, IMF, *International Financial Statistics*.

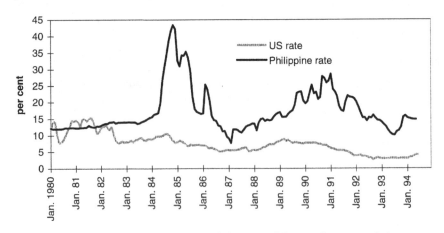

Fig. A4.1.19. The Philippines and the United States, three-month interest
rates, January 1980–January 1994

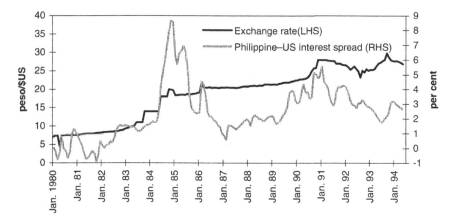

Fig. A4.1.20. The Philippines, exchange rate and interest differential,
January 1980–January 1994

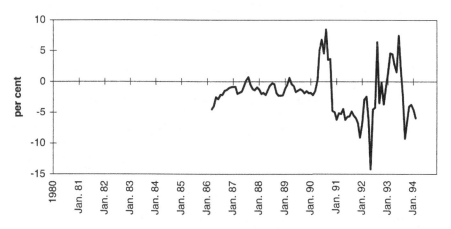

Fig. A4.1.21. The Philippines, three-month uncovered interest differential,
January 1980–January 1994

Singapore (figures A4.1.22–A4.1.24)

Domestic interest rate: the three-month interbank offer Singapore dollar
interest rate on the last Friday of the month, Monetary Authority of
Singapore, *Statistical Bulletin*.

Foreign interest rate: the three-month interbank offer US dollar interest rate
in the Singapore market (SIBOR) on the last Friday of the month, Monetary
Authority of Singapore, *Statistical Bulletin*.

Forward discount and spot rate depreciation: calculated from the mid-rate of
the end-month spot and three-month-forward Singapore dollar/US dollar
exchange rate, Monetary Authority of Singapore.

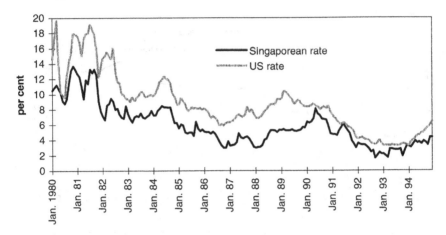

Fig. A4.1.22. Singapore and the United States, three-month interest rates,
January 1980–January 1994

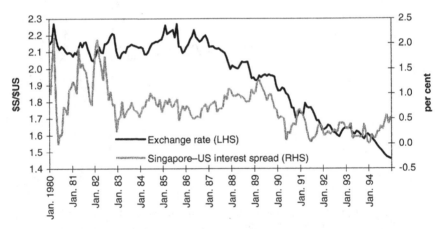

Fig. A4.1.23. Singapore, exchange rate and interest differential, January
1980–January 1994

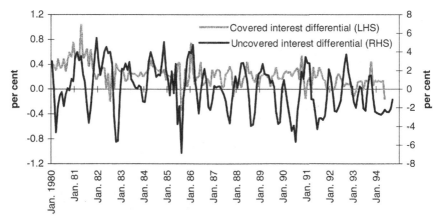

Fig. A4.1.24. Singapore, covered and uncovered interest differential,
January 1980–January 1994

Taiwan (figures A4.1.25–A4.1.27)

Domestic interest rate: alternatively, the end-month ten-30-day Taiwan interbank rate, and the one–90-day Taiwan secondary market NCD market rate, Central Bank of China on Taiwan.

Foreign interest rate: alternatively, the one-month US secondary market CD rate, Bank of International Settlements, unpublished series, and three-month SIBOR on the last Friday of the month, Monetary Authority of Singapore, *Statistical Bulletin*.

Forward discount and spot rate depreciation: alternatively, calculated from the mid-rate of the end-month spot and one-month-forward exchange rate, Central Bank of China on Taiwan, and the calculated from the mid-rate of the end-month spot and three-month-forward exchange rate, Central Bank of China on Taiwan.

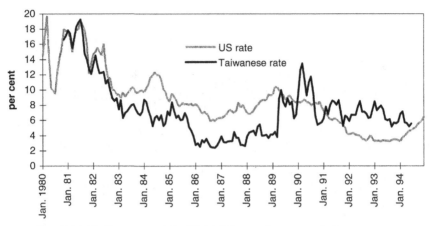

Fig. A4.1.25. Taiwan and the United States, three-month interest rates,
January 1980–January 1994

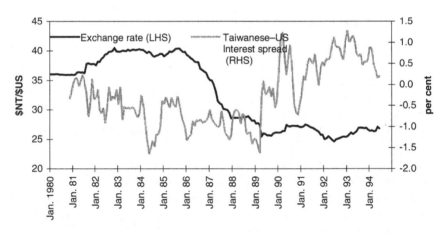

Fig. A4.1.26. Taiwan, exchange rate and interest spread, January
1980–January 1994

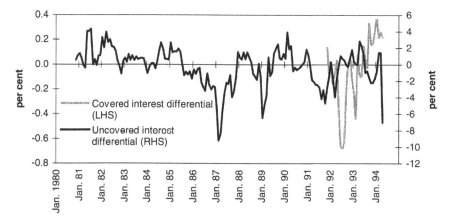

Fig. A4.1.27. Taiwan, covered and uncovered interest differential, January
1980–January 1994

Thailand (figures A4.1.28–A4.1.30)

Domestic interest rate: the weighted monthly average of the Thai interbank
market rate, Bank of Thailand.

Foreign interest rate: the monthly average of the eurodollar rate quoted in
the London market, Bank of Thailand.

Forward discount and spot rate depreciation: monthly average of the forward
discount on the baht/US dollar spot and one-month-forward exchange
rates, Bank of Thailand, unpublished series. Spot rate is from IMF,
International Financial Statistics.

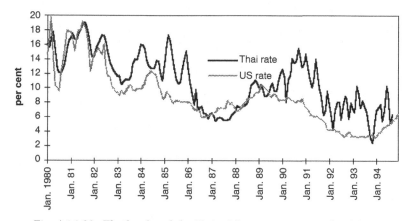

Fig. A4.1.28. Thailand and the United States, money market interest rates,
January 1980–January 1994

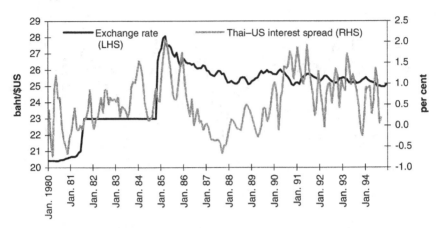

Fig. A4.1.29. Thailand, Exchange rate and interest differential, January
1980–January 1994

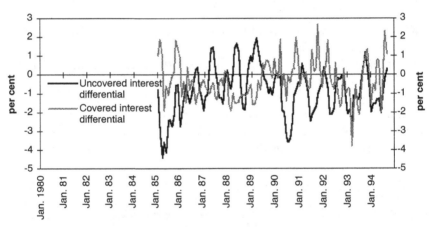

Fig. A4.1.30. Thailand, covered and uncovered interest differential,
January 1980–January 1994

Appendix 4.2: The Solution for McCallum's (1994) Model

The notation used in this chapter differs slightly from McCallum (1994). The interest differential, x in McCallum's notation, over the period t to $t+k$ is called $id_{t,t+k}$ in this chapter but it is assumed that k is only one period so $t+k$ is $t+1$ and so this second subscript is dropped for simplicity. The depreciation of the exchange rate over the period $t-k$ to t is denoted $\Delta s_{t,k}$ but since k is one period the second subscript is again dropped for simplicity. The expected depreciation of the exchange rate over the period t to $t+k$ is denoted $\Delta s^e_{t,t+k}$ and is written as $\Delta s^e_{t,t+1}$ since k is one period but the second subscript is retained to emphasise that it is forward-looking and different to the actual past depreciations.

The evolution rule for the interest differential, given the central bank objective function, is

$$id_t = \lambda \Delta s_t + \sigma id_{t-1} + \zeta_t, \tag{A4.2.1}$$

which is (4.12) in the text. The uncovered interest parity is written with an error term, ξ

$$\Delta s^e_{t,t+1} = id_t - \xi_t, \tag{A4.2.2}$$

which is (4.13) in the text. The error term is autoregressive, indicating persistence in the deviation from uncovered parity,

$$\xi_t = \rho \xi_{t-1} + v_t, \tag{A4.2.3}$$

which is (4.14) in the text. Combining these equations yields,

$$\Delta s^e_{t,t+1} = \lambda \Delta s_t + \sigma id_{t-1} + \zeta_t - v_t - \rho \xi_{t-1}. \tag{A4.2.4}$$

The state variables for the rational expectations solution of the exchange rate depreciation, Δs_t, are id_{t-1}, ξ_t, ξ_{t-1} and v_t and the solution is assumed to be of the linear form,

$$\Delta s_t = \phi_1 id_{t-1} + \phi_2 \xi_t + \phi_3 \zeta_{t-1} + \phi_4 v_t. \tag{A4.2.5}$$

Taking one-period-ahead expectations of (A4.2.5) yields,

$$\Delta s^e_{t,t+1} = \phi_1 id_t + \phi_3 \rho \zeta_{t-1} + \phi_3 v_t. \tag{A4.2.6}$$

and substituting (A4.2.1) for id_t and (A4.2.5) for Δs_t in (A4.2.1) yields,

$$\Delta s^e_{t,t+1} = [\phi_1^2 \lambda + \phi_1 \sigma] id_t + [\phi_1 \phi_2 \lambda + \phi_1] \xi_t + [\phi_1 \phi_3 \lambda + \rho] \zeta_{t-1} + [\phi_1 \phi_4 \lambda + 1] v_t. \tag{A4.2.7}$$

Equating (A4.2.7) to (A4.2.4), substituting (A4.2.5) for Δs_t, and setting the expression equal to zero yields,

$$0 = [\phi_1^2\lambda + \phi_1\sigma - \phi_1\lambda - \sigma]id_{t-1} + [\phi_1\phi_2\lambda + \phi_1 - \phi_2\lambda - 1]\xi_t$$
$$+ [\phi_1\phi_3\lambda + \phi_3\rho - \phi_3\lambda + \rho]\zeta_{t-1} + [\phi_1\phi_4\lambda + \phi_3 - \phi_4\lambda + 1]v_t. \tag{A4.2.8}$$

Excluding the trivial solution by which the variables are set to zero, the solution is obtained by setting each of the bracketed terms to zero and solving for the undetermined coefficients, yielding,

$$\phi_1 = -\sigma/\lambda$$
$$\phi_2 = -1/\lambda$$
$$\phi_3 = \rho/\lambda + \sigma - \rho$$
$$\phi_4 = 1/\lambda + \sigma - \rho \tag{A4.2.9}$$

Substituting these coefficients into (A4.2.5) yields the interim solution,

$$\Delta s_t = -\frac{\sigma}{\lambda}id_{t-1} - \frac{1}{\lambda}\xi_t + \frac{\rho}{\lambda + \sigma - \rho}\zeta_{t-1} + \frac{1}{\lambda + \sigma - \rho}v_t. \tag{A4.2.10}$$

Substituting (A4.2.10) into the evolution rule for the interest differential in (A4.2.1) yields the expression for the interest differential,

$$id_t = \frac{\lambda}{\lambda + \sigma - \rho}\zeta_t, \tag{A4.2.11}$$

which, if true at time t, is also true at time $t-1$,

$$id_{t-1} = \frac{\lambda}{\lambda + \sigma - \rho}\zeta_{t-1}. \tag{A4.2.12}$$

Multiplying both sides by $\rho/(\rho - \sigma)$ and adding and subtracting σ in the numerator of the left-hand side expression yields,

$$\left(1 + \frac{\sigma}{\rho - \sigma}\right)id_{t-1} = \frac{\lambda\rho}{(\rho - \sigma)(\lambda + \sigma - \rho)}\zeta_{t-1}. \tag{A4.2.13}$$

Taking the second term in brackets on the left-hand side over to the right-hand side and multiplying it by λ/λ yields,

$$id_{t-1} = \frac{-\lambda\sigma}{\lambda(\rho - \sigma)}id_{t-1} + \frac{\lambda\rho}{(\rho - \sigma)(\lambda + \sigma - \rho)}\zeta_{t-1}. \tag{A4.2.14}$$

Multiplying both sides by $(\rho - \sigma)/\lambda$ yields

$$\frac{\rho - \sigma}{\lambda}id_{t-1} = \frac{-\sigma}{\lambda}id_{t-1} + \frac{\rho}{(\lambda + \sigma - \rho)}\zeta_{t-1}. \tag{A4.2.15}$$

Substituting this into (A4.2.10) yields the solution which appears in the text as (4.16) and is equivalent to McCallum's (1994: 125) (25),

$$\Delta s_t = [(\rho - \sigma)/\lambda]id_{t-1} - (1/\lambda)\zeta_t + [1/(\lambda + \sigma - \rho)]v_t. \tag{A4.2.16}$$

Appendix 4.3: Time-varying estimates of beta

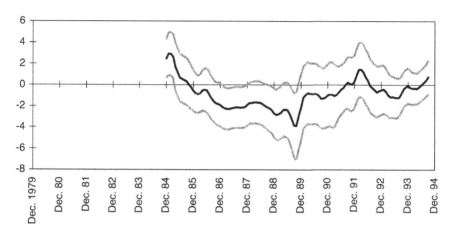

Fig. A4.3.1. Australia, rolling regression of beta with standard errors, December 1979–December 1994

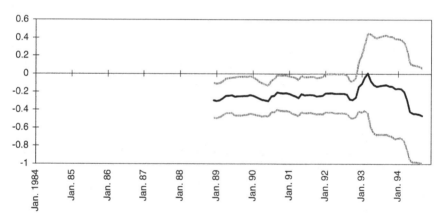

Fig. A4.3.2. Hong Kong, rolling regression of beta with standard errors, January 1984–January 1994

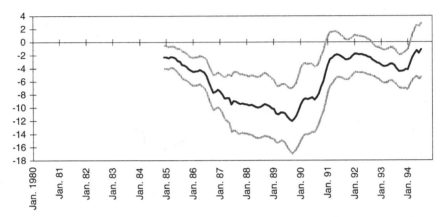

Fig. A4.3.3.　Japan, rolling regression of beta with standard errors, January 1980–January 1994

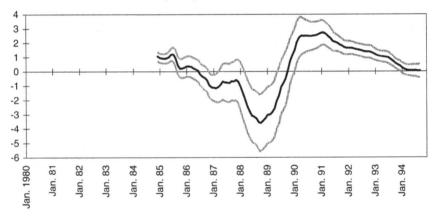

Fig. A4.3.4.　Korea, rolling regression of beta with standard errors, January 1980–January 1994

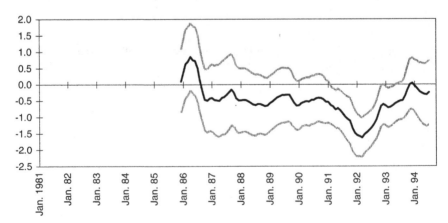

Fig. A4.3.5.　Malaysia, rolling regression of beta with standard errors, January 1981–January 1994

Fig. A4.3.6. Singapore, rolling regression of beta with standard errors,
January 1980–January 1994

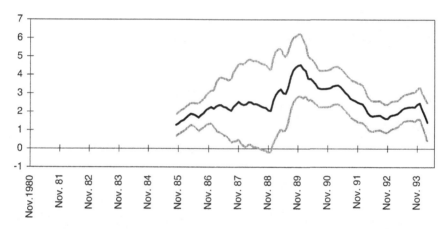

Fig. A4.3.7. Taiwan, rolling regression of beta with standard errors,
November 1980–November 1994

Appendix 5.1: Summary of deregulation in banking and in deposit and loan markets

Australia

Date	Banking sector	Deposit market	Loan market
1972 February			Maximum interest rate on overdrafts and housing loans over $A50,000 removed
1975 January	Banks' agreement to maintain uniform fee structure discontinued since it was contrary to Trade Practices Act		
1976 February			Limit extended to $A100,000
1980 December		Interest rate ceilings on all bank deposits removed	
1982 June			Reserve Bank of Australia ceased quantitative lending guidance
1984 August		All remaining controls on deposits (terms and conditions) removed	
1985 February April	Entry of 16 foreign banks		Remaining ceilings on interest rates removed, except for owner-occupied housing loans under $A100,000

1986
April

Interest rate ceiling on new owner-occupied housing loans removed, existing loans still subject to maximum rate of 13.5 per cent

1992
February

Further entry by foreign banks approved

1994
February–June

Foreign banks have choice of operating as branch or locally incorporated subsidiary; foreign bank branches not allowed to conduct retail banking business

Sources: Battellino and McMillan (1989); Reserve Bank of Australia, *Annual Report* (1994).

Hong Kong

Date	Banking sector	Deposit market	Loan market
1981 July		Banks required to observe rates set by the Hong Kong Association of Banks (HKAB) which sets the maximum interest rate payable on deposits up to $HK500,000 with a maturity less than 15 months	Banks required to observe rates set by HKAB which sets the prime lending rate (cf. Hong Kong Monetary Authority 1994, which states that the prime rate is determined by individual banks but, by convention, they follow the note-issuing banks)
1989 March	Three-tier system of banking reformed, comprising licensed banks (LBs), restricted license banks (RLBs = merchant banks) and deposit-taking institutions (DTIs)	Only LBs required to follow rates set by the HKAB, but RLBs and DTCs subject to minimum deposit requirements and DTCs excluded from short-term deposit market	
1994 October		Interest rates on deposits fixed for more than one month liberalised	
1995 January		Interest rates on deposits fixed for more than seven days liberalised	
April		Interest rates on deposits fixed for more than 24 hours on call liberalised	
Second half		Interest rates on deposits fixed for more than 24 hours liberalised	

Sources: Ho (1991); Hong Kong Monetary Authority, *Quarterly Bulletin* (November 1994).

Indonesia

Date	Banking sector	Deposit market	Loan market
1974 April		Stabilisation package including continued regulation of state bank deposit interest rates	Stabilisation package including introduction of credit ceilings for all banks; continued regulation of state bank lending interest rates; extension of provision of liquidity credits to state banks and of direct credits to priority sectors
1983 June		Removal of interest rate ceilings on time deposits by state banks (but banks entered into an agreement of understanding to avoid undue competition)	Removal of interest rate ceilings on loans by state banks (and introduction of money market instruments); abolition of credit ceilings; reduction in liquidity credits to state banks and direct credit credits to priority shifts to non-oil exports
1988 October	Prudential system overhauled; foreign banks allowed access to Tabanas and Taska rupiah savings schemes; entry and branch establishment requirements eased for domestic and foreign banks; restrictions on ATMs and mobile cash units eased	Tax-free status of interest earned on time deposits removed	
1990 January			Substantial reduction in scale and scope of liquidity credits
1991 February	Bank supervision policy overhauled; domestic banks permitted to establish branches overseas; restrictions on bank mergers eased		
1992	Foreigners allowed to buy up to 49 per cent of publicly listed shares in banks		

Sources: Bank Indonesia, *Annual Report* (various years); MacIntyre (1993); APEG (1995).

Japan

Date	Banking sector	Deposit market	Loan market
1972 April			Long-term prime rate freed and set at 90 basis points above the subscribers' yield on five-year debentures issued by long-term credit banks
1985 March		Introduction of money market certificates (MMC), Y50mn minimum deposit requirements and period of one–six months	
October		Interest rates on time deposits of three months to two years with minimum deposit of Y1bn liberalised; minimum deposit requirements to one month to one year	
1986 March		Minimum deposit requirement on free-time deposits cut to Y500mn	
September		Minimum deposit requirement on MMCs cut to Y30mn; minimum deposit requirement on free-time deposits cut to Y300mn	
1987 April		Minimum deposit requirement on MMCs cut to Y20mn; minimum deposit requirement on free-time deposits cut to Y100mn	
October		Minimum deposit requirement on MMCs cut to Y10mn; period on free-time deposits extended to one month to two years	
1988 April		Minimum deposit requirement on free-time deposits cut to Y50mn	
November		Minimum deposit requirement on free-time deposits cut to Y20mn	

1989	January	While the maximum short-term prime rate remains set at 15 per cent under the Temporary Interest Rate Adjustment Law, the rate freed from the ODR and determined by bank funding costs and expenses
	June	Small MMC introduced with minimum deposit requirement of Y3mn
	October	Minimum deposit requirement on free-time deposits cut to Y10mn; MMC merged into large–denomination time deposits
1990	April	Minimum deposit requirement on small MMC cut to Y1mn
1991	April	Minimum deposit requirement on small MMC cut to Y500,000mn
	November	Minimum deposit requirement on free-time deposits cut to Y3mn
1992	June	Minimum deposit requirement on small MMC abolished
1993	June	Minimum deposit requirement and period on time deposits abolished; small MMCs merged into time deposits
1994	October	Interest rates on demand deposits freed (though payment of interest on current deposits remains prohibited)

Long-term prime rate set at a spread above short-term prime rate

Source: Bank of Japan, *Quarterly Bulletin* (November 1994).

Korea

Date	Banking sector	Deposit market	Loan market
1981 June	Privatisation of the four government-owned commercial banks (taking total of private commercial banks to five) Lowering of entry barriers to domestic and foreign banks		
1982 December	Maximum ownership of bank by one shareholder set to 8 per cent Elimination of discriminatory tax on NBFI deposit interest lowering of entry barriers to NBFIs		
1985		Banks allowed to establish high-yielding savings deposits	
1988 December		Interest rates on time deposits of more than two years liberalised	Interest rates on loans from banks and NBFIs, other than interest rates on loans subsidised by government, fully liberalised; introduction of a prime rate system; interest rates on money market instruments fully liberalised
1989 April	Three new commercial banks established	December 1988 reform reversed	December 1988 reform reversed

1990 October	Facilitation of NBFI conversion to bank status		
1991 July	Restrictions on foreign banks concerning branching, limits on capital, access to local funding and participation in trust business eased considerably		
November		Rates on deposit >three year liberalised	Short-term rates on bank over-draft loans, commercial and trade bill discounts liberalised
1993 November		Rates on deposits >two years liberalised	Rates on all bank lending (excluding loans financed by the official sector) liberalised; export financing incentives and government-directed funds for capital investment, housing funds and agricultural funds remain
1994 November		Rates on deposits >one year liberalised	
1995			Plan to liberalised all lending rates
1996		Plan to liberalise rates on all deposits except demand deposits, introduce products linked to money market rates	
1997		Plan to set up plan to deregulate demand deposits	

Sources: Lee (1992); Bank of Korea, *Quarterly Economic Review,* various years.

Malaysia

Date	Banking sector	Deposit market	Loan market
1978 October		Commercial banks allowed to set interest rates on deposits of one year or less	Commercial banks allowed to set base lending rates (BLR) under guidance of Bank Negara Malaysia
1983 March			Bank lending rates pegged to banks' declared BLR
1985 October		Pegged interest rate agreement whereby rates on deposits of one year or less are aligned to two lead banks' rates	
1987 February		Pegged interest rate agreement disbanded	Margin of lending rates over BLR restricted to four percentage points
1991 February			BLR freed from Bank Negara Malaysia's administrative control

Sources: Bank Negara Malaysia, *Quarterly Bulletin* (various years); Abidin (1986).

The Philippines

Date	Banking sector	Deposit market	Loan market
1981 July		Interest rate ceilings removed	Interest rate ceilings removed except on loans for up to one year
1983 January			Interest rate ceiling on loans up to one year removed
Early 1980s			25 per cent of loanable funds directed to agriculture and agrarian reform credits
1985 November			Major reduction in subsidy element of central bank refinancing; interest rate ceilings removed
1989	Lifting of moratorium on the establishment of new banks		
1991 April–May	Bank branching and ATM restrictions liberalised		
1993 June	Restructuring of central bank		
1994 May	Foreign bank entry allowed (as a full branch, as local subsidiary or by acquisition of an existing domestic institution); ten foreign banks granted full branch status		5–10 per cent of loanable funds directed to small and medium cottage enterprises

Sources: Bangko Sentral ng Pilipinas, *Annual Report* (various years); Hutchcroft (1993).

Singapore

Date	Banking sector	Deposit market	Loan market
1975 July		Domestic interest rate cartel abolished, all banks free to quote their own interest rates	Domestic interest rates cartel abolished, all banks free to quote their own interest rates

Sources: Money Authority of Singapore, *Annual Report* (various years); APEG (1995).

Taiwan

Date	Banking sector	Deposit market	Loan market
1975			Central Bank of China authorises Interest Rate Committee of the Banks' Association to set ceiling and floor lending rates
1980 November			Prescribed interest rate band widened; interest rates on bank debentures, NCDs, FX deposits and interbank call loans liberalised
1983 December	Offshore banking allowed		
1984 April	Banks allowed to increase branches by 3 each year (up from two each year)		

1985			
March			Local banks free to set prime rate according to market pressures and customers' credit rating but within the prescribed band
September			Prime rate system available to all banks
November			Interest Rate Control Statute abolished, giving financial institutions more autonomy in setting interest rates
1986			
January		Categories of deposits simplified from 13 to four interest rate floor abolished	
1986–7	Restrictions on foreign bank business, $NT financing and branches moderately eased		
1987			Decontrol of foreign exchange outflow, reducing the privilege of foreign banks to import cheap capital
1989			
July	Lifting of ban on establishment of private banks (new banks limited to five branches to deal in foreign exchange and, for the first three years of operation, securities)	Ceiling on interest rates removed	Band on interest rates removed
1989–93	Privatisation of state-owned commercial banks announced		
1994		Non-residents allowed to open $NT accounts	

Sources: Chen (1990); Yang (1991); Cheng (1993); Asia Pacific Economic Group (1995).

Thailand

Date	Banking sector	Deposit market	Loan market
1983			18 per cent ceiling on growth in private bank credit
1984			Ceiling on private bank credit growth abolished
1985	Bank of Thailand to conduct on-site bank examinations, remove bank directors and officers, restrict transactions between directors and their banks and bring action against shareholders		
1989 June		Interest rate ceiling on fixed deposits >one year removed	
1990 March		Interest rate ceiling on fixed deposits <one year removed	
1992 Early 1992	Banks permitted to underwrite public securities and provide financial consultation and information services		
January		Interest rate ceiling on savings deposits removed	
June			Interest rate ceiling on loans by banks, finance companies and credit fonciers removed (excl. some housing loans), but some lending restrictions remain

1993 January	Banks required to maintain BIS asset asset and liability ratios
1994	Further prudential measures
1996 April–May	Five new foreign bank and 20 new offshore bank licences issued foreign banks opened two new branches (one outside Bangkok)

Sources: Wibulswasdi and Tanvanich (1992); Doner and Unger (1993); Kirakul, Jantarangs and Chantanahom (1993).

Appendix 5.2: Definitions, sources and graphs of money, deposit and loan rate data

Australia (figure A5.2.1)

Money market rate: average 90-day bank bill rate for week ending last Wednesday of the month, Reserve Bank of Australia, *Bulletin*.

Deposit rate: bank three-month deposit rate, Reserve Bank of Australia, *Bulletin*.

Lending rate: bank minimum prime rate, Reserve Bank of Australia, *Bulletin*.

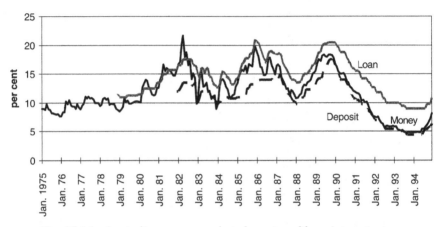

Fig. A5.2.1. Australia, money market, deposit and loan interest rates
January 1975–January 1994

Canada (figure A5.2.2)

Money market rate: average of the seven days ending the last Wednesday of the month of overnight money market financing rate, IMF, *International Financial Statistics*.

Deposit rate: last Wednesday of the month chartered banks' rates on 90-day $C deposits, IMF, *International Financial Statistics*.

Lending rate: last Wednesday of the month chartered banks, rates on loans to the most creditworthy large businesses, IMF, *International Financial Statistics*.

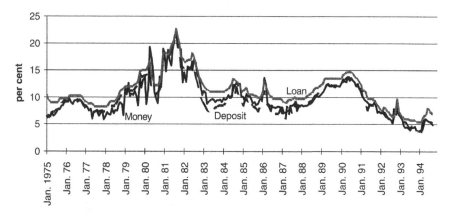

Fig. A5.2.2. Canada, money market, deposit and loan interest rates, January 1975–January 1994

Hong Kong (figure A5.2.3)

Money market rate: end-month three-month Hong Kong dollar interbank offered interest rate, *Hong Kong Monthly Digest of Statistics*.

Deposit rate: end-month maximum interest rate paid by licensed banks under the HK Association of Banks' interest rules on three-month time deposits, *Hong Kong Monthly Digest of Statistics*.

Lending rate: end-month Hong Kong Shanghai Bank's quoted best lending interest rate, *Hong Kong Monthly Digest of Statistics*.

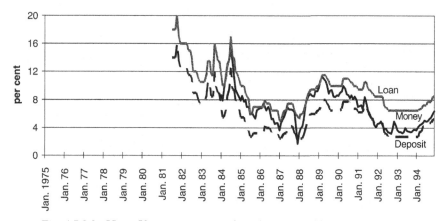

Fig. A5.2.3. Hong Kong, money market, deposit and loan interest rates, January 1975–January 1994

Indonesia (figure A5.2.4)

Money market rate: weighted average of all maturities, Bank Indonesia, *Indonesian Financial Statistics*.
Deposit rate: six-month deposit rate at deposit money banks, Bank Indonesia, *Indonesian Financial Statistics*.
Lending rate: average working capital lending rate at deposit money banks, Bank Indonesia, *Indonesian Financial Statistics*.

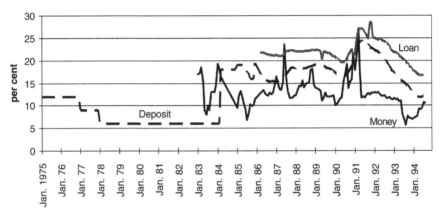

Fig. A5.2.4. Indonesia, money market, deposit and loan interest rates, January 1975–January 1994

Japan (figure A5.2.5)

Money market rate: monthly average collateralised overnight Tokyo call money rate, IMF, *International Financial Statistics Monthly*
Deposit rate: before June 1992, the guideline rate set by the Bank of Japan on three-month time deposits, from June 1992, monthly average deposit rate set by city banks on three- to six-month time deposits (so-called small money market certificates), Bank of Japan, *Economic Statistics Monthly*.
Lending rate: before 23 January 1989, rate on discount and loans on bills of especially high credit, from 23 January 1989, short-term prime lending rate set by a majority of the city banks, Bank of Japan *Economic Statistics Monthly*.

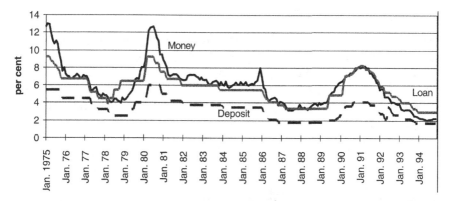

Fig. A5.2.5. Japan, money market, deposit and loan interest rates, January
1975–January 1994

Korea (figure A5.2.6)

Money market rate: average daily rate on call money, weighted by volume
of transactions, Bank of Korea, *Monthly Statistical Bulletin*.

Deposit rate: maximum guideline rate set by the Bank of Korea for deposits
of three months to one year with deposit money banks, Bank of Korea,
Monthly Statistical Bulletin.

Lending rate: maximum rate charged to general enterprises by deposit
money banks on loans of general funds for up to one year, Bank of Korea,
Monthly Stastistical Bulletin.

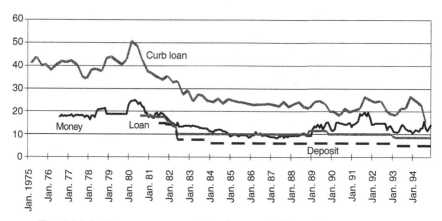

Fig. A5.2.6. Korea, money market, deposit and loan interest rates, January
1975–January 1994

Malaysia (figure A5.2.7)

Money market rate: daily average overnight lending rates of ten banks for the last week of the month, IMF, *International Financial Statistics*.

Deposit rate: mode of the range of quotes quoted on three-month deposits, IMF, *International Financial Statistics*.

Lending rate: mode of a range of quotes for the base lending rate, IMF, *International Financial Statistics*.

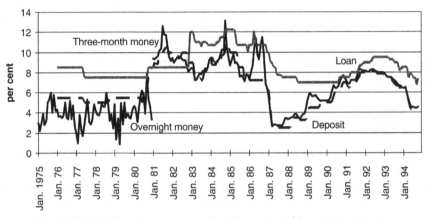

Fig. A5.2.7. Malaysia, money market, deposit and loan interest rates, January 1975–January 1994

The Philippines (figure A5.2.8)

Money market rate: rate at 91-day Treasury Bills, IMF, *International Financial Statistics*.

Deposit rate: rate on 61 to 90-day time deposits, IMF, *International Financial Statistics*.

Lending rate: average commercial lending rate, IMF, *International Financial Statistics*.

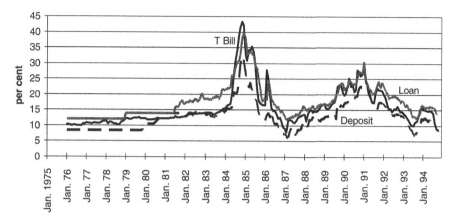

Fig. A5.2.8. The Philippines, Treasury Bill, deposit and loan interest rates,
January 1975–January 1994

Singapore (figure A5.2.9)

Money market rate: mode of the three-month interbank rate quoted by brokers on the last Friday (or closest working day thereto) of the month, IMF, *International Financial Statistics.*

Deposit rate: average of three-month deposit rates quoted by the ten leading commercial banks, IMF, *International Financial Statistics.*

Lending rate: average minimum lending rates quoted by the ten leading commercial banks, IMF, *International Financial Statistics.*

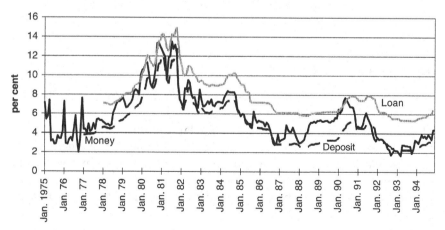

Fig. A5.2.9. Singapore, money market, deposit and loan interest rates,
January 1975–January 1994

Taiwan (figure A5.2.10)

Money market rate: weighted average interbank lending rate, Central Bank of China, *Financial Statistics Monthly*.
Deposit rate: until November 1985, the maximum rate on three-month time deposits, and after that the three-month time deposit rate offered by First Commercial Bank, Central Bank of China, *Financial Statistics Monthly*.
Lending rate: from 1975 to 1979, the maximum rate on unsecured loans, from 1980 to December 1989, the maximum rate on unsecured loans of maturities one year or less, from January 1990, the Bank of Taiwan prime rate, Central Bank of China, *Financial Statistics Monthly*.

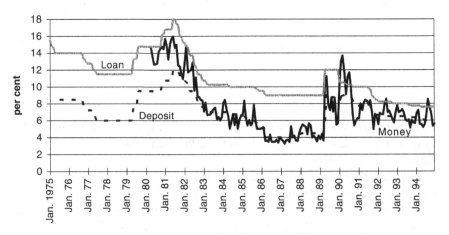

Fig. A5.2.10. Taiwan, money market, deposit and loan rates, January
1975–January 1994

Thailand (figure 5.2.11)

Money market rate: weighted average interbank lending rate, Bank of Thailand *Monthly Bulletin*.
Deposit rate: maximum offered rate by the largest four commecial banks on three- to six-month savings deposits, Bank of Thailand, *Monthly Bulletin*.
Lending rate: from 1975 to 1984, the maximum rate charged by commercial banks for priority (export-related) loans, from 1985 to 1994, the minimum prime loan rate charged by commercial banks, Bank of Thailand, *Monthly Bulletin*.

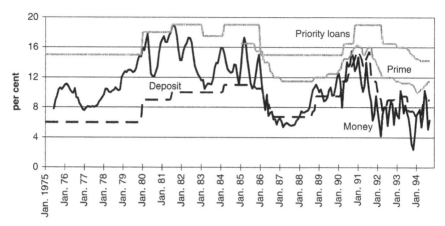

Fig. A5.2.11. Thailand, money market, deposit and loan interest rates,
January 1975–January 1994

The United States (figure A5.2.12)

Money market rate: calendar month average of federal funds rate, IMF,
International Financial Statistics.
Deposit rate: monthly business day average of three-month CDs in the secondary market, IMF, *International Financial Statistics.*
Lending rate: monthly average of prime rates offered to most creditworthy
customers of the largest banks, IMF, *International Financial Statistics.*

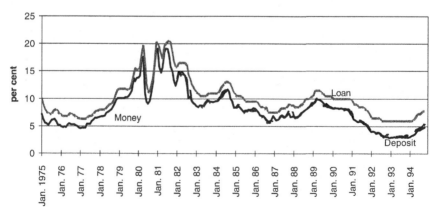

Fig. A5.2.12. The United States, money market, deposit and loan interest
rates, January 1975–January 1994

Appendix 5.3 Augmented Dickey–Fuller test statistics

The ADF statistics are estimated using Microfit 386 excluding trend unless otherwise specified. Critical values, indicated by *, are the 5 per cent level from MacKinnon (1992).

Table A5.3.1. *Interest rate unit root test statistics, Australia, 1980–94*

Interest rate	Period	Levels			First differences		
		ADF(1)	ADF(4)	ADF(6)	ADF(1)	ADF(4)	ADF(6)
Money rate	Full	−1.52	−1.97	−1.42	−9.37*	−5.40*	−4.30*
	1980–4	−1.93	−2.85	−2.54	−5.07*	−2.82	−2.89
	1985–9	−1.70	−1.67	−1.93	−4.75*	−3.22*	−2.77
	1990–4	−3.92*	−3.24*	−2.80	−2.60	−1.28	−0.03
Deposit rate	Full	−0.73	−1.37	−1.44	−7.76*	−4.17*	−4.30*
	1980–4	−1.75	−1.53	−1.57	−5.06*	−2.99*	−2.65
	1985–9	−0.54	−2.20	−2.02	−4.40*	−2.15	−2.04
	1990–4	−4.37*	−4.30*	−4.29*	−3.23*	−2.97*	−2.40−
Loan rate	Full	−1.32	−1.86	−1.62	−7.72*	−5.64*	−4.48*
	1980–4	−2.10	−2.60	−1.86	−5.83*	−4.24*	−4.00
	1985–9	−1.67	−1.88	−2.30	−3.59*	−2.93*	−2.55
	1990–4	−3.72*	−3.21*	−3.18*	−4.62*	−2.15	−1.49

Note:
In all tables: − = not available.

Table A5.3.2. *Interest rate unit root test statistics, Hong Kong, 1985–94*

Interest rate	Period	Levels			First differences		
		ADF(1)	ADF(4)	ADF(6)	ADF(1)	ADF(4)	ADF(6)
Money rate	Full	−2.13	−2.23	−2.04	−6.14*	−5.53*	−4.66*
	1985–9	−1.85	−2.16	−1.83	−4.62*	−4.01*	−3.29*
	1990–4	−1.54	−1.47	−1.50	−5.52*	−3.37*	−2.45
Deposit rate	Full	−2.09	−2.20	−2.17	−5.72*	−4.67*	−4.16*
	1985–9	−1.75	−1.74	−1.58	−3.87*	−3.44*	−2.84
	1990–4	−1.17	−1.17	−1.24	−4.33*	−3.02*	−2.58
Loan rate	Full	−2.29	−2.30	−2.34	−6.57*	−4.99*	−4.05*
	1985–9	−1.89	−1.76	−1.77	−4.62*	−3.60*	−2.81
	1990–4	−1.20	−1.22	−1.24	−4.67*	−3.06*	−2.45

Table A5.3.3. *Interest rate unit root test statistics, Indonesia, 1985–94*

Interest rate	Period	Levels			First differences		
		ADF(1)	ADF(4)	ADF(6)	ADF(1)	ADF(4)	ADF(6)
Money rate	Full	− 3.20*	− 2.26	− 1.91	− 8.91*	− 5.50*	− 4.66*
	1985–9	− 3.38*	− 2.06	− 2.54	− 5.85•	− 3.33*	− 2.96*
	1990–4	− 2.15	− 1.77	− 1.25	− 6.50*	− 3.33	− 2.96*
Deposit rate	Full	− 1.30	− 2.41	− 1.51	− 2.77	− 2.73	− 2.83
	1985–9	− 1.64	− 2.28	− 1.73	− 1.97	− 1.89	− 1.76
	1990–4	0.80	− 1.77	− 0.98	− 2.04	− 2.02	− 2.12
Loan rate	Full	− 1.23	− 0.78	− 1.14	− 8.36*	− 4.01*	− 2.49
	1985–9	− 2.04	− 1.64	− 1.46	− 6.02*	− 3.00*	− 2.28
	1990–4	− 0.93	− 0.45	− 0.82	− 6.50*	− 2.92*	− 1.79

Table A5.3.4. *Interest rate unit root test statistics, Japan, 1975–94*

Interest rate	Period	Levels			First differences		
		ADF(1)	ADF(4)	ADF(6)	ADF(1)	ADF(4)	ADF(6)
Money rate	Full	− 2.97*	− 2.66	− 3.29	− 7.97*	− 5.13*	− 4.44*
	1975–9	− 3.17*	− 1.93	− 2.08	− 3.94*	− 1.06	− 0.64
	1980–4	− 1.64	− 2.16	− 1.96	− 3.56*	− 2.87	− 2.63
	1985–9	− 1.52	− 1.36	− 1.46	− 4.49*	− 3.61*	− 2.77
	1990–4	− 0.21	− 1.55	− 1.89	− 3.96*	− 2.21	− 1.97
Deposit rate	Full	− 1.98	− 2.24	− 2.46	− 11.11*	− 5.77*	− 4.60*
	1975–9	− 1.60	− 1.82	− 1.88	− 5.29*	− 2.58	− 2.04
	1980–4	− 1.48	− 1.87	− 1.82	− 4.95*	− 2.96	− 2.02
	1985–9	− 1.74	− 1.71	− 1.78	− 3.94*	− 2.68	− 2.21
	1990–4	− 1.02	− 0.89	− 1.32	− 6.56*	− 2.83	− 2.22
Loan rate	Full	− 2.10	− 2.43	− 2.40	− 9.40*	− 5.79*	− 4.50*
	1975–9	− 2.49	− 2.38	− 2.42	− 2.62*	− 2.35	− 1.86
	1980–4	− 1.40	− 1.70	− 1.31	− 4.96*	− 3.58*	− 2.65
	1985–9	− 1.49	− 1.56	− 1.58	− 4.87*	− 3.02*	− 2.25
	1990–4	− 0.37	− 0.84	− 1.19	− 4.30*	− 2.33	− 1.62

Table A5.3.5. *Interest rate unit root test statistics, Malaysia, 1980–94*

Interest rate	Period	Levels			First differences		
		ADF(1)	ADF(4)	ADF(6)	ADF(1)	ADF(4)	ADF(6)
Money rate	Full	− 2.00	− 2.39	− 2.80	− 8.96*	− 4.76*	− 5.10*
	1980–4	− 1.93	− 1.16	− 1.14	− 1.35	− 1.04	− 1.88
	1985–9	− 1.75	− 2.08	− 1.82	− 6.06*	− 2.47	− 2.83
	1990–4	− 1.31	− 1.48	− 1.63	− 4.40*	− 2.26	− 1.98
Deposit rate	Full	− 1.31	− 1.85	− 1.83	− 7.59•	− 4.68*	− 4.45*
	1980–4	− 1.16	− 1.49	− 1.65	− 4.30*	− 1.60	− 1.73
	1985–9	− 2.01	− 2.03	− 1.99	− 4.46*	− 2.90*	− 2.73
	1990–4	− 0.88	− 1.40	− 1.36	− 3.44*	− 2.57	− 1.66
Loan rate	Full	− 1.31	− 1.27	− 1.49	− 8.89*	− 5.38*	− 4.46*
	1980–4	− 1.35	− 1.04	− 1.88	− 4.24*	− 3.03*	− 2.93*
	1985–9	− 1.44	− 1.42	− 1.46	− 5.77*	− 3.54*	− 2.64
	1990–4	− 1.08	− 1.13	− 1.69	− 5.80*	− 1.87	− 1.01

Table A5.3.6. *Interest rate unit root test statistics, the Philippines, 1975–94*

Interest rate	Period	Levels			First differences		
		ADF(1)	ADF(4)	ADF(6)	ADF(1)	ADF(4)	ADF(6)
Money rate	Full	−2.87*	−2.24	−2.41	−9.41*	−6.75*	−5.28*
	1975–9	−0.95	−1.00	−0.98	−4.89*	−3.47*	−2.33
	1980–4	−2.04	−2.05	−1.37	−2.29*	−3.52*	−1.61
	1985–9	−3.49*	−3.34*	−3.15*	−5.59*	−4.58*	−3.99*
	1990–4	−1.02	−0.66	−0.57	−5.62*	−3.75*	−2.78
Deposit rate	Full	−1.30	−2.41	−1.51	−2.77	−2.73	−2.83
	1975–9	−	−	−	−	−	−
	1980–4	−1.90	−2.23	−2.44	−7.17*	−4.74*	−4.14*
	1985–9	−4.62*	−4.21*	−4.50*	−5.02*	−4.19*	−3.34*
	1990–4	0.54	−0.83	−0.49	−3.30*	−2.87	−2.80
Loan rate	Full	−1.97	−2.24	−2.41	−9.24*	−6.09*	−4.97*
	1975–9	−0.53	−0.46	−0.40	−4.74*	−2.90	−2.39
	1980–4	4.40	3.21	2.05	−4.23*	0.43	1.97
	1985–9	−3.46*	−3.34*	−3.46*	−5.22*	−3.84*	−3.35*
	1990–4	−0.93	−0.87	−0.54	−5.22*	−4.18*	−3.70*

Table A5.3.7. *Interest rate unit root test statistics, Singapore, 1975–94*

Interest rate	Period	Levels			First differences		
		ADF(1)	ADF(4)	ADF(6)	ADF(1)	ADF(4)	ADF(6)
Money rate	Full	−2.05	−1.69	−1.12	−9.47*	−8.67*	−6.49*
	1975–9	−2.02	−1.65	−1.16	−7.94*	−7.65*	−5.50*
	1980–4	−1.91	−1.31	−0.65	−4.89*	−5.61*	−3.72*
	1985–9	−2.12	−2.11	−2.18	−5.55*	−3.30*	−3.02*
	1990–4	−1.42	−1.44	−1.11	−5.27*	−3.39*	−3.20*
Deposit rate	Full	−1.96	−1.21	−0.98	−9.56*	−9.31*	−5.11*
	1975–9	−1.79	−1.02	−0.77	−8.35*	−8.12*	−4.42*
	1980–4	−2.22	−1.27	−0.94	−5.28*	−5.41*	−2.96*
	1985–9	−0.23	−2.46	−2.14	−4.19*	−3.01*	−2.52
	1990–4	−1.14	−1.49	−1.28	−2.90	−2.83	−2.24
Loan rate	Full	−1.59	−1.09	−1.09	−8.25*	−7.45*	−4.21*
	1975–9	1.15	1.32	1.27	−2.43	−1.55	−0.81
	1980–4	−1.97	−1.25	−1.22	−4.87*	−4.47*	−2.23
	1985–9	−4.22*	−3.19*	−3.11*	−5.09*	−2.47	−2.29
	1990–4	−1.26	−1.53	−1.33	−2.97*	−3.01*	−2.26

Table A5.3.8. *Interest rate unit root test statistics, Taiwan, 1980–94*

Interest rate	Period	Levels			First differences		
		ADF(1)	ADF(4)	ADF(6)	ADF(1)	ADF(4)	ADF(6)
Money rate	Full	−2.86	−2.13	−2.44	−11.78*	−7.75*	−6.91*
	1980–4	−0.73	−0.54	−0.71	−6.19*	−4.57*	−3.15*
	1985–9	−2.79	−1.93	−2.37	−7.32*	−4.24*	−3.55*
	1990–4	−3.65*	−2.10	−2.49	−7.31*	−3.95*	−4.54*
Deposit rate	Full	−	−	−	−	−	−
	1980–4	−0.12	−0.56	−1.02	−4.05*	−2.05	−1.62
	1985–9	−0.79	−0.94	−1.00	−5.33*	−3.16*	−2.61
	1990–4	−1.04	−0.98	−0.93	−4.52*	−3.16*	−4.34*
Loan rate	Full	−	−	−	−	−	−
	1980–4	−0.27	−0.76	−1.17	−3.62*	−2.11	−1.84
	1985–9	−0.62	−0.74	−0.78	−5.36*	−3.31*	−2.75
	1990–4	−2.08	−1.97	−1.93	−2.84	−2.65	−2.71

Table A5.3.9. *Interest rate unit root test statistics, Thailand, 1980–94*

Interest rate	Period	Levels			First differences		
		ADF(1)	ADF(4)	ADF(6)	ADF(1)	ADF(4)	ADF(6)
Money rate	Full	−2.90*	−1.99	−1.97	−12.04*	−7.36*	−7.14*
	1980–4	−2.73	−1.73	−1.40	−4.63*	−3.92*	−3.07*
	1985–9	−1.81	−1.08	−1.04	−5.07*	−3.69*	−3.35*
	1990–4	−2.31	−1.23	−1.56	−7.94*	−4.02*	−3.23*
Deposit rate	Full	−1.99	−2.28	−2.72	−8.92*	−5.43*	−4.01*
	1980–4	−8.12*	−7.75*	−8.16*	−5.57*	−2.98*	−2.85
	1985–9	−1.83	−1.79	−1.86	−3.29*	−3.47*	−2.45
	1990–4	−1.32	−1.45	−1.93	−4.68*	−2.71	−1.79
Loan rate	Full	−1.78	−2.27	−2.07	−5.14*	−3.67*	−2.40
	1980–4	−	−	−	−	−	−
	1985–9	−3.17*	−5.31*	−2.62	−4.15*	−2.29	−1.37
	1990–4	−0.86	−1.02	−1.43	−3.43*	−2.62	−1.87

Table A5.3.10. *Interest rate unit root test statistics, Canada, 1975–94*

Interest rate	Period	Levels			First differences		
		ADF(1)	ADF(4)	ADF(6)	ADF(1)	ADF(4)	ADF(6)
Money rate	Full	−2.64	−1.95	−1.72	−12.93*	−9.71*	−7.10*
	1975–9	−0.85	−0.36	−0.58	−7.33*	−2.81	−2.33
	1980–4	−2.24	−1.54	−1.39	−6.64*	−5.26*	−3.72*
	1985–9	−1.79	−1.25	−0.97	−6.31*	−4.65*	−3.67*
	1990–4	−1.06	−1.05	−0.97	−5.08*	−3.80*	−3.01*
Deposit rate	Full	−1.83	−2.03	−2.12	−9.41*	−6.57*	−6.11*
	1975–9	−0.35	−0.49	−0.05	−5.13*	−1.89	−1.33
	1980–4	−1.26	−1.46	−1.43	−4.11*	−3.28*	−3.48*
	1985–9	−0.81	−0.26	−0.65	−6.70*	−4.02*	−3.01*
	1990–4	−1.17	−1.15	−1.08	−4.85*	−3.77*	−2.71
Loan rate	Full	−1.82	−1.78	−1.76	−9.18*	−6.92*	−6.28*
	1975–9	−0.76	−0.57	−0.33	−4.62*	−2.08	−1.72
	1980–4	−1.43	−1.39	−1.31	−4.09*	−3.52*	−3.65*
	1985–9	−0.93	−0.66	−0.64	−5.77*	−3.86*	−2.78
	1990–4	−1.30	−1.22	−1.21	−5.74*	−3.31*	−2.34

Table A5.3.11. *Interest rate unit root test statistics, the United States, 1975–94*

Interest rate	Period	Levels			First differences		
		ADF(1)	ADF(4)	ADF(6)	ADF(1)	ADF(4)	ADF(6)
Money rate	Full	−2.50	−1.54	−1.32	−11.14*	−7.94*	−7.64*
	1975–9	−2.06	−2.02	−2.00	−4.36*	−2.82	−1.93
	1980–4	−2.58	−1.43	−1.16	−5.89*	−4.27*	−4.30*
	1985–9	−1.26	−1.18	−1.47	−5.97*	−3.69*	−3.39*
	1990–4	−1.85	−1.63	−1.58	−2.76	−2.52	−1.12
Deposit rate	Full	−3.00*	−2.58	−2.42	−6.72*	−4.34*	−4.41*
	1975–9	−	−	−	−	−	−
	1980–4	−2.14	−2.72	−3.14*	−2.97*	−1.65	−2.91
	1985–9	−1.56	−1.45	−1.60	−5.36*	−3.42*	−2.74
	1990–4	−1.66	−1.56	−1.52	−3.30*	−1.59	−0.54
Loan rate	Full	−2.58	−1.57	−1.26	−10.27*	−7.10*	−6.10*
	1975–9	−0.19	−1.04	−1.47	−5.26*	−3.94*	−2.23
	1980–4	−2.41	−1.31	−0.93	−5.37*	−3.64*	−3.16*
	1985–9	−1.33	−1.32	−1.60	−4.45*	−3.00*	−2.40
	1990–4	−1.85	−1.88	−1.87	−3.69*	−2.35	−1.12

Appendix 5.4 Error-correction model of institutional interest rates

The error-correction model is estimated using Microfit 386. Standard errors are Newey–West corrected using a Parzen window of six lags when significant serial correlation or heteroscedasticity are reported. The original specification is six lags in the ADL (that is, five lags in the ECM). When the fifth lag in the ECM is significant, additional lags are added to ascertain that a longer lag specification is unnecessary.

Dynamic lags are generally eliminated only if they are singly and jointly statistically insignificant: see the 'restriction' Lagrange multiplier statistic. However, in some cases dynamic lags are eliminated if they are 'wrongly' signed or have no economic significance – for example, if two consecutive lag coefficients are both significant and of similar absolute value but of opposite sign. The modelling process also involves obtaining economically meaningful results. The resulting adjustment coefficients and cointegration vectors do not appear to be significantly affected by such eliminations, even though the joint hypothesis that the eliminated coefficients are zero is rejected.

As discussed in the text, there is a tendency for residuals to be non-normally distributed. The primary causes of non-normality are sharp movements in institutional rates, particularly in regulated regimes. In general, dummies are not included in the regression equation at these times, even though their inclusion tends to render the distribution process normal and make the residuals homoscedastic. While this increases the error in the equations and biases the parameter estimates, the effect does not appear to be generally significant. Dummies are included only when there is a series break, as for Japanese deposit rates (table A5).

The serial correlation is the Lagrange multiplier test using 12 lags; the functional form test is the Ramsey reset test using squares of the fitted value; the normality test is the Bera–Jarque test based on the skewness and kurtosis of the residuals; the heteroscedaticity test is the Ramsey reset test regressing the squared residuals on the squared fitted values of the regression (see Maddala 1989). The figures in parentheses following the diagnostic statistics are the marginal significance of the statistic.

Table A5.4.1. Australia, 1981M12–1994M12

A Deposit-rate error-correction model

	1981M12–1994M11		1981M12–1984M12	1985M1–1989M12	1990M1–1994M12
Constant	0.04 (0.10)	—	1.08 (0.59)	−0.24 (0.44)	0.08 (0.06)
Deposit rate $(t-1)$	−0.20* (0.04)	—	−0.29* (0.08)	−0.15* (0.05)	−0.51* (0.10)
Bill rate $(t-1)$	0.17* (0.03)	—	0.18* (0.03)	0.15* (0.15)	0.45* (0.09)
ΔBill rate (t)	0.24* (0.07)	—	0.18* (0.03)	—	0.35* (0.08)
$\bar{R}^2$	0.396	—	0.856	0.159	0.688
Standard error	0.414	—	0.271	0.478	0.197
Restriction	$\chi^2(10) = 11.1\ (0.35)$	—	$\chi^2(10) = 13.7\ (0.19)$	$\chi^2(11) = 11.8\ (0.38)$	$\chi^2(10) = 8.3\ (0.60)$
Serial correlation	$\chi^2(12) = 14.3\ (0.28)$	—	$\chi^2(12) = 17.1\ (0.15)$	$\chi^2(12) = 13.4\ (0.34)$	$\chi^2(12) = 13.9\ (0.31)$
Functional form	$\chi^2(1) = 41.1^*\ (0.00)$	—	$\chi^2(1) = 0.4\ (0.54)$	$\chi^2(1) = 7.0^*\ (0.01)$	$\chi^2(1) = 7.0^*\ (0.01)$
Normality	$\chi^2(2) = 236^*\ (0.00)$	—	$\chi^2(2) = 3.5\ (0.17)$	$\chi^2(2) = 10.5^*\ (0.01)$	$\chi^2(2) = 1.4\ (0.50)$
Heteroscedasticity	$\chi^2(1) = 43.3^*\ (0.00)$	—	$\chi^2(1) = 0.3\ (0.59)$	$\chi^2(1) = 1.4\ (0.23)$	$\chi^2(1) = 3.1\ (0.08)$

B Loan-rate error-correction model

	1978M12–1994M11		1980M1–1984M12	1985M1–1989M12	1990M1–1994M12
Constant	0.334 (0.16)	—	0.83 (0.50)	0.84* (0.35)	2.62* (0.35)
Loan rate $(t-1)$	−0.10* (0.03)	—	−0.17* (0.06)	−0.45* (0.06)	−0.56* (0.09)
Bill rate $(t-1)$	0.09* (0.05)	—	0.12* (0.04)	0.46* (0.04)	0.49* (0.08)
ΔBill rate (t)	0.17* (0.05)	—	0.09* (0.04)	0.40* (0.05)	—
ΔBill rate $(t-1)$	0.24* (0.03)	—	0.19* (0.05)	—	—
$\bar{R}^2$	0.333	—	0.544	0.839	0.549
Standard error	0.366	—	0.424	0.237	0.262
Restriction	$\chi^2(9) = 20.9^*\ (0.01)$	—	$\chi^2(9) = 21.5^*\ (0.00)$	$\chi^2(10) = 15.5\ (0.11)$	$\chi^2(11) = 11.4\ (0.41)$
Serial correlation	$\chi^2(12) = 20.2\ (0.06)$	—	$\chi^2(12) = 17.8\ (0.12)$	$\chi^2(12) = 6.1\ (0.91)$	$\chi^2(12) = 9.4\ (0.67)$
Functional form	$\chi^2(1) = 0.6\ (0.43)$	—	$\chi^2(1) = 1.5\ (0.23)$	$\chi^2(1) = 0.3\ (0.57)$	$\chi^2(1) = 0.0\ (0.35)$
Normality	$\chi^2(2) = 46.5^*\ (0.00)$	—	$\chi^2(2) = 0.9\ (0.65)$	$\chi^2(2) = 1.5\ (0.48)$	$\chi^2(2) = 0.2\ (0.91)$
Heteroscedasticity	$\chi^2(1) = 10^*\ (0.00)$	—	$\chi^2(1) = 0.9\ (0.34)$	$\chi^2(1) = 5.5^*\ (0.02)$	$\chi^2(1) = 8.0^*\ (0.01)$

Note:
In all tables: * = statistical significance at the 5 per cent level.
— = not available.

Table A5.4.2. *Hong Kong, 1985M1–1994M2*

A Deposit-rate error-correction model

	1985M1–1989M12	1990M1–1994M12
Constant	−0.21 (0.19)	0.08 (0.09)
Deposit rate $(t-1)$	−0.21* (0.08)	−0.23* (0.07)
Interbank rate $(t-1)$	0.17* (0.07)	0.21* (0.06)
ΔInterbank rate (t)	0.30* (0.06)	0.47* (0.08)
ΔInterbank rate $(t-1)$	0.25* (0.07)	—
$\bar{R}^2$	0.567	0.515
Standard error	0.340	0.267
Restriction	$\chi^2(9) = 13.4\ (0.14)$	$\chi^2(10) = 3.9\ (0.27)$
Serial correlation	$\chi^2(12) = 19.2\ (0.08)$	$\chi^2(12) = 6.7\ (0.88)$
Functional form	$\chi^2(1) = 2.1\ (0.15)$	$\chi^2(1) = 1.4\ (0.23)$
Normality	$\chi^2(2) = 6.5^*\ (0.04)$;	$\chi^2(2) = 14.3^*\ (0.00)$
Heteroscedasticity	$\chi^2(1) = 0.3\ (0.57)$	$\chi^2(1) = 8.8^*\ (0.00)$

B Loan-rate error-correction model

	1985M1–1989M12	1990M1–1994M12
Constant	0.77* (0.27)	0.71* (0.25)
Loan rate $(t-1)$	−0.45* (0.08)	−0.20* (0.07)
Interbank rate $(t-1)$	0.40* (0.07)	0.17* (0.06)
ΔInterbank rate (t)	0.41* (0.07)	0.44* (0.08)
$\bar{R}^2$	0.500	0.510
Standard error	0.426	0.256
Restriction	$\chi^2(10) = 10.8\ (0.37)$;	$\chi^2(10) = 4.7\ (0.91)$
Serial correlation	$\chi^2(12) = 8.7\ (0.73)$	$\chi^2(12) = 8.8\ (0.72)$
Functional form	$\chi^2(1) = 1.3\ (0.26)$	$\chi^2(1) = 0.3\ (0.58)$
Normality	$\chi^2(2) = 16.1^*\ (0.00)$	$\chi^2(2) = 20.1^*\ (0.00)$
Heteroscedasticity	$\chi^2(1) = 1.9\ (0.16)$	$\chi^2(1) = 13.8^*\ (0.00)$

Table A5.4.3. *Indonesia, 1986M5–1994M7*

A Deposit-rate error-correction model

	1986M5–1989M7	1986M5–1989M12	1990M1–1994M7
Constant	0.06 (0.17)	−0.66 (0.37)	−0.30 (0.22)
Deposit rate $(t-1)$	−0.03* (0.01)	−0.03 (0.02)	−0.05* (0.01)
Interbank rate $(t-1)$	0.05* (0.02)	0.03* (0.01)	0.10* (0.02)
ΔInterbank rate (t)	0.06* (0.02)	—	0.10* (0.03)
ΔInterbank rate $(t-1)$	0.04 (0.02)	—	—
ΔInterbank rate $(t-2)$	0.01 (0.02)	—	—
ΔInterbank rate $(t-3)$	0.04* (0.02)	—	—
ΔInterbank rate $(t-4)$	0.04* (0.01)	—	—
ΔInterbank rate $(t-5)$	0.04* (0.01)	—	—
ΔDep rate $(t-1)$	—	0.54* (0.13)	—
ΔDep rate $(t-2)$	0.32* (0.08)	—	0.41* (0.12)
ΔDep rate $(t-3)$	0.27* (0.09)	—	—
$\bar{R}^2$	0.779	0.503	0.727
Standard error	0.210	0.163	0.281
Restriction	$\chi^2(3) = 6.3$ (0.10)	$\chi^2(10) = 14.6$ (0.15)	$\chi^2(9) = 28.3$* (0.00)
Serial correlation	$\chi^2(12) = 18.0$ (0.12)	$\chi^2(12) = 13.3$ (0.35)	$\chi^2(12) = 17.3$ (0.14)
Functional form	$\chi^2(1) = 19.6$* (0.00)	$\chi^2(1) = 2.4$ (0.12)	$\chi^2(1) = 8.8$* (0.00)
Normality	$\chi^2(2) = 16.1$* (0.00)	$\chi^2(2) = 4.8$ (0.09)	$\chi^2(2) = 17.2$* (0.00)
Heteroscedasticity	$\chi^2(1) = 36.4$* (0.00)	$\chi^2(1) = 0.2$ (0.67)	$\chi^2(1) = 7.3$* (0.01)

B Loan-rate error-correction model

	1986M5–1989M7	1986M5–1989M12	1990M1–1994M7
Constant	0.57 (0.42)	—	0.52 (0.49)
Loan rate $(t-1)$	−0.08* (0.03)	—	−0.10* (0.03)
Interbankl rate $(t-1)$	0.10* (0.02)	—	0.12* (0.02)
$\bar{R}^2$	0.138		0.175
Standard error	0.738	$F(13,24) = 1.13$ (0.38)	0.890
Restriction	$\chi^2(11) = 24$* (0.01)	—	$\chi^2(11) = 35$* (0.00)
Serial correlation	$\chi^2(12) = 30$* (0.00)	—	$\chi^2(12) = 28$* (0.00)
Functional form	$\chi^2(1) = 0.40$ (0.53)	—	$\chi^2(1) = 0.9$ (0.35)
Normality	$\chi^2(2) = 851$* (0.00)	—	$\chi^2(2) = 255$* (0.00)
Heteroscedasticity	$\chi^2(1) = 0.6$ (0.43)	—	$\chi^2(1) = 0.2$ (0.67)

Table A5.4.4. Japan, 1975M12–1994M10

A Deposit-rate error-correction model

	1975M12–1994M10	1975M1–1979M12	1980M1–1984M12	1985M1–1989M12	1990M1–1994M10
Constant	0.02 (0.03)	0.08 (0.10)	0.63* (0.16)	−0.02 (0.01)	−0.30* (0.16)
Deposit rate ($t-1$)	−0.10* (0.03)	−0.24* (0.06)	−0.63* (0.15)	—	−0.47* (0.09)
Interbank rate ($t-1$)	0.06* (0.01)	0.13* (0.03)	0.27* (0.07)	0.12* (0.04)	0.28* (0.06)
ΔInterbank rate (t)	0.24* (0.06)	0.30* (0.07)	—	0.19* (0.06)	0.49* (0.07)
ΔInterbank rate($t-1$)	0.13* (0.04)	—	—	—	—
D92M6	1.39* (0.02)	—	—	—	1.41* (0.14)
D92M7–94M10	—	—	—	—	0.46* (0.13)
$\bar{R}^2$	0.512	0.310	0.453	0.516	0.812
Standard error	0.164	0.204	0.189	0.425	0.124
Restriction	$\chi^2(9) = 14.2\ (.12)$	$\chi^2(10) = 13.5\ (0.20)$	$\chi^2(11) = 27.0\ (0.00)$	$\chi^2(9) = 11\ (0.27)$	$\chi^2(10) = 10.1\ (0.44)$
Serial correlation	$\chi^2(12) = 15.3\ (.23)$	$\chi^2(12) = 8.8\ (0.72)$	$\chi^2(12) = 15.7\ (0.21)$	$\chi^2(12) = 16.5\ (0.17)$	$\chi^2(12) = 17.9\ (0.12)$
Functional form	$\chi^2(1) = 0.3\ (.57)$	$\chi^2(1) = 5.4^*\ (0.02)$	$\chi^2(1) = 0.3\ (0.57)$	$\chi^2(1) = 16.1^*\ (0.00)$	$\chi^2(1) = 0.6\ (0.44)$
Normality	$\chi^2(2) = 199^*\ (.00)$	$\chi^2(2) = 17^*\ (0.00)$	$\chi^2(2) = 28^*\ (0.00)$	$\chi^2(2) = 8.9^*\ (0.01)$	$\chi^2(2) = 31.9^*\ (0.00)$
Heteroscedasticity	$\chi^2(1) = 3.4\ (.06)$	$\chi^2(1) = 27^*\ (0.00)$	$\chi^2(1) = 19^*\ (0.00)$	$\chi^2(1) = 17.9^*\ (0.00)$	$\chi^2(1) = 0.0\ (0.80)$

B Loan-rate error-correction model

	1975M12–1994M10	1975M1–1979M12	1980M1–1984M12	1985M1–1989M12	1990M1–1994M10
Constant	0.14* (0.06)	0.03 (0.04)	0.81* (0.37)	0.33 (0.190)	0.79* (0.09)
Loan rate (-1)	−0.07* (0.03)	—	−0.34* (0.14)	−0.30 (0.15)	−0.69* (0.06)
Interbank rate ($t-1$)	0.04* (0.02)	—	0.19* (0.08)	0.19 (0.10)	0.60* (0.05)
ΔInterbank rate (t)	0.42* (0.07)	0.25* (0.10)	0.55* (0.12)	0.34* (0.15)	0.71* (0.04)
$\bar{R}^2$	0.283	0.097	0.547	0.271	0.821
Standard error	0.260	0.320	0.232	0.198	0.134
Restriction	$\chi^2(10) = 13.6\ (0.19)$	$\chi^2(12) = 17.9\ (0.12)$	$\chi^2(10) = 22.9^*\ (0.02)$	$\chi^2(10) = 7.8\ (0.65)$	$\chi^2(10) = 4.8^*\ (0.91)$
Serial correlation	$\chi^2(12) = 15.5\ (0.22)$	$\chi^2(12) = 13.6\ (0.33)$	$\chi^2(12) = 15.7\ (0.21)$	$\chi^2(12) = 10.9\ (0.54)$	$\chi^2(12) = 7.1\ (0.85)$
Functional form	$\chi^2(1) = 1.95\ (0.16)$	$\chi^2(1) = 1.2\ (0.27)$	$\chi^2(1) = 5.9^*\ (0.02)$	$\chi^2(1) = 3.2\ (0.08)$	$\chi^2(1) = 0.0\ (0.98)$
Normality	$\chi^2(2) = 541^*\ (0.00)$	$\chi^2(2) = 40.8^*\ (0.00)$	$\chi^2(2) = 8.1^*\ (0.02)$	$\chi^2(2) = 981^*\ (0.00)$	$\chi^2(2) = 1.5\ (0.48)$
Heteroscedasticity	$\chi^2(1) = 30.8^*\ (0.00)$	$\chi^2(1) = 2.72\ (0.10)$	$\chi^2(1) = 32.3\ (0.00)$	$\chi^2(1) = 21.1\ (0.00)$	$\chi^2(1) = 0.1\ (0.71)$

Table A5.4.5. *Malaysia, 1981M12–1994M10*

A Deposit-rate error-correction model

	1981M12–1994M10	1975M1–1979M12	1981M12–1984M12	1985M1–1989M12	1990M1–1994M10
Constant	−0.10 (0.9)	—	0.78 (0.53)	0.06 (0.14)	−0.34* (0.19)
Deposit rate ($t-1$)	−0.14* (0.06)	—	−0.37* (0.08)	−0.18* (0.05)	−0.48* (0.06)
Interbank rate ($t-1$)	0.14* (0.07)	—	0.28* (0.06)	0.14* (0.05)	0.50* (0.07)
ΔInterbank rate (t)	0.19* (0.08)	—	—	—	0.53* (0.11)
ΔInterbank rate ($t-1$)	0.16* (0.05)	—	—	—	—
$\bar{R}^2$	0.311	F (13,28) = 1.68 (0.12)	0.316	0.164	0.663
Standard error	0.331		0.367	0.043	0.143
Restriction	$\chi^2(9) = 12.7$ (0.18)		$\chi^2(11) = 8.2$ (0.70)	$\chi^2(11) = 17.3$ (0.10)	$\chi^2(10) = 12.8$ (0.24)
Serial correlation	$\chi^2(12) = 19.6$ (0.08)		$\chi^2(12) = 7.6$ (0.81)	$\chi^2(12) = 6.2$ (0.90)	$\chi^2(12) = 8.0$ (0.79)
Functional form	$\chi^2(1) = 39^*$ (0.00)		$\chi^2(1) = 0.3$ (0.57)	$\chi^2(1) = 0.3$ (0.60)	$\chi^2(1) = 10.3^*$ (0.00)
Normality	$\chi^2(2) = 155^*$ (0.00)		$\chi^2(2) = 23.3^*$ (0.00)	$\chi^2(2) = 12.1^*$ (0.00)	$\chi^2(2) = 6.7^*$ (0.03)
Heteroscedasticity	$\chi^2(1) = 36^*$ (0.00)		$\chi^2(1) = 0.02$ (0.90)	$\chi^2(1) = 15.5$ (0.06)	$\chi^2(1) = 6.0^*$ (0.01)

B Loan-rate error-correction model

	1981M12–1994M10	1975M1–1979M12	1981M12–1984M12	1985M1–1989M12	1990M1–1994M10
Constant	0.27 (0.18)	—	—	0.51* (0.21)	0.47 (0.27)
Loan rate (−1)	−0.08* (0.03)	—	—	−0.11* (0.03)	−0.17* (0.05)
Interbankl rate ($t-1$)	0.06* (0.02)	—	—	0.06* (0.02)	0.13* (0.04)
ΔInterbank rate ($t-1$)	0.14* (0.05)	—	—	—	—
$\bar{R}^2$	0.080	F (13,28) = 1.21 (0.32)	F (13,28) = 0.43 (0.95)	0.063	0.168
Standard error	0.397			0.371	0.248
Restriction	$\chi^2(10) = 7.1$ (0.72)			$\chi^2(11) = 17.2$ (0.10)	$\chi^2(8) = 28^*$ (0.00)
Serial correlation	$\chi^2(12) = 11.3$ (0.50)			$\chi^2(12) = 19.8$ (0.07)	$\chi^2(12) = 23.8^*$ (0.02)
Functional form	$\chi^2(1) = 0.8$ (0.37)			$\chi^2(1) = 4.1^*$ (0.04)	$\chi^2(1) = 8.3^*$ (0.00)
Normality	$\chi^2(2) = 8301^*$ (0.00)			$\chi^2(2) = 77^*$ (0.00)	$\chi^2(2) = 35^*$ (0.00)
Heteroscedasticity	$\chi^2(1) = 0.1^*$ (0.76)			$\chi^2(1) = 1.6$ (0.20)	$\chi^2(1) = 2.2$ (0.14)

Table A5.4.6. *The Philippines, 1981M10–1994M10*

A Deposit-rate error-correction model

	1981M10–1994M10	1975M1–1979M12	1981M10–1984M12	1985M1–1989M12	1990M1–1994M10
Constant	0.59* (0.29)	—	2.42* (0.41)	1.42* (0.42)	−0.77* (0.30)
Deposit rate ($t-1$)	−0.18* (0.05)	—	−0.49* (0.08)	−0.54* (0.09)	−0.45* (0.05)
TB rate ($t-1$)	0.11* (0.04)	—	0.30* (0.07)	0.31* (0.07)	0.41* (0.05)
ΔTB rate (t)	0.25* (0.05)	—	0.35* (0.11	0.21* (0.06)	0.23* (0.05)
ΔTB rate ($t-1$)	0.18* (0.06)	—			
ΔTB rate ($t-3$)	0.12* (0.06)	—			
$\bar{R}^2$	0.417	Perfect linearity	0.548	0.492	0.644
Standard error	1.066	no regression	0.013	1.118	0.590
Restriction	$\chi^2(8) = 18.4^*$ (0.02)	—	$\chi^2(10) = 26^*$ (0.00)	$\chi^2(11) = 12.9$ (0.23)	$\chi^2(10) = 10.0$ (0.44)
Serial correlation	$\chi^2(12) = 17.7$ (0.13)	—	$\chi^2(12) = 22.9^*$ (0.03)	$\chi^2(12) = 13.1$ (0.37)	$\chi^2(12) = 13.7$ (0.32)
Functional form	$\chi^2(1) = 0.0$ (0.93)	—	$\chi^2(1) = 0.3$ (0.58)	$\chi^2(1) = 0.2$ (0.67)	$\chi^2(1) = 1.6$ (0.21)
Normality	$\chi^2(2) = 6.7^*$ (0.04)	—	$\chi^2(2) = 4.6$ (0.10)	$\chi^2(2) = 2.2$ (0.34)	$\chi^2(2) = 3.0$ (0.23)
Heteroscedasticity	$\chi^2(1) = 15.7^*$ (0.00)	—	$\chi^2(1) = 17.4^*$ (0.00)	$\chi^2(1) = 0.1$ (0.74)	$\chi^2(1) = 0.4$ (0.52)

B Loan-rate error-correction model

	1981M6–1994M10	1975M1–1979M12	1981M6–1984M12	1985M1–1989M12	1990M1–1994M10
Constant	1.48* (0.40)	—	1.43* (0.71)	2.52* (0.38)	2.30* (0.74)
Loan rate (−1)	−0.25* (0.07)	—	0.23* (0.08)	−0.63* (0.05)	−0.54* (0.10)
TB rate ($t-1$)	0.20* (0.06)	—	0.23* (0.05)	0.52* (0.05)	0.46* (0.09)
ΔTB rate (t)	0.19* (0.09)	—		0.15* (0.05)	0.49* (0.08)
ΔTB rate ($t-1$)	0.27* (0.09)	—			
$\bar{R}^2$	0.468	$F (13,28) = 1.5$ (0.18)	0.328	0.709	0.564
Standard error	0.980	—	1.127	0.894	1.021
Restriction	$\chi^2(10) = 17.1^*$ (0.05)	—	$\chi^2(11) = 17.3$ (0.10)	$\chi^2(10) = 11.7$ (0.31)	$\chi^2(8) = 20.7^*$ (0.22)
Serial correlation	$\chi^2(12) = 28^*$ (0.01)	—	$\chi^2(12) = 22.4^*$ (0.03)	$\chi^2(12) = 7.4$ (0.83)	$\chi^2(12) = 15.4$ (0.02)
Functional form	$\chi^2(1) = 0.7$ (0.40)	—	$\chi^2(1) = 0.3$ (0.56)	$\chi^2(1) = 5.0^*$ (0.03)	$\chi^2(1) = 4.3^*$ (0.04)
Normality	$\chi^2(2) = 55.6^*$ (0.00)	—	$\chi^2(2) = 23.4^*$ (0.00)	$\chi^2(2) = 2.1$ (0.34)	$\chi^2(2) = 0.03$ (0.99)
Heteroscedasticity	$\chi^2(1) = 1.0$ (0.32)	—	$\chi^2(1) = 1.2$ (0.27)	$\chi^2(1) = 1.1$ (0.30)	$\chi^2(1) = 2.4$ (0.12)

Table A5.4.7. Singapore, 1977M1–1994M12

A Deposit-rate error-correction model

	1977M1–1994M9	1977M1–1979M12	1980M1–1984M12	1985M1–1989M12	1990M1–1994M12
Constant	−0.11* (0.05)	—	−0.17 (0.18)	−0.14 (0.09)	0.12 (0.07)
Deposit rate $(t-1)$	−0.14* (0.04)	—	−0.60* (0.13)	−0.11* (0.22)	−0.21* (0.03)
Interbank rate $(t-1)$	0.14* (0.03)	—	0.55* (0.12)	0.10* (0.03)	0.15* (0.02)
ΔInterbank rate (t)	0.33* (0.09)	—	0.44* (0.09)	0.11* (0.04)	0.10 (0.05)
ΔInterbank rate $(t-1)$	0.22* (0.04)	—			
$\bar{R}^2$	0.570	$F_{(13,16)} = 1.31$ (0.30)	0.743	0.519	0.526
Standard error	0.287		0.395	0.097	0.145
Restriction	$\chi^2(9) = 24.4^*$ (.00)		$\chi^2(10) = 13.2$ (0.21)	$\chi^2(10) = 16.3$ (0.09)	$\chi^2(10) = 13.6$ (0.17)
Serial correlation	$\chi^2(12) = 30^*$ (.00)		$\chi^2(12) = 11.9$ (0.46)	$\chi^2(12) = 15.1$ (0.24)	$\chi^2(12) = 6.3$ (0.90)
Functional form	$\chi^2(1) = 38.6^*$ (.00)		$\chi^2(1) = 23.3^*$ (0.00)	$\chi^2(1) = 29.8^*$ (0.00)	$\chi^2(1) = 4.7^*$ (0.03)
Normality	$\chi^2(2) = 3132^*$ (.00)		$\chi^2(2) = 12.5^*$ (0.00)	$\chi^2(2) = 11^*$ (0.00)	$\chi^2(2) = 15^*$ (0.00)
Heteroscedasticity	$\chi^2(1) = 75.5^*$ (.00)		$\chi^2(1) = 24.6^*$ (0.00)	$\chi^2(1) = 13.4^*$ (0.00)	$\chi^2(1) = 12^*$ (0.00)

B Loan-rate error-correction model

	1977M1–1994M9	1977M1–1979M12	1980M1–1984M12â	1985M1–1989M12	1990M1–1994M12
Constant	0.13 (0.08)	—	0.81* (0.20)	0.45* (0.17)	0.68* (0.14)
Loan rate (-1)	−0.07* (0.02)	—	−0.36* (0.04)	−0.12* (0.03)	−0.18* (0.03)
Interbank rate $(t-1)$	0.07* (0.02)	—	0.35* (0.03)	0.07* (0.02)	0.12* (0.02)
ΔInterbank rate (t)	0.25* (0.05)	—	0.32* (0.03)	0.09* (0.05)	
ΔInterbank rate $(t-1)$	0.17* (0.03)				
ΔInterbank rate $(t-2)$	0.07* (0.02)				
ΔInterbank rate $(t-3)$	0.07 (0.04)				
ΔInterbank rate $(t-4)$	0.06* (0.03)				
$\bar{R}^2$	0.645	$F_{(13,4)} = 1.5$ (0.36)	0.831	0.299	0.471
Standard error	0.202		0.228	0.154	0.133
Restriction	$\chi^2(6) = 18.3^*$ (0.01)		$\chi^2(10) = 27.2^*$ (0.00)	$\chi^2(10) = 17.2$ (0.07)	$\chi^2(11) = 15.3$ (0.17)
Serial correlation	$\chi^2(12) = 30.1^*$ (0.00)		$\chi^2(12) = 16.5$ (0.17)	$\chi^2(12) = 19.1$ (0.09)	$\chi^2(12) = 8.7$ (0.73)
Functional form	$\chi^2(1) = 3.0$ (0.08)		$\chi^2(1) = 1.2$ (0.27)	$\chi^2(1) = 8.1^*$ (0.00)	$\chi^2(1) = 3.5$ (0.06)
Normality	$\chi^2(2) = 92^*$ (0.00)		$\chi^2(2) = 0.4$ (0.82)	$\chi^2(2) = 760^*$ (0.00)	$\chi^2(2) = 17.2^*$ (0.00)
Heteroscedasticity	$\chi^2(1) = 16.4^*$ (0.00)		$\chi^2(1) = 0.1$ (0.73)	$\chi^2(1) = 9.8^*$ (0.00)	$\chi^2(1) = 0.6$ (0.45)

Table A5.4.8. *Taiwan, 1975M1–1994M12*

A Deposit-rate error-correction model

	1975M1–1979M12	1980M4–1984M12	1985M1–1989M12	1990M1–1994M12
Constant	—	0.43* (0.18)	−0.01 (0.12)	0.22 (0.11)
Deposit rate $(t-1)$	—	−0.19* (0.05)	−0.16* (0.07)	−0.08* (0.03)
Interbank rate $(t-1)$	—	0.11* (0.03)	0.17* (0.06)	0.04* (0.02)
ΔInterbank rate (t)	—	0.10* (0.03)	0.31* (0.11)	0.05* (0.01)
ΔInterbank rate $(t-1)$	—	—	—	0.04* (0.02)
$\bar{R}^2$	—	0.256	0.527	0.449
Standard error	—	0.262	0.361	0.120
Restriction	—	$\chi^2(10)=14.6$ (0.15)	$\chi^2(10)=12.6$ (0.25)	$\chi^2(9)=10.5$ (0.31)
Serial correlation	—	$\chi^2(12)=20.1$ (0.07)	$\chi^2(12)=24^*$ (0.02)	$\chi^2(12)=8.9$ (0.71)
Functional form	—	$\chi^2(1)=0.7$ (0.40)	$\chi^2(1)=40^*$ (0.00)	$\chi^2(1)=0.5$ (0.49)
Normality	—	$\chi^2(2)=41^*$ (0.00)	$\chi^2(2)=111^*$ (0.00)	$\chi^2(2)=79^*$ (0.00)
Heteroscedasticity	—	$\chi^2(1)=2.8$ (0.09)	$\chi^2(1)=56$ (0.00)	$\chi^2(1)=4.1^*$ (0.04)

B Loan-rate error-correction model

	1975M1–1979M12	1980M4–1984M12	1985M1–1989M12	1990M1–1994M12
Constant	—	1.00* (0.25)	0.57 (0.45)	−0.02 (0.01)
Loan rate (-1)	—	−0.23* (0.05)	−0.11 (0.07)	—
Interbank rate $(t-1)$	—	0.19* (0.05)	0.09* (0.04)	—
ΔInterbank rate (t)	—	0.17* (0.06)	0.23 (0.10)	0.05* (0.02)
ΔLoan rate $(t-2)$	—	—	—	0.52* (0.12)
$\bar{R}^2$	—	0.214	0.508	0.220
Standard error	—	0.392	0.279	0.119
Restriction	—	$\chi^2(10)=15.8$ (0.10)	$\chi^2(10)=15.6$ (0.11)	—
Serial correlation	—	$\chi^2(12)=19.9$ (0.07)	$\chi^2(12)=22^*$ (0.04)	$\chi^2(12)=5.7$ (0.93)
Functional form	—	$\chi^2(1)=0.1$ (0.81)	$\chi^2(1)=50.8^*$ (0.00)	$\chi^2(1)=4.6^*$ (0.03)
Normality	—	$\chi^2(2)=5.6$ (0.06)	$\chi^2(2)=301^*$ (0.00)	$\chi^2(2)=770^*$ (0.00)
Heteroscedasticity	—	$\chi^2(1)=4.1^*$ (0.04)	$\chi^2(1)=59.6^*$ (0.00)	$\chi^2(1)=2.8$ (0.12)

Table A5.4.9. *Thailand, 1975M6–1994M9*

A Deposit-rate error-correction model

	1975M6–1994M9	1975M6–1979M12	1980M1–1984M12	1985M1–1989M12	1990M1–1994M9
Constant	0.05 (0.16)	—	—	0.74* (0.36)	0.52 (0.31)
Deposit rate $(t-1)$	−0.047 (0.025)	—	—	−0.21* (0.10)	−0.21* (0.05)
Interbank rate $(t-1)$	0.035* (0.012)	—	—	0.11* (0.05)	0.18* (0.04)
$\bar{R}^2$	0.055	Perfect linearity	$F_{(13,46)} = 2.7$ (0.01)	0.179	0.216
Standard error	0.484	no regression	but not sensible	0.351	0.722
Restriction	$\chi^2(11) = 20.7^*$ (0.04)	—	—	$\chi^2(11) = 16.8$ (0.14)	$\chi^2(11) = 12.7$ (0.31)
Serial correlation	$\chi^2(12) = 17.2$ (0.45)	—	—	$\chi^2(12) = 5.2$ (0.95)	$\chi^2(12) = 17.9$ (0.11)
Functional form	$\chi^2(1) = 8.7^*$ (0.00)	—	—	$\chi^2(1) = 3.0^*$ (0.08)	$\chi^2(1) = 3.4$ (0.06)
Normality χ^2	$\chi^2(2) = 2218^*$ (0.00)	—	—	$\chi^2(2) = 249$ (0.00)	$\chi^2(2) = 24.0^*$ (0.00)
Heteroscedasticity	$\chi^2(1) = 29.1^*$ (0.00)	—	—	$\chi^2(1) = 9.4$ (0.00)	$\chi^2(1) = 9.1^*$ (0.00)

B Loan-rate error-correction model

	1975M6–1979M12	1980M1–1984M12	1985M1–1989M12	1990M1–1994M12
Constant	—	6.39* (3.03)	0.90* (0.35)	0.76* (0.25)
Loan rate (-1)	—	−0.39* (0.17)	−0.12* (0.04)	−0.13* (0.03)
Interbank rate $(t-1)$	—	0.06* (0.03)	0.06* (0.02)	0.10* (0.01)
$\bar{R}^2$	Perfect linearity	0.361	0.273	0.317
Standard error	no regression	0.393	0.287	0.329
Restriction	—	$\chi^2(11) = 12.7$ (.32)	$\chi^2(11) = 16.2$ (0.13)	$\chi^2(11) = 16.4$ (0.13)
Serial correlation	—	$\chi^2(12) = 8.8$ (.72)	$\chi^2(12) = 10.4$ (0.58)	$\chi^2(12) = 7.7$ (0.81)
Functional form	—	$\chi^2(1) = 27.7^*$ (.00)	$\chi^2(1) = 1.2$ (0.27)	$\chi^2(1) = 0.2$ (0.68)
Normality	—	$\chi^2(2) = 79.0^*$ (.00)	$\chi^2(2) = 161^*$ (0.00)	$\chi^2(2) = 7^*$ (0.03)
Heteroscedasticity	—	$\chi^2(1) = 47.7^*$ (.00)	$\chi^2(1) = 12.3^*$ (0.00)	$\chi^2(1) = 5.4^*$ (0.02)

Table A5.4.10. *Canada, 1975M1–1994M9*

A Deposit-rate error-correction model

	1975M1–1994M9	1975M1–1979M12	1980M1–1984M12	1985M1–1989M12	1990M1–1994M9
Constant	0.003 (0.49)	0.10 (0.5)	−0.06 (0.16)	0.06 (0.80)	0.54* (0.22)
Deposit rate $(t-1)$	—	—	—	−0.46* (0.17)	−1.01* (0.15)
Interbank rate $(t-1)$	—	—	—	0.44* (0.21)	0.94* (0.15)
ΔInterbank rate (t)	0.23* (0.05)	0.23* (0.07)	0.20* (0.07)	0.62* (0.12)	0.83* (0.15)
$\bar{R}^2$	0.123	0.371	0.118	0.225	0.477
Standard error	0.878	0.387	1.219	0.840	0.589
Restriction	$\chi^2(12) = 31.2^*$ (0.00)	$\chi^2(12) = 6.44$ (0.89)	$\chi^2(12) = 9.4$ (0.67)	$\chi^2(10) = 29.8^*$ (0.00)	$\chi^2(11) = 12.4$ (0.26)
Serial correlation	$\chi^2(12) = 26.7^*$ (0.00)	$\chi^2(12) = 10.5$ (0.58)	$\chi^2(12) = 8.3$ (0.76)	$\chi^2(12) = 32.4^*$ (0.00)	$\chi^2(12) = 4.6$ (0.97)
Functional form	$\chi^2(1) = 2.6$ (0.11)	$\chi^2(1) = 1.0$ (0.31)	$\chi^2(1) = 2.4$ (0.13)	$\chi^2(1) = 0.4$ (0.53)	$\chi^2(1) = 9.8^*$ (0.00)
Normality	$\chi^2(2) = 32.9^*$ (0.00)	$\chi^2(2) = 2.2$ (0.34)	$\chi^2(2) = 4.7$ (0.09)	$\chi^2(2) = 3.2$ (0.20)	$\chi^2(2) = 11.3^*$ (0.00)
Heteroscedasticity	$\chi^2(1) = 10.3^*$ (0.00)	$\chi^2(1) = 16.3^*$ (0.00)	$\chi^2(1) = 2.4$ (0.12)	$\chi^2(1) = 1.2$ (0.27)	$\chi^2(1) = 1.0$ (0.32)

B Loan-rate error-correction model

	1975M1–1994M9	1975M1–1979M12	1980M1–1984M12	1985M1–1989M12	1990M1–1994M9
Constant	−0.02 (0.04)	0.10 (0.06)	−0.05 (0.14)	0.60 (0.38)	0.87* (0.25)
Loan rate (-1)	—	—	—	−0.28* (0.09)	−0.59* (0.12)
Interbank rate $(t-1)$	—	—	—	0.26* (0.08)	0.56* (0.12)
ΔInterbank rate $(t-1)$	0.20* (0.04)	0.11* (0.05)	0.19* (0.06)	0.44* (0.06)	0.57* (0.11)
$\bar{R}^2$	0.175	0.122	0.170	0.440	0.412
Standard error	0.613	0.357	0.941	0.e344	0.481
Restriction	$\chi^2(6) = 18.6$ (0.10)	$\chi^2(12) = 11.4$ (0.49)	$\chi^2(12) = 11.4$ (0.53)	$\chi^2(10) = 12.3$ (0.27)	$\chi^2(10) = 13.9$ (0.18)
Serial correlation	$\chi^2(12) = 13.4$ (0.34)	$\chi^2(12) = 12.5$ (0.41)	$\chi^2(12) = 9.9$ (0.63)	$\chi^2(12) = 13.8$ (0.32)	$\chi^2(12) = 14$ (0.30)
Functional form	$\chi^2(1) = 8.2^*$ (0.01)	$\chi^2(1) = 7.6^*$ (0.01)	$\chi^2(1) = 4.5^*$ (0.03)	$\chi^2(1) = 3.6$ (0.06)	$\chi^2(1) = 1.1$ (0.30)
Normality	$\chi^2(2) = 358^*$ (0.00)	$\chi^2(2) = 10.0^*$ (0.01)	$\chi^2(2) = 16.5^*$ (0.00)	$\chi^2(2) = 1.7$ (0.43)	$\chi^2(2) = 4.9$ (0.09)
Heteroscedasticity	$\chi^2(1) = 26.2^*$ (0.00)	$\chi^2(1) = 8.2^*$ (0.00)	$\chi^2(1) = 6.0^*$ (0.02)	$\chi^2(1) = 0.2$ (0.65)	$\chi^2(1) = 2.3$ (0.13)

Table A5.4.11. *The United States, 1982M10–1994M9*

A Deposit-rate error-correction model

	1982M10–194M9		1982M10–1984M12	1985M1–1989M12	1990M1–1994M9
Constant	0.11 (0.06)	—	−0.14 (0.38)	0.10 (0.21)	0.12 (0.07)
Deposit rate ($t-1$)	−0.45* (0.07)	—	−0.71* (0.17)	−0.33* (0.09)	−0.36* (0.12)
Interbank rate ($t-1$)	0.44* (0.07)	—	0.70* (0.17)	0.31* (0.09)	0.35* (0.12)
ΔInterbank rate (t)	0.94* (0.05)	—	0.94* (0.10)	0.96* (0.16)	0.91* (0.10)
$\bar{R}^2$	0.712	—	0.768	0.589	0.602
Standard error	0.255	—	0.398	0.228	0.152
Restriction	$\chi^2(10) = 20.1^*\ (0.03)$	—	$\chi^2(10) = 17.8\ (0.06)$	$\chi^2(10) = 6.7\ (0.76)$	$\chi^2(10) = 15.2\ (0.12)$
Serial correlation	$\chi^2(12) = 13.4\ (0.34)$	—	$\chi^2(12) = 12.7\ (0.39)$	$\chi^2(12) = 6.2\ (0.91)$	$\chi^2(12) = 12.3\ (0.43)$
Functional form	$\chi^2(1) = 0.0\ (0.99)$	—	$\chi^2(1) = 0.5\ (0.47)$	$\chi^2(1) = 7.8^*\ (0.01)$	$\chi^2(1) = 0.2\ (0.63)$
Normality	$\chi^2(2) = 90^*\ (0.00)$	—	$\chi^2(2) = 6.2^*\ (0.05)$	$\chi^2(2) = 6.8^*\ (0.03)$	$\chi^2(2) = 7.4^*\ (0.02)$
Heteroscedasticity	$\chi^2(1) = 2.8^*\ (0.10)$	—	$\chi^2(1) = 0.0\ (0.99)$	$\chi^2(1) = 5.7\ (0.02)$	$\chi^2(1) = 0.1\ (0.79)$

B Loan-rate error-correction model

	1975M10–194M10	1975M1–1979M12	1980M1–1984M12	1985M1–1989M12	1990M1–1994M10
Constant	0.67* (0.17)	0.02 (0.02)	0.67* (0.28)	0.52* (0.26)	0.55* (0.20)
Loan rate (-1)	−0.35* (0.08)	—	−0.61* (0.09)	−0.44* (0.10)	−0.15* (0.06)
Interbank rate ($t-1$)	0.35* (0.09)	0.47* (0.06)	0.66* (0.10)	0.47* (0.11)	0.13* (0.05)
ΔInterbank rate (t)	0.58* (0.05)	0.65* (0.02)	0.55* (0.04)	0.55* (0.10)	0.78* (0.15)
ΔInterbank rate ($t-1$)	—	—	—	—	—
$\bar{R}^2$	0.740	0.876	0.888	0.471	0.633
Standard error	0.346	0.142	0.411	0.217	0.128
Restriction	$\chi^2(10) = 101^*\ (0.00)$	$\chi^2(11) = 15.5\ (0.16)$	$\chi^2(10) = 9.6\ (0.48)$	$\chi^2(10) = 9.7\ (0.47)$	$\chi^2(10) = 17.4\ (0.07)$
Serial correlation	$\chi^2(12) = 96^*\ (0.00)$	$\chi^2(12) = 19.9\ (0.07)$	$\chi^2(12) = 10\ (0.623)$	$\chi^2(12) = 13.9\ (0.31)$	$\chi^2(12) = 25.3^*\ (0.01)$
Functional form	$\chi^2(1) = 15.3^*\ (0.00)$	$\chi^2(1) = 0.47\ (0.49)$	$\chi^2(1) = 5.1^*\ (0.02)$	$\chi^2(1) = 1.0\ (0.32)$	$\chi^2(1) = 1.6\ (0.21)$
Normality	$\chi^2(2) = 416^*\ (0.00)$	$\chi^2(2) = 8.2^*\ (0.02)$	$\chi^2(2) = 4.6\ (0.10)$	$\chi^2(2) = 9.4^*\ (0.01)$	$\chi^2(2) = 11.3\ (0.00)$
Heteroscedasticity	$\chi^2(1) = 43.8^*\ (0.00)$	$\chi^2(1) = 0.2\ (0.67)$	$\chi^2(1) = 12^*\ (0.00)$	$\chi^2(1) = 8.6^*\ (0.00)$	$\chi^2(1) = 8.3^*\ (0.00)$

Appendix 5.5 Speed of adjustment

The error-correction model of the institutional interest rate is

$$\Delta i_t = \mu - \beta_1 i_{t-1} + \beta_2 m_{t-1} - \sum_{j=1}^{n-1} \pi_j \Delta i_{t-j} + \sum_{j=1}^{n-1} \theta_j \Delta m_{t-j}. \tag{A5.5.1}$$

which is (5.14) in the text. In all cases apart from the Indonesian deposit rate, lags of the dependent variable are not statistically significant. In the remaining cases, apart from the Australian loan rate from 1980M1 to 1984M12, the parsimonious regression includes at most only the error-correction term and the contemporaneous change in the money market rate. In the case of the Australian loan rate from 1980M1 to 1984M12, the first lag of the change in the money market rate is also statistically significant. Short-run dynamics are fast and speed up the adjustment to equilibrium as they eliminate the disequilibrium that exists between the money and institutional rate.

The parsimonious equation is

$$\Delta i_t = \mu - \beta_1(i_{t-1} - \beta m_{t-1}) + \theta_0 \Delta m_t + \theta_1 \Delta m_{t-1} \tag{A5.5.2}$$

where

$$\beta = \left(\frac{\beta_2}{\beta_1}\right)$$

Assuming that the series have been demeaned and that the money market rate rises by one percentage point, the cumulative adjustment after n-periods, $n \geq 2$ is

$$\gamma + (1 - \gamma) \sum_{j=2}^{n} \beta_1(1 - \beta_1)^{j-2} \tag{A5.5.3}$$

where $\gamma = \left(\frac{\beta_1}{\beta_2}\right)(\beta_2 + \theta_0(1 - \beta_1) + \theta_1)$.

Note that γ sums the adjustment that occurs in the contemporaneous and first period. When the dynamics terms are statistically insignificant, the error-correction alone drives the changes in the institutional rate and (A5.5.3) reduces to

$$\sum_{j=1}^{n} \beta_1(1 - \beta_1)^{j-1}. \tag{A5.5.4}$$

Appendix 6.1 Derivation of the consumption equation

There are two countries with a represenative infinitely lived consumer in each country. The real exchange rate, z, is defined as the relative price of the foreign good, $z_t = p^*/p$, so a rise in z is a depreciation of the real exchange rate. The budget constraint evolves as

$$\dot{b}_t = z_t^{1-\beta} c_t + r_t b_t - y_t \qquad (A6.1.1)$$

where b is the *per capita* stock of foreign liabilities, r is the real interest rate and y is income in terms of the home good. Total consumption, c, is determined by the representative household maximising its utility over an infinite horizon,

$$u = \int_t^\infty u(c(s)) e^{-\theta(s-t)} dt \qquad (A6.1.2)$$

subject to foreign debt accumulation, (A6.1.1), with y defined as returns to factors, $rqk + w$,

$$\dot{b}_t = z_t^{1-\beta} c_t + r_t b_t - r_t q_t k_t - w_t \qquad (A6.1.3)$$

where q is the price of capital relative to the home good. Defining and maximising the present-value Hamiltonian,

$$\max_c H = \ln c_t + \lambda [r_t b_t + z_t^{1-\beta} c_t - r_t q_t k_t - w_t], \qquad (A6.1.4)$$

with respect to consumption, yields the first order conditions,

$$\lambda = -c^{-1} z^{\beta-1}$$

$$\dot{\lambda} = (\theta - r)\lambda \qquad (A6.1.5)$$

Re-arranging and substitution yields the evolution rule for consumption,

$$\dot{c} = (r - \theta)c, \qquad (A6.1.6)$$

which implies that $r = \theta$ in the steady state. Equation (A6.1.6) can be written as

$$\dot{c} e^{-r(s-t)} = (r - \theta) c e^{-r(s-t)}. \qquad (A6.1.7)$$

Since

$$\frac{d[c_s e^{-r(s-t)}]}{ds} = \dot{c}_s e^{-r(s-t)} - r c_s e^{-r(s-t)},$$

(A6.1.7) can be rewritten and then integrated to yield

$$\int_t^\infty \frac{d[c_s e^{-r(s-t)}]}{ds} ds = -\theta \int_t^\infty c_s e^{-r(s-t)} ds. \qquad (A6.1.8)$$

The budget constraint in (A6.1.3) can be rewritten as

$$be^{-r(s-t)} = rbe^{-r(s-t)} + cz^{1-\beta}e^{-r(s-t)} - rqke^{-r(s-t)} - we^{-r(s-t)}.$$ (A6.1.9)

This can be simplified and integrated as

$$\int_t^\infty \frac{d[b_s e^{-r(s-t)}]}{ds} ds = \int_t^\infty z_s^{1-\beta} c_s e^{-r(s-t)} ds - \int_t^\infty r_s q_s k_s e^{-r(s-t)} ds$$

$$- \int_t^\infty w_s e^{-r(s-t)} ds.$$ (A6.1.10)

Evaluating (A6.1.10) yields

$$-b_t = \int_t^\infty z_s^{1-\beta} c_s e^{-r(s-t)} ds - \int_t^\infty r_s q_s k_s e^{-r(s-t)} ds - \int_t^\infty w_s e^{-r(s-t)} ds.$$ (A6.1.11)

In the steady state, the interest rate, the relative price of capital, the capital stock and human wealth are determined variables. Human wealth,

$$W_t = \int_t^\infty w_s e^{-r(s-t)} ds,$$

evolves as

$$\dot{W} = r_t W_t - w_t.$$ (A6.1.12)

Linear homogeneity in the production functions implies that $w = f(k) - f'(k)k$, and so steady-state human wealth is a simple function of the capital stock,

$$W = \frac{(1-\alpha)k^\alpha}{r}.$$ (A6.1.13)

Human wealth is an increasing function of the physical capital stock since wages are increasing in capital ($\frac{\partial w}{\partial k} = -f''(k)k > 0$). Evaluating (A6.1.11) for steady-state wealth yields

$$-b_t = \int_t^\infty z_s^{1-\beta} c_s e^{-r(s-t)} ds - qk - \frac{(1-\alpha)k^\alpha}{r}.$$ (A6.1.14)

Substituting (A6.1.14) into (A6.1.8) yields,

$$\int_t^\infty \frac{d[c_s e^{-r(s-t)}]}{ds} ds = -\theta z_t^{\beta-1}(q_t k_t + W_t - b_t).$$ (A6.1.15)

Evaluating (A6.1.15), yields the solution,

$$c_t = \theta z_t^{\beta-1}(q_t k_t + W_t - b_t),$$ (A6.1.16)

which is (6.12) in the text.

Appendix 7.1 Definitions, sources and graphs of consumption and its determinants

Australia (figures A7.1.1–A7.1.3)

Consumption: non-durables expenditure and total private expenditure 1990 constant prices, Australian Bureau of Statistics (ABS).

Income: household disposable income, ABS, deflated by the total private expenditure deflator.

Deposit rate: three-month fixed deposit rate at June, 1960–90, Reserve Bank of Australia, *Australian Economic Statistics*, and from 1991, RBA, *Bulletin*.

Loan rate: maximum overdraft rate at June, 1960–85, Reserve Bank of Australia, *Australian Economic Statistics*, from 1991, small and medium-sized business rate, RBA, *Bulletin*.

Money market rate: 26-week T-note rate at June, 1960–90, Reserve Bank of Australia, *Australian Economic Statistics*, from 1991, RBA, *Bulletin*.

Inflation: deflator(t)/deflator$(t-1)-1$ from the total private expenditure deflator.

Population statistics: RBA, *Australian Economic Statistics*, table 4.2 and ABS.

Money: currency and deposits with banks (M3), RBA, *Bulletin*.

Credit: consumer credit, other personal credit adjusted for breaks, unpublished series, Reserve Bank of Australia from 1976; before 1976 calendar years are backcast with financial year growth in housing credit, Reserve Bank of Australia, *Australian Economic Statistics*.

Residential property prices: established house prices in Australian capital cities, index 1989/90 = 100, Reserve Bank of Australia unofficial series comprising Treasury unpublished series from 1960 to June 1978, REIA series from September 1978 to June 1986 and ABS official series from September 1986 onwards.

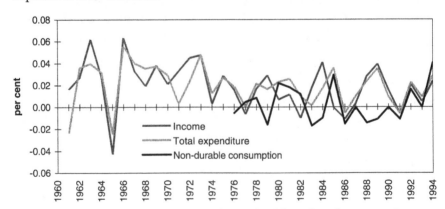

Fig. A7.1.1. Australia, income and non-durable and total consumption, 1960–1994

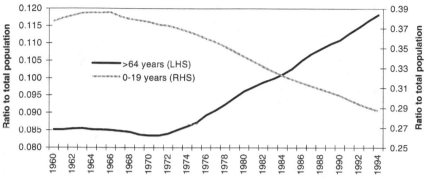

Fig. A7.1.2. Australia, demographic transition, 1960–1994

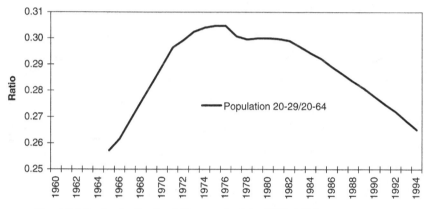

Fig. A7.1.3. Australia, liquidity constraints, 1960–1994

Hong Kong (figures A7.1.4–A7.1.5)

Consumption: non-durables expenditure and total private consumption expenditure 1990 constant prices, provided courtesy of the Hong Kong Monetary Authority.

Income: gross domestic product, World Bank Tables, IEDB Database, ANU.

Deposit rate: annual average six-month deposit rate 1970–93, Asian Development Bank (ADB), *Key Indicators*.

Loan rate: commercial bill rate 1970–93, ADB, *Key Indicators*.

Inflation: deflator(t)/deflator($t-1$) -1 from the total private expenditure deflator.

Population statistics: total population and dependancy ratio, World Bank Tables, IEDB Database, ANU; proportion aged 64 and over estimated from Keyfitz and Flieger (1990).

Money: currency and deposits with banks (M2 + NCDs), ABD, *Key Indicators*.

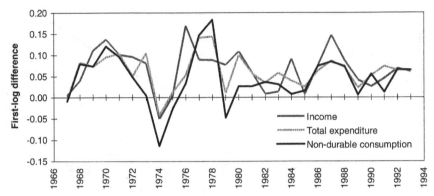

Fig. A7.1.4. Hong Kong, income and non-durable and total consumption, 1966–1994

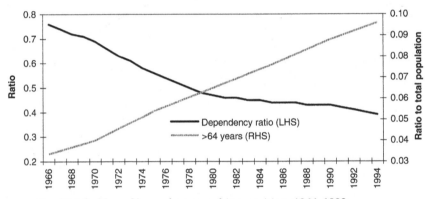

Fig. A7.1.5. Hong Kong, demographic transition, 1966–1993

Japan (figures A7.1.6–A7.1.8)

Consumption: non-durables expenditure and total private expenditure 1985 constant prices, Nikkei database.

Income: household disposable income, Nikkei database, deflated by the total private expenditure deflator

Deposit rate: annual average three-month fixed deposit rate, IMF, *International Financial Statistics*.

Loan rate: annual average loan rate, IMF, *International Financial Statistics*.

Money market rate: annual average collateralised overnight call money rate, IMF, *International Financial Statistics*.

Inflation: deflator(t)/deflator($t-1$) -1 from the total private expenditure deflator.

Population statistics: Nikei database.

Money: M2 + CDs, IMF, *International Financial Statistics*.

Credit: consumer credit from city and regional banks and mutual loan and saving institutions, Nikei database.

Residential property prices: residential property prices in Japan, Datastream database.

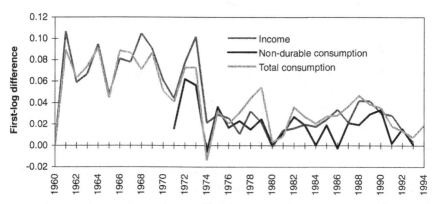

Fig. A7.1.6. Japan, income and non-durable and total consumption, 1960–1994

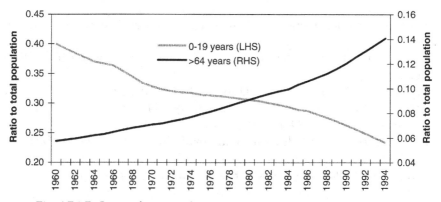

Fig. A7.1.7. Japan, demographic transition, 1960–1994

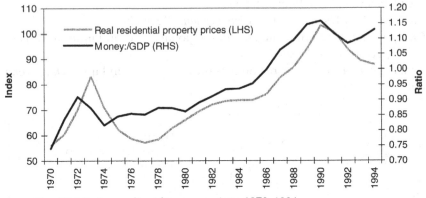

Fig. A7.1.8. Japan, liquidity constraints, 1970–1994

Korea (figures A7.1.9–A7.1.11)

Consumption: non-durables expenditure and total private expenditure 1990 constant prices, Bank of Korea, *Annual Statistical Bulletin*.

Income: national factor income, Bank of Korea, *Annual Statistical Bulletin*, deflated by the total private expenditure deflator.

Deposit rate: annual average one-year deposit rate, IMF, *International Financial Statistics*.

Loan rate: annual average curb loan rate, unpublished series, Bank of Korea.

Inflation: deflator(t)/deflator($t-1$) -1 from the total private expenditure deflator.

Population statistics: total population and dependency ratio, World Bank Tables, IEDB Database, ANU; proportion aged 64 and over estimated from Keyfitz and Flieger (1990).

Money: currency and deposits with banks. IMF, *International Financial Statistics*.

Credit: household loans, Bank of Korea, *Annual Statistical Bulletin*.

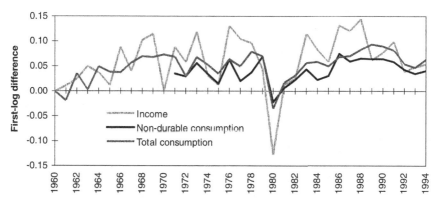

Fig. A7.1.9. Korea, income and non-durable and total consumption, 1960–1994

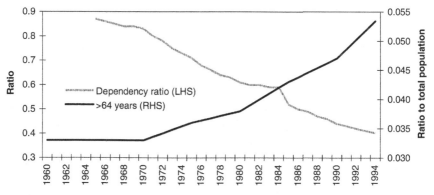

Fig. A7.1.10. Korea, demographic transition, 1960–1994

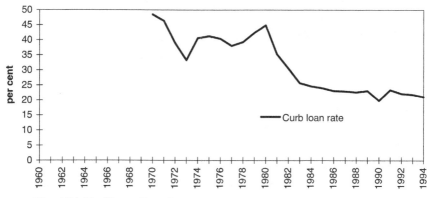

Fig. A7.1.11. Korea, liquidity constraints, 1960–1994

Singapore (figures A7.1.12–A7.1.14)

Consumption: non-durables expenditure and total private expenditure 1985 constant prices, Department of Statistics, Singapore.

Income: gross domestic product, Department of Statistics, Singapore, deflated by the total private expenditure deflator.

Deposit rate: annual average six-month fixed deposit rate, *Singapore Yearbook of Statistics* and ADB, *Key Indicators*.

Loan rate: annual average indicator lending rate, *Singapore Yearbook of Statistics* and IMF, *International Financial Statistics*.

Money market rate: annual average three-month interbank market rate, *Singapore Yearbook of Statistics* and IMF, *International Financial Statistics*.

Inflation: deflator(t)/deflator($t-1$) -1 from the total private expenditure deflator.

Population statistics: total population, World Bank Tables, IEDB Database, ANU; age classifications, *Singapore Annual Statistics*.

Money: currency and deposits with banks, IMF, *International Financial Statistics*.

Credit: end-year loans to professional and private individuals. Monetary Authority of Singapore, *Statistical Bulletin*.

Residential property prices: spliced index of average annual residential property prices 1975–93, *Singapore Yearbook of Statistics* and *Monthly Digest of Statistics Singapore*, and index of accommodation costs from the CPI 1970–4, *Singapore Yearbook of Statistics*.

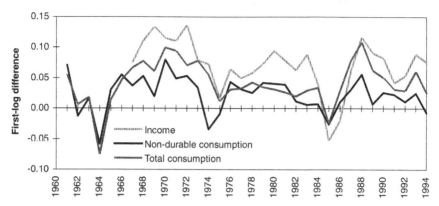

Fig. A7.1.12. Singapore, income and non-durable and total consumption, 1960–1994

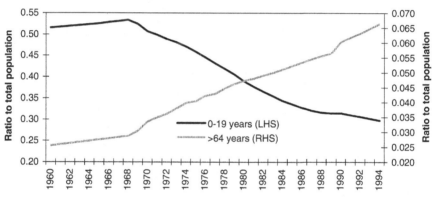

Fig. A7.1.13. Singapore, demographic transition, 1960–1994

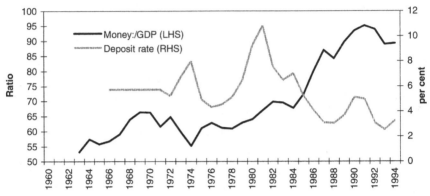

Fig. A7.1.14. Singapore, liquidity constraints, 1960–1994

Taiwan (figures A7.1.15–A7.1.17)

Consumption: non-durables expenditure and total private expenditure 1991 constant prices, *Statistical Yearbook of the Republic of China*.

Income: factor income, *Statistical Yearbook of the Republic of China*, deflated by the total private expenditure deflator.

Deposit rate: end-year three-month fixed deposit rate, *Taiwan Statistical Data Book*.

Loan rate: end-year secured loan rate, *Taiwan Statistical Data Book*.

Inflation: deflator(t)/deflator$(t-1)-1$ from the total private expenditure deflator.

Population statistics: *Taiwan Statistical Data Book*, adjusted for break in 1969.

Money: currency and deposits with banks, IMF, *International Financial Statistics*.

Credit: end-year loans and discounts of all banks to individuals and others, *Taiwan Statistical Data Book*.

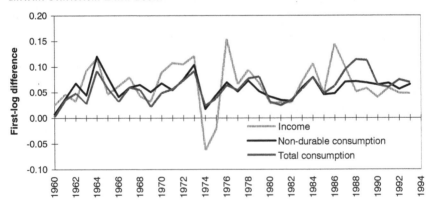

Fig. A7.1.15. Taiwan, income and non-durable and total consumption, 1960–1994

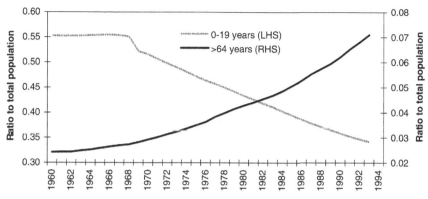

Fig. A7.1.16. Taiwan, demographic transition, 1960–1994

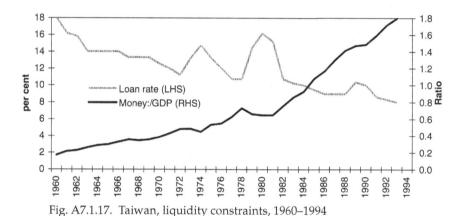

Fig. A7.1.17. Taiwan, liquidity constraints, 1960–1994

Thailand (figures A7.1.18–A7.1.20)

Consumption: non-durables expenditure and total private expenditure 1988 constant prices, *Statistical Yearbook Thailand*, ADB, *Key Indicators* and United Nations, *National Accounts*.

Income: personal disposable income, *Statistical Yearbook Thailand*, deflated by the total private expenditure deflator.

Deposit rate: annual average three- to six-month fixed deposit rate, Bank of Thailand, *Monthly Statistical Bulletin* and ADB, *Key Indicators*.

Loan rate: annual average maximum lending rate, Bank of Thailand, *Monthly Statistical Bulletin* and ADB, *Key Indicators*.

Money market rate: annual average weighted interbank market rate, Bank of Thailand, *Monthly Statistical Bulletin*.

Inflation: deflator(t)/deflator($t-1$) -1 from the total private expenditure deflator.

Population statistics: total population and dependency ratio, World Bank Tables, IEDB Database, ANU; proportion aged 64 and over estimated from Keyfitz and Flieger (1990).

Money: currency and deposits with banks, IMF, *International Financial Statistics*.

Credit: end-year loans for personal consumption, Bank of Thailand, *Monthly Statistical Bulletin*.

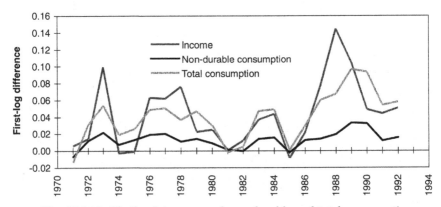

Fig. A7.1.18. Thailand, income and non-durable and total consumption, 1960–1994

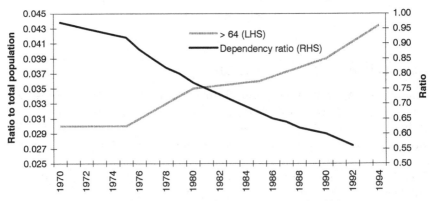

Fig. A7.1.19. Thailand, demographic transition, 1960–1994

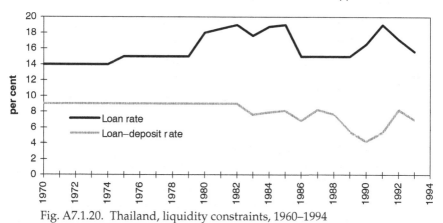

Fig. A7.1.20. Thailand, liquidity constraints, 1960–1994

Appendix 7.2 Estimating (7.10)

Table A7.2.1. *Australia, non-durable and total consumption growth, 1965–94*

	Non-dur (PFC def), constraint defined as income growth (1970–94) (1)	Non-dur and services, constraint defined as income growth (1975–94) (2)	Total consumption constraint defined as income growth (1965–94) (3)	Total consumption constraint defined as income growth (1965–94) (4)	Total consumption constraint defined as income growth (1965–94) (5)
Constant	1.61–1.52	0.012* (0.003)	−0.25 (0.17)	−0.01 (0.13)	−0.14 (0.18)
Log income (t−1)	0.14* (0.05)		0.44* (0.17)	0.19# (0.10)	0.38* (0.17)
Log consumption (t−1)	−0.37 (0.22)		−0.41* (0.15)	−0.18# (0.09)	−0.37* (0.16)
Inflation rate (t)			−0.30* (0.12)		−0.24# (0.13)
Age 20–29/age 20–64 (t)		0.32# (0.163)		−0.34# (0.19)	
Liquidity constraint (t)	0.55* (0.24)		0.43* (0.12)	0.56* (0.12)	0.41* (0.16)
Liquidity constraint (t)(70s)	0.38 (0.30)				0.66* (0.24)
Liquidity constraint (t)(80s)					
$\bar{R}^2$	0.186	0.198	0.511	0.480	0.563
Standard error	0.0151		0.0098	0.0100	0.092
Misspecification	$\chi^2(10)=4.2$ (0.939)	$\chi^2(4)=1.0$ (0.918)	$\chi^2(10)=15$ (0.120)	$\chi^2(11)=18$# (0.092)	$\chi^2(6)=2.7$ (0.841)
Serial correlation ($\chi^2(1)$)	1.10 (0.294)	1.98 (0.159)	2.05 (0.152)	0.09 (0.765)	0.26 (0.612)
Functional form ($\chi^2(1)$)	0.00 (0.968)	0.32 (0.574)	0.00 (0.999)	0.93 (0.335)	0.01 (0.915)
Normality ($\chi^2(2)$)	0.24 (0.886)	0.79 (0.674)	1.52 (0.469)	0.12 (0.943)	1.02 (0.600)
Heteroscedasticity ($\chi^2(1)$)	0.41 (0.520)	0.01 (0.904)	1.57 (0.219)	0.69 (0.405)	0.20 (0.658)

Notes:
Value in parenthesis after estimated coefficient is standard error, value in parenthesis after chi-square diagnostic statistic is marginal significance level. # = statistical significance at the 10 per cent level; * = statistical significance at the 5 per cent level.

Table A7.2.2. *Hong Kong, non-durable consumption growth*

	Constraint defined as loan rate (1)
Constant	1.16 (0.70)
Log income (t–1)	0.24# (0.12)
Log consumption (t–1)	-0.38# (0.19
Liquidity constraint (t)	-0.95* (0.43)
$\bar{R}^2$	0.234
Standard error	0.0534
Misspecification	$\chi^2(7) = 11.37$ (0.123)
Serial corrtelation ($\chi^2(1)$)	6.32 (0.012)
Functional form ($\chi^2(1)$)	0.36 (0.547)
Normality ($\chi^2(2)$)	1.02 (0.601)
Heteroscedasticity ($\chi^2(1)$)	0.00 (0.995)

Notes:
Value in parenthesis after estimated coefficient is standard error, value in parenthesis after chi-square diagnostic statistic is marginal significance level. # = statistical significance at the 10 per cent level; * = statistical significance at the 5 per cent level.

Table A7.2.3. *Japan, non-durable consumption growth*

	Constraint defined as income growth (1)	Constraint defined as money/GDP (2)	Constraint defined as real land prices (3)	Constraint defined as income growth (4)	Constraint defined as real land prices (5)
Constant	1.32* (0.25)	1.95* (0.31)	2.18* (0.26)	0.95* (0.32)	2.35* (0.29)
Log income $(t-1)$	0.32* (0.10)	0.16 (0.11)	0.32* (0.08)	0.37* (0.11)	0.39* (0.09)
Log consumption $(t-1)$	−0.60* (0.15)	−0.53* (0.16)	−0.76* (0.13)	−0.66* (0.18)	−0.86 (0.14)
Real deposit rate (t)	0.24* (0.07)	0.24* (0.08)	0.39* (0.07)	0.26* (0.08)	0.39* (0.07)
ddepend (t)	−5.18# (2.45)	−4.59# (2.59)	−3.04 (2.11)		
Liquidity constraint (t)	0.36* (0.15)	0.13* (0.05)	0.001* (0.0002)		
Liquidity constraint (t)(70s)				0.55* (0.13)	0.0010* (0.0002)
Liquidity constraint (t)(80s)				0.40# (0.20)	0.0011* (0.0002)
$\bar{R}^2$	0.762	0.716	0.829	0.660	0.803
Standard error	0.0074	0.0081	0.0062	0.0088	0.0067
Misspecification	$\chi^2(5) = 3.20$ (0.669)	$\chi^2(6) = 6.50$ (0.370)	$\chi^2(6) = 6.32$ (0.388)	$\chi^2(12) = 7.4$ (0.687)	$\chi^2(12) = 10$ (0.615)
Serial correlation $(\chi^2(1))$	0.51 (0.475)	0.04 (0.844)	0.17 (0.684)	0.84 (0.559)	0.10 (0.741)
Functional form $(\chi^2(1))$	0.00 (0.991)	0.22 (0.642)	0.02 (0.879)	0.71 (0.400)	0.35 (0.556)
Normality $(\chi^2(2))$	1.47 (0.479)	1.15 (0.563)	1.12 (0.572)	0.14 (0.934)	0.87 (0.647)
Heteroscedasticity $(\chi^2(1))$	0.10 (0.757)	2.97# (0.085)	0.73 (0.392)	1.03 (0.311)	0.92 (0.337)

Notes:
Value in parenthesis after estimated coefficient is standard error, value in parenthesis after chi-square diagnostic statistic is marginal significance level. # = statistical significance at the 10 per cent level; * = statistical significance at the 5 per cent level.

Table A7.2.4. Korea, non-durable consumption growth

	Constraint defined as income growth (1)	Constraint defined as loan rate (2)	Constraint defined as income growth (3)
Constant	0.52* (0.23)	1.13* (0.38)	0.49* (0.23)
Log income ($t-1$)	0.18* (0.06)	0.23* (0.09)	0.19* (0.06)
Log consumption ($t-1$)	−0.29* (0.11)	−0.43* ((0.16)	−0.29* (0.10)
Liquidity constraint (t)	0.20* (0.09)	−0.22* (0.08)	
Liquidity constraint (t)(70s)			0.39* (0.08)
Liquidity constraint (t)(80s)			0.35* (0.08)
$\bar{R}^2$	0.654	0.337	0.685
Standard error	0.0137	0.0189	0.0130
Misspecification	$\chi^2(5) = 1.20$ (0.945)	n/a	$\chi^2(6) = 8.34$ (0.214)
Serial correlation ($\chi^2(1)$)	0.59 (0.443)	0.78 (0.378)	0.50 (0.478)
Functional form ($\chi^2(1)$)	2.42 (0.120)	0.00 (0.953)	3.15# (0.076)
Normality ($\chi^2(2)$)	1.28 (0.526)	0.24 (0.889)	6.44* (0.040)
Heteroscedasticity ($\chi^2(1)$)	0.28 (0.594)	2.24 (0.134)	1.35 (0.245)

Notes:
Value in parenthesis after estimated coefficient is standard error, value in parenthesis after chi-square diagnostic statistic is marginal significance level. # = statistical significance at the 10 per cent level; * = statistical significance at the 5 per cent level.

Table A7.2.5. *Singapore, non-durable consumption growth*

	Liquidity constraint defined as income growth (1)	Liquidity constraint defined as money / GDP ratio (2)	Liquidity constraint defined as the deposit rate (3)	Liquidity constraint defined as income growth (4)
Constant	2.57* (0.71)	0.72 (0.89)	−0.20 (1.02)	2.15* (0.75)
Log income ($t-1$)	0.19* (0.06)	−0.04 (0.08)	−0.08 (0.08)	0.18* (0.06)
Log consumption ($t-1$)	−0.56* (0.16)	−0.05 (0.20)	0.13 (0.23)	−0.46* (0.17)
Real interest rate (t)	0.34* (0.08)	0.30* (0.12)	0.38* (0.13)	0.35* (0.09)
Liquidity constraint (t)	0.56* (0.09)	0.16* (0.07)		
Log constraint ($t-1$)			−0.74* (0.32)	
Liquidity constraint (t)(70s)				0.60* (0.17)
Liquidity constraint (t)(80s)				0.46* (0.10)
$\bar{R}^2$	0.723	0.465	0.388	0.716
Standard error	0.0140	0.0199	0.0204	0.0144
Misspecification	$\chi^2(5) = 4.46$ (0.486)	—	—	$\chi^2(10) = 9.94$ (0.446)
Serial correlation ($\chi^2(1)$)	0.42 (0.518)	1.01 (0.314)	1.45 (0.228)	0.31 (0.579)
Functional form ($\chi^2(1)$)	2.43 (0.119)	0.36 (0.549)	0.36 (0.547)	0.12 (0.725)
Normality ($\chi^2(2)$)	0.87 (0.646)	0.30 (0.860)	0.45 (0.798)	15.87* (0.000)
Heteroscedasticity ($\chi^2(1)$)	0.95 (0.329)	2.45 (0.115)	2.17 (0.140)	2.09 (.491)

Notes:
Value in parenthesis after estimated coefficient is standard error, value in parenthesis after chi-square diagnostic statistic is marginal significance level. # = statistical significance at the 10 per cent level; * = statistical significance at the 5 per cent level.

Table A7.2.6. *Taiwan, non-durable consumption growth*

	Liquidity constraint defined as income growth (1)	Liquidity constraint defined as money/GDP ratio (2)	Liquidity constraint defined as the deposit rate (3)	Liquidity constraint defined as income growth (4)
Constant	1.99* (0.51)	1.77* (0.58)	1.42* (0.43)	1.58* (0.45)
Log income ($t-1$)	0.27* (0.06)	0.22* (0.07)	0.19* (0.08)	0.28* (0.06)
Log consumption ($t-1$)	−0.49* (0.11)	−0.43* (0.13)	−0.34* (0.12)	−0.46* (0.11)
Δdependency ratio (t)	5.21* (1.45)		1.87 (1.42)	4.70* (1.57)
Loan-deposit rates (t)	−1.34* (0.55)			0.78* (0.38)
Liquidity constraint (t)	0.34* (0.08)	0.06* (0.03)	−0.80* (0.31)	
Liquidity constraint (t)(60s)				0.38* (0.14)
Liquidity constraint (t)(70s)				0.36* (0.06)
Liquidity constraint (t)(80s)				0.15 (0.10)
$\bar{R}^2$	0.625	0.350	0.390	0.653
Standard error	0.0145	0.0191	0.0185	0.0140
Misspecification	$\chi^2(8) = 6.46$ (0.596)	$\chi^2(9) = 8.09$ (0.525)	$\chi^2(11) = 17.20$ (0.102)	$\chi^2(22) = 16.22$ (0.805)
Serial correlation ($\chi^2(1)$)	1.33 (0.249)	0.00 (0.970)	0.67 (0.411)	1.56 (0.212)
Functional form ($\chi^2(1)$)	0.32 (0.572)	0.44 (0.508)	2.63 (0.105)	0.39 (0.533)
Normality ($\chi^2(2)$)	0.00 (1.000)	1.02 (0.599)	1.79 (0.409)	0.48 (0.785)
Heteroscedasticity ($\chi^2(1)$)	0.54 (0.462)	0.26 (0.609)	0.00 (0.980)	0.59 (0.320)

Notes:
Value in parenthesis after estimated coefficient is standard error, value in parenthesis after chi-square diagnostic statistic is marginal significance level. # = statistical significance at the 10 per cent level; * = statistical significance at the 5 per cent level.

Table A7.2.7. *Thailand, non-durable consumption growth*

	Liquidity constraint defined as current income growth (1)	Liquidity constraint defined as money/GDP ratio (2)	Liquidity constraint defined as loan rate (3)	Liquidity constraint defined as loan-deposit rate (4)	Liquidity constraint defined as current income growth (5)
Constant	1.94* (0.41)	0.38 (0.68)	1.17* (0.52)	0.09* (0.03)	1.99* (0.41)
Log income (t–1)	0.50* (0.09)	0.41* (0.12)	0.37* (0.12)		0.51* (0.09)
Log consumption (t–1)	–0.77* (0.14)	–0.52* (0.19)	–0.52* (0.19)		–0.78* (0.14)
ΔAge ratio (t)	14.92* (6.66)			—	16.00# (8.18)
Real interest rate (t)	0.15* (0.06)	0.31* (0.11)	0.16# (0.09		0.15* (8.18)
Liquidity constraint (t)	0.32* (0.06)	2.13* (0.029)	–0.62* (0.26)	–0.71* (0.34)	
Liquidity constraint (t)(70s)					0.30* (0.12)
Liquidity constraint (t)(80s)					0.30* (0.07)
$\bar{R}^2$	0.800	0.581	0.588	0.261	0.786
Standard error	0.0093	0.0136	0.0134	0.0180	0.0097
Misspecification	$\chi^2(7) = 7.94$ (0.338)	$\chi^2(7) = 8.19$ (0.899)	$\chi^2(7) = 11.3$ (0.126)	$\chi^2(6) = 9.03$ (0.172)	$\chi^2(10) = 12$ (0.259)
Serial correlation ($\chi^2(1)$)	2.29 (0.130)	0.02 (0.316)	0.00 (0.957)	1.21 (0.272)	2.59 (0.107)
Functional form ($\chi^2(1)$)	0.44 (0.507)	0.44 (0.505)	2.02 (0.155)	0.56 (0.454)	0.06 (0.811)
Normality ($\chi^2(2)$)	0.67 (0.716)	1.47 (0.479)	1.05 (0.593)	0.85 (0.654)	0.74 (0.691)
Heteroscedasticity ($\chi^2(1)$)	0.01 (0.927)	1.05 (0.306)	0.44 (0.507)	0.42 (0.517)	0.04 (0.834)

Notes:
Value in parenthesis after estimated coefficient is standard error, value in parenthesis after chi-square diagnostic statistic is marginal significance level. # = statistical significance at the 10 per cent level; * = statistical significance at the 5 per cent level.

References

Abidin, A.Z. (1986). 'Financial Reform and the Role of Foreign Banks in Malaysia', chapter 21 in H.S. Cheng (ed.) *Financial Policy and Reform in Pacific Basin Countries*, Lexington MA: Lexington Books

Ahn, S.I. (1994). 'Interest Rate Deregulation and Financial Policy in Developing Countries', Centre for Pacific Basin Monetary and Economic Studies, Economic Research Department, Federal Reserve Bank of San Francisco, Pacific Basin Working Paper, 94–07

Andersen, P.S. (1993). 'Economic Growth and Financial Markets: The Experience of Four Asian Tigers', chapter 4 in R. O'Brien (ed.), *Finance and the International Economy*, The Amex Review Prize Essays, vol. 7, Oxford: Oxford University Press, 67–91

Andersen, P.S. and D. Gruen (1995). 'Macroeconomic Policies and Growth', *Productivity and Growth*, Reserve Bank of Australia: 279–319

Argy, V. (1989). 'International Financial Deregulation – Some Macroeconomic Implications', Australian National University, Research School of Pacific and Asian Studies, Australia–Japan Research Centre, *Pacific Economic Paper*, 168

(1996). 'The Integration of World Capital Markets: Some Economic and Social Implications', *Economic Papers*, 15(2): 1–19

Arif, M., B.K. Kapur, and A. Tyabji (1995). 'Money Markets in Singapore', chapter 7 in D.C. Cole, H.S. Scott and P.A. Wellons (eds.), *Asian Money Markets*, New York: Oxford University Press: 349–87

Asia Pacific Economic Group (APEG) (1995). *Asia Pacific Profiles*, Canberra

Asian Development Bank (ADB) (1977) *Asian Development Outlook*, Oxford: Oxford University Press

Attanasio, O.P. and G. Weber (1989). 'Intertemporal Substitution, Risk Aversion and the Euler Equation for Consumption', *Economic Journal*, 99: 59–73

Attfield, C.L.F., D. Demery and N.W. Duck (1985). *Rational Expectations in Macroeconomics*, New York, Basil Blackwell

Bacchetta, P. (1992). 'Liberalization of Capital Movements and of the Domestic Financial System', *Economica*, 59: 465–74

Backus, D.K. and G.W. Smith (1993). 'Consumption and Real Exchange Rates in Dynamic Economies with Non-traded Goods', *Journal of International Economies*, 35: 297–316

Bailey, R.W., R.T. Baillie and P.C. McMahon (1984). 'Interpreting Economic Evidence on Efficiency in the Foreign Exchange Market', *Oxford Economic Papers*, 36: 67–85

Baldwin, R.E. (1992). 'Discussion on "International Finance and Economic Development"', chapter 2 in A. Giovannini (ed.), *Finance and Development: Issues and Experience,* Cambridge: Cambridge University Press: 24–6

Baltensperger, E. (1980). 'Alternative Approaches to the Theory of the Banking Firm', *Journal of Monetary Economics,* 6: 1–37

Bank of Japan (1994). 'Characteristics of Interest Rate Indicators', *Bank of Japan Quarterly Bulletin,* November: 35–61

Bannerjee, A., J. Dolado, J.W. Galbraith and D.F. Hendry (1993). *Co-integration, Error-correction, and the Econometric Analysis of Non-stationary Data,* Oxford: Oxford University Press

Barro, R.J. (1996). 'Determinants of Economic Growth: A Cross-country Empirical Study', NBER, Cambridge Working Paper, 5698

Barro, R.J. and X. Sala-i-Martin (1995). *Economic Growth,* New York: McGraw-Hilll International Editions

Barro, R.J., N.G. Mankiw and X. Sala-i-Martin (1995). 'Capital Mobility in Neoclassical Models of Growth', *American Economic Review,* 85(1): 103–15

Battellino, R. and N. McMillan (1989). 'Changes in the Behaviour of Banks and their Implications for Financial Aggregates', Reserve Bank of Australia, Research Discussion Paper, 8904

Bayoumi, T. (1990). 'Saving-investment Correlations: Immobile Capital Government Policy or Endogenous Behaviour?', *IMF Staff Papers,* 37(3): 361–87

Bayoumi, T. and P. Koujianou (1989). 'The Effects of Financial Deregulation on Consumption', IMF Working Paper 88

(1990). 'Consumption, Liquidity Constraints and Financial Deregulation', *Greek Economic Review,* 12: 195–210

Bayoumi, T. and R. McDonald (1994a). 'Consumption, Income, and International Capital Market Integration', IMF Working Paper, 94/120

(1994b). 'On the Optimality of Consumption Across Canadian Provinces', Centre for Economic Policy Research, Discussion Paper, 1030

Baxter, M. and M.J. Crucini (1993). 'Explaining Savings/investment Correlations', *American Economic Review,* 83

Beng, G.W. (1989). 'Testing International Parity Conditions for a Small Open Development Economy: The Case of Malaysia', Malaysian Institute of Economic Research, Discussion Paper, 28

Bernanke, B. S. (1985). 'Adjustment Costs, Durables, and Aggregate Consumption', *Journal of Monetary Economics,* 15: 41–68

Bisagnano, J. (1989). 'Financial Interdependence and External Adjustment: Some Problems Posed by US Federal Government Indebtedness', chapter 11 in D.E. Fair and C. de Boissieu (eds.), *The International Adjustment Process,* Dordrecht: Kluwer Academic: 177–205

Blanchard, O.J. and S. Fischer (1989). *Lectures on Macroeconomics,* Cambridge, MA: MIT Press

Blinder, A.S. and A. Deaton (1985). 'The Time Series Consumption Function Revisited', *Brookings Papers on Economic Activity,* 2: 465–521

Blundell-Wignall, A., F. Browne and A. Tarditi (1995). 'Financial Liberalisation and the Permanent Income Hypothesis', *Manchester Journal of Economics,* 63(2): 125–44

Borio, C.E.V. and W. Fritz (1995). 'The Response of Short-term Bank Lending Rates to Policy Rates: A Cross-country Comparison', *Bank for International Settlements Working Paper*, May

Bollerslev, T., R.F. Engle and D.B.Nelson (1994). 'ARCH Models', chapter 49 in R.F. Engle and D.L. McFadden (eds.), *Handbook of Econometrics*, Amsterdam: Elsevier Science: 2959–3038

Branson, W.E. (1992). 'Discussion on 'International Finance and Economic Development", chapter 2 in A. Giovannini (ed.), *Finance and Development: Issues and Experience*, Cambridge: Cambridge University Press: 24–6

Caballero, R.J. (1990). 'Expenditure on Durable Goods: A Case for Slow Adjustment', *Quarterly Journal of Economics*, 105(3): 727–43

Caballero, R.J. and E.M.R.A. Engel (1993). 'Microeconomic Adjustment Hazards and Aggregate Dynamics', *Quarterly Journal of Economics*, 108(2): 359–83

Campbell, J.Y. and N.G. Mankiw (1987). 'Permanent Income, Current Income, and Consumption', NBER Working Paper, 2436

(1989). 'Consumption, Income, and Interest Rates: Reinterpreting the Time Series Evidence', *NBER Macroeconomic Review*, 4: 185–245

(1991). 'The Response of Consumption to Income', *European Economic Review*, 35: 723–67

Campos, J. and N.R. Ericsson (1990). 'Econometric Modeling of Consumers' Expenditure in Venezuela', Board of Governors of the Federal Reserve System, *International Finance Discussion Paper*, 325

Canova, F. and M.O. Ravn (1994). 'International Consumption Risk Sharing', Centre for Economic Policy Research, Discussion Paper, 1074

Caprio Jr., G., I. Atiyas and J.A. Hanson (1994). 'Policy Issues in Reforming Finance: Lessons and Strategies', chapter 13 in G. Caprio. Jr., I. Atiyas and J.A. Hanson (eds.), *Financial Reform: Theory and Experience*, Cambridge: Cambridge University Press: 413–36

Carroll, C. and L.H. Summers (1989). 'Consumption Growth Parallels Income Growth: Some New Evidence', NBER Working Paper, 3090

Chah, E.Y., V.A. Ramey and R.M. Starr (1991). 'Liquidity Constraints and Intertemporal Consumer Optimization: Theory and Evidence from Durable Goods', NBER Working Paper, 3907

Chaiyasoot, N. (1993). 'Commercial Banking', chapter 7 in P.G. Warr (ed.) *The Thai Economy in Transition*, Cambridge: Cambridge University Press

Checchi, D. (1992). 'What Are the Real Effects of Liberalising International Capital Movements?', *Open Economies Review*, 3: 83–125

Chen, M.T. (1990). 'The Financial System and Financial Policy in the Republic of China', The International Commercial Bank of China, *Economic Review*, 256, July–August

Cheng, T.J. (1993). 'Guarding the Commanding Heights: The State as Banker in Taiwan', chapter 3 in S. Haggard, C.H. Lee and S. Maxfield (eds.), *The Politics of Finance in Developing Countries*, Ithaca: Cornell University Press: 55–92

Chinn, M.D. and J.A. Frankel (1992). 'Financial Links Around the Pacific Rim: 1982–1992', in R. Glick (ed.) *Exchange Rate Policies in Pacific Basin Countries*, Conference at the Reserve Bank of San Francisco, 16–18 September

(1994a). 'Financial Barriers in the Pacific Basin: 1982–1992', *Journal of Economic Integration*, 9(1): 62–79

(1994b). 'The Relative Influence of US and Japan on Real Interest Rates Around the Pacific Rim: 1982–1992', University of California Santa Cruz, Working Paper, 302

Cho, Y.J. (1988). 'The Effect of Financial Liberalisation on the Efficiency of Credit Allocation: Some Evidence from Korea', *Journal of Development Economics*, 29(1): 101–10

Choi, B.S. (1993). 'Financial Policy and Big Business in Korea: The Perils of Financial Regulation', chapter 2 in S. Haggard, C.H. Lee and S. Maxfield (eds.) *The Politics of Finance in Developing Countries*, Ithaca: Cornell University Press: 23–54

Chou, T.C. (1991). 'Government, Financial Systems and Economic Development in Taiwan', Institute of Economics, National Chung-Hsing University, Taipei, mimeo

Clarida, R.H. (1991). 'Aggregate Stochastic Implications of the Life-cycle Hypothesis', *Quarterly Journal of Economics*, 106: 851–67

Cochrane, J.H. (1991). 'A Simple Test of Consumption Insurance', *Journal of Political Economy*, 99(5): 957–76

Cohen, D. (1994). 'Foreign Finance and Economic Growth: An Empirical Analysis', chapter 8 in L. Leiderman and A. Razin (eds.), *Capital Mobility: The Impact on Consumption, Investment and Growth*, Cambridge: Cambridge University Press: 217–34

Cole, D.C., H.S. Scott and P.A. Wellons (1995a). *Asian Money Markets*, New York: Oxford University Press

(1995b). 'Asian Money Markets: An Overview', chapter 1 in D.C. Cole, H.S. Scott and P.A. Wellons (eds.), *Asian Money Markets*, New York: Oxford University Press: 3–38

Cole, D.C. and B.F. Slade (1995). 'Money Markets in Indonesia', chapter 3 in D.C. Cole, H.S. Scott and P.A. Wellons (eds.), *Asian Money Markets*, New York: Oxford University Press: 95–158

Cooper, R. (1974). 'Worldwide Regional Integration: Is there an Optimal Size of the Integrated Area?', Yale Economic Growth Center, *Discussion Paper*, 220, reprinted in R. Garnaut and P. Drysdale (eds.), *Asia Pacific Regionalism: Readings in International Economic Relations*, Sydney: HarperEducational: 11–19

Cottarelli, C. and A. Kourelis (1994). 'Financial Structure, Bank Lending Rates, and the Transmission Mechanism of Monetary Policy', IMF Working Paper, 94/39

Cox, D. and T. Jappelli (1993). 'The Effect of Borrowing Constraints on Consumer Liabilities', *Journal of Money, Credit, and Banking*, 25: 197–213

Crockett, A. (1993). 'Monetary Policy Implications of Increased Capital Flows', *Bank of England Quarterly Bulletin*, November: 492–504

Cumby, R.E. and F.S. Mishkin (1986). 'The International Linkage of Real Interest Rates: the European–US Connection', *Journal of International Money and Finance*, 5(1): 5–23

Cumby, R.E. and M. Obstfeld (1984). 'International Interest Rate and Price Level Linkages Under Flexible Exchange Rates', chapter 3 in J.F.O. Bilson and R. Marston (eds.), *Exchange Rate Theory and Practice*, Chicago: University of Chicago Press:, 121–51

Cushing, M.J. (1992). 'Liquidity Constraints and Aggregate Consumption Behaviour', *Economic Inquiry*, 30: 134–53

Cutler, D., J. Poterba and L. Summers (1990a). 'Speculative Dynamics', NBER, Cambridge Working Paper, 3242

(1990b). 'Speculative Dynamics and the role of Feedback Traders', NBER Working paper, 3243

Dalla, I. and D. Khatkhate (1996). 'The Emerging East Asian Bond Market', *Finance and Development*, March: 11–13

Das Gupta, D. and B. Das Gupta (1994). 'Interest Rates in Open Economies: Real Interest Rate Parity, Exchange Rates, and Country Risk in Industrial and Developing Countries', World Bank, Policy Research Working Paper, 1283

Davidson, I., J. Okunev and M. Tippett (1996). 'Some Further Evidence in Relation to Short-terminism of Stock Prices', School of Finance and Economics, University of Technology, Sydney, Working Paper, 57

Deaton, A. (1992). *Understanding Consumption*, Oxford: Clarendon Press

Debelle, G. and B. Preston (1995). 'Consumption, Investment and International Linkages', Reserve Bank of Australia, Research Discussion Paper, 9512.

de Brouwer, G.J. (1995). 'Summary of Discussion', chapter 13 in E.K.Y. Chen and P. Drysdale (eds.), *Corporate Links and Foreign Direct Investment in Asia and the Pacific*, proceedings from the 21st Pacific Trade and Development (PAFTAD) conference in Hong Kong, June 1994, Sydney: HarperEducational: 275–89

(1996). 'Deregulation and the Structure of Japan's Money Market' chapter 11 in P. Sheard (ed.) *Japanese Firms, Finance and Markets*, Sydney: HarperEducational; previously published as 'An Analysis of the Japanese Money Market', *Pacific Economic Papers*, 211 (1992)

de Brouwer, G.J., Ng, I. and R. Subbaraman (1993). 'New Tests on an Old Topic', Reserve Bank of Australia, Research Discussion Paper, 9314

de Brouwer, G.J and B. Preston (1996). 'Consumption in Australian States: What's Income Got to do with it?', Reserve Bank of Australia, mimeo

Doner, R. and D. Unger (1993). 'The Politics of Finance in Thai Economic Development', chapter 4 in S. Haggard, C.H. Lee and S. Maxfield (eds.) *The Politics of Finance in Developing Countries*, Ithaca, Cornell University Press: 93–122

Dooley, M. (1996). 'The Tobin Tax: Good Theory, Weak Evidence, Questionable Policy', chapter 3 in M. ul Haq, I. Kaul and I. Grunberg (eds.) *The Tobin Tax: Coping with Financial Volatility*, New York: Oxford University Press: 83–106

Dooley, M.P., J.A. Frankel and J. Mathieson (1987). 'International Capital Mobility: What Do Saving–Investment Correlations Tell Us?', *IMF Staff Papers*, 34(3): 871–83

Dooley, M.P. and Isard, P. (1980). 'Capital Controls, Political Risk, and Deviations from Interest-rate Parity', *Journal of Political Economy*, 88(2): 370–84

Dooley, M.P. and D.J. Mathieson (1994). 'Exchange Rate Policy, International Capital Mobility, and Monetary Policy Instruments', chapter 4 in R. Glick and W.M. Mathieson (eds.), *Exchange Rate Policy and Interdependence*, Cambridge: University Press: 68–95

Dornbusch, R. (1976). 'Expectations and Exchange Rate Dynamics', *Journal of Political Economy*, 84(6): 1161–76

Dornbusch, R. and T.C. Park (1994). 'Financial Integration in a Second Best World: Are We Still Sure about Our Classical Prejudices?', Korea Institute of Finance, *Policy Issue Series*, 94–1, February

Dwyer, J. and P. Lowe (1993). 'Alternative Concepts of the Real Exchange Rate: A Reconciliation', Reserve Bank of Australia, Research Discussion Paper, 9309

Edey, M. and K. Hviding (1995). 'An Assessment of Financial Reform in OECD Countries', OECD Economics Department, Working Paper, 154

Edwards, S. (1989). 'Tariffs, Capital Controls, and Equilibrium Real Exchange Rates', *Canadian Journal of Economics*, 22(1): 79–92

Edwards, S. and M. Khan (1985). 'Interest Rate Determination in Developing Countries: A Conceptual Framework', *IMF Staff Papers*, 32(3): 377–403

Emery, R. (1988). 'Monetary Policy in Taiwan, China', in H.S. Cheng (ed.), *Monetary Policy in Pacific Basin Countries*, Boston: Kluwer Academic Publishers: 381–99

(1991). *The Money Markets of Developing East Asia*, New York: Praeger

Enders, W. (1995). *Applied Econometric Time Series*, Wiley Series in Probability and Mathematical Statistics, New York: John Wiley

Engel, C. (1995). 'Accounting for US Real Exchange Rate Changes', NBER Working Paper, 5394

Engle, R.F. and C.W.J. Granger (1987). 'Co-integration and Error Correction: Representation, Estimation and Testing', *Econometrica*, 55: 251–276

Epstein, L.G. and S.E. Zin (1989). 'Substitution, Risk Aversion, and the Temporal Behaviour of Consumption and Asset Returns: A Theoretical Framework', *Econometrica*, 57(4): 937–69

(1991). 'Substitution, Risk Aversion, and the Temporal Behaviour of Consumption and Asset Returns: An Empirical Analysis', *Journal of Political Economy*, 99(2): 263–86

Ericsson, N. (1992). 'Cointegration, Exogeneity, and Policy Analysis: An Overview', *Journal of Policy Modelling*, 14: 251–80

Euromoney (1994). *Euromoney Supplement: Singapore*, September

Fama, E.F. (1984). 'Forward and Spot Exchange Rates', *Journal of Monetary Economics*, 14: 319–38

Faruquee, H. (1992). 'Dynamic Capital Mobility in Pacific Basin Developing Economies', *IMF Staff Papers*, 39(3): 706–17

Faruquee, H., D. Laxton and S. Symansky (1995). 'Government Debt, Life-cycle Income and Liquidity Constraints: Beyond Approximate Ricardian Equivalence', mimeo

Feldstein, M.S. (1983). 'Domestic Saving and International Capital Movements in the Long-run and the Short-run', *European Economic Review*, 21: 129–51

(1988). 'Thinking about International Policy Co-ordination', *Journal of Economic Perspectives*, 2(2): 3–13

Feldstein, M.S. and P. Bacchetta (1989). 'National Saving and International Investment', NBER Working Paper, 3164

Feldstein, M.S. and C. Horioka (1980). 'Domestic Saving and International Capital Flows', *Economic Journal*, 90: 314–29

Fischer, B. (1993). 'Impediments in the Domestic Banking Sector to Financial Opening', in H. Reisen and B. Fischer (eds.), *Financial Opening: Policy Issues and Experiences in Developing Countries*, Paris: OECD: 119–32

Fischer, B. and H. Reisen (1993). *Liberalising Capital Flows in Developing Countries: Pitfalls, Prerequisites and Perspectives*, Paris: Development Centre of the OECD

Fischer, S. (1994). 'International Capital Flows, the International Agencies, and Financial Stability', *Bank of Japan Monetary and Economic Studies*, 12(1): 17–27

Flavin, M.A. (1981). 'The Adjustment of Consumption to Changing Expectations about Future Income', *Journal of Political Economy*, 89: 974–1009

   (1985). 'Excess Sensitivity of Consumption to Current Income: Liquidity Constraints or Myopia?', *Canadian Journal of Economics*, 189: 117–36

Fleming, J.M. (1962). 'Domestic Financial Policies under Fixed and Floating Exchange Rates', *IMF Staff Papers*, 9(3): 369–79

Folkerts-Landau, D. (1990). 'The Case for International Coordination of Financial Policy', chapter 7 in W.H. Branson, J.A. Frenkel and M. Goldstein (eds.), *International Policy Coordination and Exchange Rate Fluctuations*, Chicago: University of Chicago Press: 279–303

Frankel, J.A. (1993a). 'Quantifying International Capital Mobility in the 1980s', chapter 2 in *On Exchange Rates*, Cambridge, MA: MIT Press

   (1993b). 'Tests of Rational Expectations in the Forward Exchange Market', chapter 8 in J.A. Frankel, *On Exchange Rates*, Cambridge, MA: MIT Press

   (1993c). 'The Diversifiability of Exchange Risk', chapter 9 in J.A. Frankel, *On Exchange Rates*, Cambridge, MA: MIT Press

Frankel, J.A. and K.A Froot (1993). 'Using Survey Data to Test Standard Propositions Regarding Exchange Rate Expectations', chapter 13 in J.A. Frankel, *On Exchange Rates*, Cambridge, MA: MIT Press; previously published in *American Economic Review*, 77(1) (1987): 33–53

Frankel, J.A. and A.T. MacArthur (1988). 'Political vs Currency premia in International Real Interest Rate Differentials', *European Economic Review*, 32(5): 1081–121

Fraser, B.W. (1995). 'Central Bank Co-operation in the Asian Region', talk by the Governor of the Reserve Bank of Australia to the 24th Conference of Economists, Adelaide, 25 September; Reserve Bank of Australia, *Bulletin*, October: 21–28

Frenkel, J.A. and R.M. Levich (1975). 'Covered Interest Arbitrage: Unexploited Profits?', *Journal of Political Economy*, 83: 325–38

Fried, J. and P. Howitt (1980). 'Credit Rationing and Implicit Contract Theory', *Journal of Money, Credit, and Banking*, 12(3): 471–87

Froot, K.A. and J.A. Frankel (1989). 'Forward Discount Bias: Is It An Exchange Risk Premium?', *Quarterly Journal of Economics*, 104(1): 139–61

Froot, K.A. and R.H. Thaler (1990). 'Anomalies: Foreign Exchange', *Journal of Economic Perspectives*, 4(3): 179–92

Fry, M. (1995). 'Financial Development in Asia: Some Analytical Issues', *Asian-Pacific Economic Literature*, 9(1): 40–57

Fukao, M. (1993). 'International Integration of Financial Markets and the Cost of Capital', *Journal of International Securities Markets*, 7: 75–90

Fukao, M. and M. Hanazaki (1986). 'Internationalization of Financial Markets: Some Implications for Macroeconomic Policy and for the Allocation of Capital', OECD Economic and Statistics Department, Working Paper, 37

Fuller, W. (1976). *Introduction to Statistical Time Series*, New York: John Wiley

Gaab, W., M. Franziol and M. Horner (1986). 'On Some International Parity Conditions: An Empirical Investigation', *European Economic Review*, 30(3): 683–713

Gali, J. (1990). Finite Horizons, Life-cycle Savings, and Time-series Evidence on Consumption', *Journal of Monetary Economics*, 26: 433–52

    (1991). 'Budget Constraints and Time-series Evidence on Consumption', *American Economic Review*, 81(5): 1238–53

Gertler, M. and A. Rose (1994). 'Finance, Public Policy, and Growth', chapter 2 in G. Caprio, Jr., I. Itiyas and J.A. Hanson (eds.), *Financial Reform: Theory and Experience*, Cambridge: Cambridge University Press: 13–48

Giovannini, A. and P. Weil (1989). 'Risk Aversion and Intertemporal Substitution in the Capital Asset pricing Model', NBER Working Paper, 2824

Glick, R. (1988). 'Financial Market Changes and Monetary Policy in Pacific Basin Countries', chapter 2 in H.S. Cheng (ed.), *Monetary Policy in Pacific Basin Countries*, Boston: Kluwer

Glick, R. and M. Hutchison (1990). 'Financial Liberalization in the Pacific Basin: Implications for Real Interest Rates', *Journal of the Japanese and International Economies*, 4: 36–48

Glick, R. and R. Moreno (1994). 'Capital Flows and Monetary Policy in East Asia', Centre for Pacific Basin Monetary and Economic Studies, Economic Research Department, Federal Reserve Bank of San Francisco, Working Paper, 94–08

Goldsborough, D. and R. Teja (1991). 'Globalization of Financial Markets and Implications for Pacific Basin Countries', IMF Working Paper, 91/34, 1991

Goldstein, M. and M. Mussa (1993). 'The Integration of World Capital Markets', IMF Working Paper, 93/95

Goodwin, B.K. and T.J. Grennes (1994). 'Real Interest Rate Equalization and the Integration of International Financial Markets', *Journal of International Money and Finance*, 13: 107–124

Goto, J. and K. Hamada (1994). 'Economic Preconditions for Asian Regional Integration', Chapter 14 in T. Ito and A.O. Krueger (eds.), *Macroeconomic Linkage. Savings, Exchange Rates and Capital Flows*, Chicago: University of Chicago Press: 359–385

Greene, W.H. (1993). *Econometric Analysis*, 2nd edn, New York: Macmillan Publishing Company

Grenville, S.A. (1995). 'Recent Capital Inflows: The Experience and Policy Response of Asian Countries', Reserve Bank of Australia, Economic Group, February, mimeo

    (1998). 'The Asian Economic Crisis', Reserve Bank of Australia, *Bulletin*, April: 9–20

Gruen, D. (1994). 'Capital Flows, Monetary and Exchange Rate Management: The Australian Experience', Reserve Bank of Australia, paper presented at the Eleventh Pacific Basin Central Bank Conference, Hong Kong, 31 October –2 November, mimeo

Gruen, D. and T. Kortian (1996). 'Why Does the Australian Dollar Move so Closely with the Terms of Trade?', Reserve Bank of Australia, Research Discussion Paper, 9601

Guciano, H. (1995). 'The Political Economy of International Money and Finance in the Asia-Pacific Region', PhD thesis, Australian National University, Research School of Pacific and Asian Studies, Australia–Japan Research Centre

Gultekin, M.N., N.B. Guletkin and A. Penati (1989). 'Capital Controls and International Capital Market Segmentation: The Evidence from the Japanese and American Stock Markets', *Journal of Finance*, 44(4): 849–69

Haggard, S., C.H. Lee and S. Maxfield (eds.) (1993). *The Politics of Finance in Developing Countries*, Ithaca: Cornell University Press

Hall, R.E. (1978). 'Stochastic Implications of the Life Cycle–Permanent Income Hypothesis: Theory and Evidence', *Journal of Political Economy*, 86: 971–87

(1989). 'Consumption', in R.J. Barro (ed.), *Modern Business Cycle Theory*, Cambridge MA: Harvard University Press: 153–77

Hall, R.E. and F.S. Mishkin (1982). 'The Sensitivity of Consumption to Transitory Income: Estimates from Panel Data on Households', *Econometrica*, 50: 461–81

Hannan, T.H. and A.N. Berger (1991). 'The Rigidity of Prices: Evidence from the Banking Industry', *American Economic Review*, (4): 938–48

Hansen, L. and R. Hodrick (1980). 'Forward Exchange Rates as Optimal Predictors of Future Spot Rates', *Journal of Political Economy*, 80(3): 829–53

Hanson, J.A. (1994). 'An Open Capital Account: A Brief Survey of the Issues and the Results', chapter 11 in G. Caprio, Jr., I. Atiyas and J.A. Hanson (eds.), *Financial Reform: Theory and Experience*, Cambridge: Cambridge University Press: 323–56

Haque, N.U. and P. Montiel (1990). 'Capital Mobility in Developing Countries – Some Empirical Tests', IMF Working Paper, 90/117

Harris, J., F. Schiantarelli and M.G. Siregar (1994). 'The Effect of Financial Liberalisation on the Capital Structure and Investment Decisions of Indonesian Manufacturing Establishments', *World Bank Economic Review*, 8(1): 17–47

Hasan, P. and D.C. Rao (1979). *Korea: Policy Issues for Long-term Development*, World Bank Mission Report, Baltimore: Johns Hopkins University Press

Hayashi, F. (1982). 'The Permanent Income Hypothesis: Estimation and Testing by Instrumental Variables', *Journal of Political Economy*, 90: 895–916

(1985). 'The Effect of Liquidity Constraints on Consumption: A Cross-Sectional Analysis', *Quarterly Journal of Economics*, 100(1): 183–206

Hendry, D.F. (1994). 'HUS Revisited', *Oxford Review of Economic Policy*, 10(2): 86–106

Hicks, J.R. (1946). *Value and Capital*, 2nd edn., Oxford: Clarendon Press

Ho, R.Y.K. (1991). 'The Regulatory Framework of the Banking Sector', chapter 5 in R.Y.K. Ho, R.H. Scott and K.A. Wong (eds.), *The Hong Kong Financial System*, Hong Kong: Oxford University Press

Ho, R.Y.K., Y.H. Lui and D.W.W. Cheung (1995). 'Money Markets in Hong Kong', chapter 2 in D.C. Cole, H.S. Scott and P.A. Wellons (eds.), *Asian Money Markets*, New York: Oxford University Press: 39–94

Hodrick, R.J. (1987). *The Empirical Evidence of the Efficiency of Forward and Futures Foreign Exchange Markets*, Chur: Harwood Academic Publishers

Hughes, H. (1987). 'The Role of Aid and Private Capital Flows in Economic Development' in Sir F. Holmes (ed.), *Economic Adjustment: Policies and Problems*, Washington, DC: IMF, 120–46

Hutchcroft, P.D. (1993). 'Selective Squander: The Politics of Preferential Credit Allocation in the Philippines', chapter 6 in S. Haggard, C.H. Lee and S. Maxfield (eds.) *The Politics of Finance in Developing Countries*, Ithaca: Cornell University Press: 165–198

International Monetary Fund (1995). *World Economic Outlook*, Washington, DC: IMF

    (1997a). 'Capital Flow Sustainability and Speculative Currency Attacks', *Finance and Development*, December: 8–11

    (1997b). *Exchange Arrangements and Exchange Restrictions*, Washington, DC: IMF

Isard, P. (1988). 'Exchange Rate Modeling: An Assessment of Alternative Approaches', chapter 8 in R.C. Bryant, D.W. Henderson, G. Holtham, P. Hooper and S. Symansky (eds.) *Empirical Macroeconomics for Interdependent Economies*, Washington, DC: Brookings Institution, 183–201

    (1995). *Exchange Rate Economics*, Cambridge: Cambridge University Press

Ishii, S. and S. Dunaway (1995). 'Portfolio Capital Flows to the Developing Country Members of APEC', chapter 2 in M.S. Khan and C.M. Reinhart (eds.), *Capital Flows in the APEC Region*, Washington, DC: IMF: 3–14

Ito, T. (1986). 'Capital Controls and Covered Interest Parity Between the Yen and the Dollar', *Economic Studies Quarterly*, 37(3): 223–41

Iwamura, M. (1992). 'The Determination of Monetary Aggregates and Interest Rates', *Bank of Japan Monetary and Economic Studies*, 10(1): 65–93

Jantarangs, J. (1994). 'Monetary Policy Conduct in Thailand', Bank of Thailand, November, mimeo

Jappelli, T. and M. Pagano (1989). 'Consumption and Capital Market Imperfections: An International Comparison', *American Economic Review*, 79: 1088–105

Johansen, J. and K. Juselius (1990). 'Maximum Likelihood Estimation and Inference on Cointegration with Application to the Demand for Money', *Oxford Bulletin of Economics and Statistics*, 52: 169–209

Johansen, S. (1988). 'Statistical Analysis of Cointegration Vectors', *Journal of Economic Dynamics and Control*, 12: 231–54

Johnston, R.B. and C. Ryan (1994). 'The Impact of Controls on Capital Movements on the Private Capital Accounts of Countries' Balance of Payments: Empirical Estimates and Policy Implications', IMF Working Paper, 94/78

Jung, W.S. (1986). 'Financial Development and Economic Growth', *Economic Development and Cultural Change*, 34(2): 333–346

Kang, M.S. (1995). 'Money Markets in Korea', chapter 4 in D.C. Cole, H.S. Scott and P.A. Wellons (eds.), *Asian Money Markets*, New York: Oxford University Press: 159–208

Kenen, P.B. (1993). 'Financial Opening and the Exchange Rate Regime', in H. Reisen and B. Fischer (eds.), *Financial Opening: Policy Issues and Experiences in Developing Countries*, Paris: OECD, Paris: 237–67

Keyfitz, N. and W. Flieger (1990). *World Population Growth and Aging: Demographic Trends in the Late Twentieth Century*, Chicago: University of Chicago Press

Khan, M.S. and C.M. Reinhart (1995). 'Macroeconomic Management in APEC Economies: The Response to Capital Inflows', chapter 3 in M.S. Khan and C.M. Reinhart (eds.), *Capital Flows in the APEC Region*, Washington, DC: IMF: 15–30

Khan, M.S. and R. Zahler (1983). 'The Macroeconomic Effects of Changes in Barriers to Trade and Capital Flows: A Simulation Analysis', IMF Staff Papers, 30(2): 223–82

Kim, E.J. and S.K. Lee (1994). 'Financial Liberalization and Internationalization in Korea', Bank of Korea, Research Paper, 94–5

Kim, K.S. (1991). 'Korea', chapter 1 in D. Papageorgiou, M. Michaely and A.M. Choksi (eds.), *Liberalizing Foreign Trade*, 2, Cambridge, MA: Basil Blackwell: 1–132

(1994). 'Survey of International Capital Mobility: Causes, Measurement and Consequences', SungKyun Kwan University, Seoul, Korea, February, mimeo

King, R.G. and R. Levine (1993a). 'Financial Intermediation and Economic Development', University of Rochester, mimeo

(1993b). 'Finance, Entrepreneurship, and Growth: Theory and Evidence', *Journal of Monetary Economics*, 32(3): 513–42

Kirakul, S., J. Jantarangs and P. Chantanahom (1993). 'Economic Development and the Role of Financial Deepening in Thailand', Bank of Thailand, *Papers on Policy Analysis and Assessment*, Bangkok

Kiriwat, E. (1995). 'Development of Asia's Emerging Capital Market: What Lies Ahead?', *Journal of Asian Economics*, 6(1): 113–17

Klein, M.A. (1971). 'A Theory of the Banking Firm', *Journal of Money, Credit and Banking*, 3: 205–18

Kohsaka, A. (1995). 'Interdependence through Capital Flows in Pacific Asia and the Role of Japan', Osaka University, mimeo

Krasker, W. (1980). 'The "Peso Problem" in Testing the Efficiency of Forward Exchange Markets', *Journal of Monetary Economics*, 6: 269–76

Kreps, D.M. and E.L. Porteus (1978). 'Temporal Resolution of Uncertainty and Dynamic Choice Theory', *Econometrica*, 46(1): 185–200

Krugman, P. (1992). 'International Finance and Economic Development', chapter 2 in A. Giovannini (ed.), *Finance and Development: Issues and Experience*, Cambridge: Cambridge University Press: 11–23

(1993). 'Recent Thinking About Exchange Rate Determination and Policy', *The Exchange Rate, International trade and the Balance of Payments*, Reserve Bank of Australia: 6–22

Kugler, P. and K. Neusser (1993). 'International Real Interest Rate Equalization: A Multivariate Time-series Approach', *Journal of Applied Econometrics*, 8: 163–74

Lattimore, R. (1994). 'Australian Consumption and Saving', *Oxford Review of Economic Policy*, 10(2): 54–70

Lahiri, A.K. (1989). 'Dynamics of Asian Savings: The Role of Growth and Age Structure', IMF Staff Papers, 36(March): 228–61

Lee, D.H. (1992). 'The Korean Economy: Prospects for Financial Reforms', Research School of Pacific and Asian Studies, Australian National University, Economics Division Working Paper: 92/2

Lee, S.Y. (1990). *Money and Finance in the Economic Development of Taiwan*, London: Macmillan

Lin, S.Y. and T.F. Chung (1995). Money Markets in Malaysia', chapter 5 in D.C. Cole, H.S. Scott and P.A. Wellons (eds.), *Asian Money Markets*, New York: Oxford University Press: 209–72

Loopesko, B. (1984). 'Relationships among Exchange Rates, Intervention and Interest Rates: An Empirical Investigation', *Journal of International Money and Finance*, 3: 257–78

Lovell, M.C. (1983). 'Data Mining', *Review of Economics and Statistics*, 65(1): 1–12

Lowe, P. (1995). 'The Link Between the Cash Rate and Market Interest Rates', Reserve Bank of Australia, Research Discussion Paper, 9504

Lowe, P. and T. Rohling (1992). 'Loan Stickiness: Theory and Evidence', Reserve Bank of Australia, Research Discussion Paper, 9206

Lucas, R.E. (1982). 'Interest Rates and Currency Prices in a Two-country World', *Journal of Monetary Economics*, 10: 335–59

MacIntyre, A.J. (1993). 'The Politics of Finance in Indonesia: Command, Confusion, and Competition', chapter 5 in S. Haggard, C.H. Lee and S. Maxfield (eds.) *The Politics of Finance in Developing Countries*, Ithaca: Cornell University Press: 123–64

MacKinnon, J.G. (1992). 'Critical Values for Cointegration Tests', in R.F. Engle and C.W.J. Granger (eds.), *Long-Run Economic Relationships: Readings in Co-Integration*, Oxford: Oxford University Press: 267–76

Maddala, G.S. (1989). *Introduction to Econometrics*, New York: Maxwell Macmillan

Makin, A.J. (1994). *International Capital Mobility and External Account Determination*, New York: St. Martin's Press

Mariger, R.P. (1987). 'A Life-cycle Consumption Model with Liquidity Constraints: Theory and Empirical Results', *Econometrica*, 55: 533–57

Mark, N. (1985). 'Some Evidence on the International Inequality of Real Interest Rates', *Journal of International Money and Finance*, 4: 189–208

Marston, R.C. (1993). 'Three Parity Conditions in International Finance', chapter 14 in H. Frisch and A. Worgötter (eds.), *Open Economy Macroeconomics*, London: Macmillan

Masson, P.R. (1992). 'Effects of Long-run Demographic Changes in a Multi-country Model', chapter 3 in C. Hargreaves (ed.), *Macroeconomic Modelling of the Long-Run*, Aldershot: Edward Elgar

Masson, P.R. and P. Agenor (1996). 'The Mexican Peso Crisis: Overview and Analysis of Credibility Factors', IMF Working Paper, 96/6

Mathieson, D.J. and L. Rojas-Suarez (1993). 'Liberalization of the Capital Account: Experiences and Issues', IMF Occasional Paper, 103

McCallum, B.T. (1989). *Monetary Economics: Theory and Policy*, New York: Macmillan

   (1994). 'A Reconsideration of the Uncovered Interest Parity Relationship', *Journal of Monetary Economics*, 33(1): 105–32

McCauley, R.N. and S.A. Zimmer (1992). 'Exchange Rates and International Differences in the Cost of Capital', paper presented to the Conference on Exchange Rate Effects on Corporate Financial Performance and Stategies, New York University Salomon Center, Leonard K. Stern School of Business, 1 May, mimeo

McCulloch, J.H. (1975). 'Operational Aspects of the Siegel Paradox: Comment', *Quarterly Journal of Economics*, 89(1): 170–72

McCulloch R. (1994). 'An Asian Capital Crunch? Implications for East Asia of a Global Capital Shortage', chapter 6 in T. Ito and A. Kreuger (eds.), *Macroeconomic Linkage: Savings, Exchange Rates and Capital Flows*, Chicago: University of Chicago Press: 167–84

McKibbin, W. J. and A.J. Richards (1988). 'Consumption and Permanent Income: The Australian Case', Reserve Bank of Australia, *Research Discussion Paper*, 8808

McKibbin, W.J. and J.D. Sachs (1991). *Global Linkages. Macroeconomic Interdependence and Cooperation in the World Economy*, Washington, DC: Brookings Institution

McNelis, P.D. and K. Schmidt-Hebbel, (1993). 'Financial Liberalization and Adjustment: the Cases of Chile and New Zealand', *Journal of International Money and Finance*, 12: 249–77

Mendoza, E.G. (1991). 'Real Business Cycles in A Small Open Economy', *American Economic Review*, 81: 797–818

(1994). 'The Robustness of Macroeconomic Indicators of Capital Mobility', chapter 4 in L. Leiderman and A. Razin (eds.), *Capital Mobility: The Impact on Consumption, Investment and Growth*, Cambridge: Cambridge University Press: 83–117

Mishkin, F.S. (1984a). 'The Real Interest Rate: A Multi-country Empirical Study', *Canadian Journal of Economics*, 17(2): 283–311

(1984b). 'Are Real Interest Rates Equal Across Countries? An Empirical Examination of International Parity Conditions', *Journal of Finance*, 39: 1345–58

Monti, M. (1972). 'Deposit, Credit and Interest Rate Determination Under Alternative Bank Objective Functions', in G.P. Szego and K. Shell (eds.), *Mathematical Methods in Investment and Finance*, Amsterdam: North-Holland: 430–54

Montiel, P.J. (1993). 'Capital Mobility in Developing Countries: Some Measurement Issues and Empirical Estimates', World Bank Debt and International Finance Policy Research, Working Paper, 1103

Muellbauer, J. (1983). 'Surprises in the Consumption Function', *Economic Journal*, 93 (Supplement): S34–S50

(1994). 'The Assessment: Consumer Expenditure', *Oxford Review of Economic Policy*, 10(2): 1–41

Muellbauer, J. and R. Lattimore (1994). 'The Consumption Function: A Theoretical and Empirical Overview', chapter 5 in M.H. Pesaran and M.R. Wickens (eds.), *Handbook of Applied Econometrics*, Oxford: Blackwell: 221–311

Mundell, R. (1963). 'Capital Mobility and Stabilization Policy under Fixed and Flexible Exchange Rates', *Canadian Journal of Economics and Political Science*, 29: 475–85

Murphy, R.G. (1984). 'Capital Mobility and the Relationship Between Saving and Investment in OECD Countries', *Journal of International Money and Finance*, 3: 327–42

Mussa, M. (1984). 'The Theory of Exchange Rate Determination', chapter 1 in J.F.O. Bilson and R.C. Marston (eds.), *Exchange Rate Theory and Practice*, Chicago: University of Chicago Press: 13–78

(1986). 'The Effects of Commercial, Fiscal, Monetary, and Exchange Rate Policies on the Real Exchange Rate', chapter 2 in S. Edwards and L. Ahamed (eds.), *Economic Adjustment and Exchange Rates in Developing Countries*, Chicago: University of Chicago Press: 43–88

Nelson, C.R. (1987). 'A Reappraisal of Recent Tests of the Permanent Income Hypothesis', *Journal of Political Economy*, 95(3): 641–6

Neusser, K. (1992). 'Intertemporal Nonseparability, Liquidity Constraints, and Seasonality of Aggregate Consumer Expenditures: An Empirical Investigation', *Empirical Economics*, 17: 363–82

Newey, W.K. and K.D. West (1987): 'A Simple, Positive Semi-definite, Heteroskedasticity and Autocorrelation Consistent Covariance Matrix', *Econometrica*, 55(3): 703–8

Niederer R. (1994). 'Emerging Capital Markets in Southeast Asia', *Economic and Financial Prospects*, 1: 1–14

Nijathaworn, B. (1993). 'Managing Foreign Capital in a Rapidly Growing Economy: Thailand's Experience and Policy Issues', Economic Research Department, Bank of Thailand, *Papers on Policy Analysis and Assessment*: 19–38

Nijathaworn, B. and T. Dejthamrong (1994). 'Capital Flows, Exchange Rate and Monetary Policy: Thailand's Recent Experience', Economic Research Department, Bank of Thailand, *Papers on Policy Analysis and Assessment*: 1–15

O'Brien, R. (1992). *Global Financial Integration: The End of Geography*, Chatham House Papers, The Royal Institute of International Affairs, London: Pinter Publishers

Obstfeld, M. (1986a). 'Capital Mobility in the World Economy: Theory and Measurement', *Carnegie–Rochester Conference Series on Public Policy*, 24: 55–104

(1986b). 'Capital Flows, the Current Account, and the Real Exchange Rate: Some Consequences of Stabilization and Liberalization', chapter 6 in S. Edwards and L. Ahamed (eds.), *Economic Adjustment and Exchange Rates in Developing Countries*, Chicago: University of Chicago Press: 201–31

(1993). 'Are Industrial-Country Risks Globally Diversified?', NBER Working Paper: 4308

(1994). 'International Capital Mobility in the 1990s', Centre for Economic Policy Research Discussion Paper, 902

Okina, K. and C. Sakuraba (1994). 'Bank Balance Sheet Adjustments and Interest Rate Policy in Japan', *National Differences in Interest Rate Transmission*, Basle: BIS, Monetary and Economic Department

Okuda, H. (1993). 'International Linkage of Interest Rates in the 1980s for Selected Southeast Asian Countries', chapter 9 in J. Teranishi and S. Fukuda (eds.), *The Asian Financial and Capital Markets – Growth and Interrelationship*, Tokyo: QUICK Research Institute Corporation

Pacific Economic Cooperation Council (PECC) (1995). *Survey of Impediments to Trade and Investment in the APEC Region*, Singapore: APEC Secretariat

Pagan, A. (1995). 'The Econometrics of Financial Markets', Australian National University, January, mimeo

Park, Y.C. (1992). 'The Role of Finance in Economic Development in South Korea and Taiwan', chapter 6 in A. Giovannini (ed.), *Finance and Development: Issues and Experience*, Cambridge: Cambridge University Press: 121–57

(1994). 'Korea: Development and Structural Change in the Financial System', chapter 4 in H.T. Patrick and Y.C. Park (eds.), *The Financial Development of Japan, Korea, and Taiwan: Growth, Recession, and Liberalization*, New York: Oxford University Press: 129–87

Patrick, H.T. (1994). 'Comparisons, Contrasts and Implications', chapter 8 in H.T. Patrick and Y.C. Park (eds.), *The Financial Development of Japan, Korea, and Taiwan: Growth, Recession, and Liberalization*, New York: Oxford University Press: 325–71

Patrick, H.T. and Y.C. Park (1994). *The Financial Development of Japan, Korea, and Taiwan: Growth, Recession, and Liberalization*, New York: Oxford University Press

Phillips, P.C.B. and B.E. Hansen (1990). 'Statistical Inference in Instrumental Variables Regression with I(1) Processes', *Review of Economic Studies*, 53: 473–95

Phylaktis, K. (1995). 'Capital Market Integration in the Pacific Basin: An Analysis of Real Interest Rate Linkages', IMF Working Paper, 95/133

Piggott, C.A. (1991). 'Introduction and Summary', in C.A. Piggott (ed.), *International Financial Integration and US Monetary Policy*, a colloquium sponsored by the Federal Reserve Bank of New York (October 1989)

(1994). 'International Interest Rate Convergence: A Survey of the Issues and Evidence', *FRBNY Quarterly Review*, Winter

Prachowny, M.F.J. (1970). 'A Note on Interest Parity and the Supply of Arbitrage Funds', *Journal of Political Economy* 78: 540–5

Razin, A. and A.K. Rose (1994). 'Business-cycle Volatility and Openness: An Exploratory Cross-Sectional Analysis', chapter 3 in L. Leiderman and A. Razin (eds.), *Capital Mobility: The Impact on Consumption, Investment and Growth*, Cambridge: Cambridge University Press: 48–82

Reisen, H. (1996). 'Developing-country Savings and the Global Capital Shortage', in *Future Global Capital Shortages. Real Threat or Pure Fiction?*, Paris: OECD: 143–60

Reisen, H. and H. Yeches (1993). 'Time-varying Estimates on the Openness of the Capital Account in Korea and Taiwan', *Journal of Development Economics*, 41: 285–305

Rivera-Batiz, F.L. and L.A. Rivera-Batiz (1994). *International Finance and Open Economy Macroeconomics*, 2nd edn, New York: Macmillan Publishing

Roubini, N. and X. Sala-i-Martin (1992). 'Financial Repression and Economic Growth', *Journal of Economic Development*, 39(1): 5–30

Sachs, J., A. Tornell and A. Velasco (1996). 'Financial Crises in Emerging Markets: the Lessons from 1995'. NBER Working Paper, 5576

Scheinkman, J.A. and L. Weiss (1986). 'Borrowing Constraints and Aggregate Economic Activity', *Econometrica*, 54: 23–45

Schmidt-Hebbel, K., S.B. Webb and G. Corsetti (1992). 'Household Saving in Developing Countries: First Cross-country Evidence', *World Bank Economic Review*, 6(3): 529–47

Sekkat, K., F. Thys-Clement and D. Van Regemorter (1994). 'Life-cycle Consumption and Liquidity Constraints: An Empirical Analysis at the EC Level', chapter 12 in M. Dewatripoint and V. Ginsburgh (eds.), *European Economic Integration*, Amsterdam: North Holland

Shea, J.D. (1994). 'Taiwan: Development and Structural Change in the Financial System', chapter 6 in H.T. Patrick and Y.C. Park (eds.), *The Financial Development of Japan, Korea, and Taiwan: Growth, Recession, and Liberalization*, New York: Oxford University Press: 222–87

Shiller, R.J. and P. Perron (1985). 'Testing the Random Walk Hypothesis', *Economics Letters*, 18: 381–86

Shintani, M. (1993). 'Excess Smoothness of Consumption', Institute of Social and Economic Research Osaka University, Discussion Paper, 299

    (1994). 'Co-integration and Tests of the Permanent Income Hypothesis: Japanese Evidence with International Comparisons', *Journal of the Japanese and International Economies*, 8: 144–72

Siegel, J.J. (1972). 'Risk, Interest Rates and the Forward Exchange', *Quarterly Journal of Economics*, 86(2): 301–9

Solow, R.M. (1986). 'Unemployment: Getting the Questions Right', *Economica*, 53: S23–S34

Spiegel, M.M. (1995). 'Sterilization of Capital Inflows through the Banking Sector: Evidence From Asia', Center for Pacific Basin Monetary and Economic Studies, Federal Reserve Bank of San Francisco, Pacific Basin Working Paper Series, Working Paper, PB95–06

Stiglitz, J.E. and A. Weiss (1981). 'Credit Rationing in Markets with Imperfect Information', *American Economic Review*, 71(3): 393–410

Summers, R. and A. Heston (1991). 'The Penn World Table (Mark 5): An Expanded Set of International Comparisons, 1950–1988', *Quarterly Journal of Economics*, 106: 327–68

Suzuki, Y. (1987). *The Japanese Financial System*, Oxford: Clarendon Press

Takahashi, W. and Y. Kitamura (1993). 'Consumer Behaviour in Japan under Financial Liberalisation and Demographic Change', Macquarie University Department of Economics Working Paper, 18

Takeda, M. (1985). 'A Theory of Loan Rate Determination in Japan', *Bank of Japan Monetary and Economic Studies*, 3(1)

Taylor, M.P. (1995). 'The Economics of Exchange Rates', *Journal of Economic Literature*, 23: 13–47

Tobin, J. (1978). 'A Proposal for International Monetary Reform', *Eastern Economic Journal*, 4(3–4): 153–9

    (1983). 'Comments on Domestic Saving and International Capital Movements in the Long-Run and the Short-run by M. Feldstein', *European Economic Review*, 21: 153–6

Truman, E.M. (1996). 'The Risks and Implications of External Financial Shocks: Lessons from Mexico', International Finance Discussion Papers, 535

Urbain, J.P. (1992). 'On Weak Exogeneity in Error-correction Models', *Oxford Bulletin of Economics and Statistics*, 54: 187–201

Vaidyanthan, G. (1993). 'Consumption, Liquidity Constraints and Economic Development', *Journal of Macroeconomics*, 15: 591–610

Van Wijnbergen, S. (1990). 'Capital Controls and the Real Exchange Rate', *Economica*, 57: 15–28

Viaene, J.M. (1992). 'Real Effects of the 1992 Financial Deregulation', *Weltwirtschaftliches Archiv*, 128: 615–37

Warr, P.G. and B. Nidhiprabha (1995). *Thailand's Macroeconomic Miracle: Stable Adjustment and Sustained Growth*, Washington, DC: World Bank

Weil, D.N. (1993) 'Demographic Change, Consumption, and Saving', Ministry of Finance, *Financial Review*, Tokyo, June

Weil, P. (1987). 'Non-expected Utility in Macroeconomics', Harvard Institute of Economic Research, Discussion Paper, 1334

Westphal, U. (1983). 'Comments on Domestic Saving and International Capital Movements in the Long-run and the Short-run by M. Feldstein', *European Economic Review*, 21: 157–9

Wibulswasdi, C. and O. Tanvanich (1992). 'Liberalization of the Foreign Exchange Market: Thailand's Experience', Bank of Thailand, *Quarterly Bulletin*, 32(4): 25–37

Wilcox, J.A. (1989). 'Liquidity Constraints on Consumption: The Real Effects of 'Real' Lending Policies', *Federal Reserve Bank of San Francisco Economic Review*, Fall

World Bank (1993). *The East Asian Miracle: Economic Growth and Public Policy*, New York: Oxford University Press

Yang, Y.H. (1991). 'An Analysis on the Structure of Interest Rates in the Banking Sector and the Curb Market', Chung-Hua Institute for Economic Research, Discussion Paper, 9105, July

Yap, J.T., M.B. Lamberte, T.S. Untalan and M.S.V. Zingapan (1995). 'Money Markets in the Philippines', chapter 6 in D.C. Cole, H.S. Scott and P.A. Wellons (eds.), *Asian Money Markets*, New York: Oxford University Press: 273–348

Yasuhara, N., K. Nishimura, S. Takada and Y. Ogawa (1995). 'International Capital Flows in Recent Years: Characteristics and Background', *EXIM Review*, 15(1): 109–66

Zeldes, S.P. (1989). 'Consumption and Liquidity Constraints: An Empirical Investigation', *Journal of Political Economy*, 97: 305–46.

Index